A HISTORICAL GUIDE TO
Ernest Hemingway

HISTORICAL GUIDES
TO AMERICAN AUTHORS

The Historical Guides to American Authors is an interdisciplinary, historically sensitive series that combines close attention to the United States' most widely read and studied authors with a strong sense of time, place, and history. Placing each writer in the context of the vibrant relationship between literature and society, volumes in this series contain historical essays written on subjects of contemporary social, political, and cultural relevance. Each volume also includes a capsule biography and illustrated chronology detailing important cultural events as they coincided with the author's life and works, while photographs and illustrations dating from the period capture the flavor of the author's time and social milieu. Equally accessible to students of literature and of life, the volumes offer a complete and rounded picture of each author in his or her America.

A Historical Guide to Ernest Hemingway
Edited by Linda Wagner-Martin

A Historical Guide to Walt Whitman
Edited by David S. Reynolds

A Historical Guide to Ralph Waldo Emerson
Edited by Joel Myerson

A
Historical Guide
to Ernest Hemingway

EDITED BY
LINDA WAGNER-MARTIN

New York   Oxford
Oxford University Press
2000

Oxford University Press

Oxford   New York

Athens   Auckland   Bangkok   Bogotá   Buenos Aires   Calcutta
Cape Town   Chennai   Dar es Salaam   Delhi   Florence   Hong Kong   Istanbul
Karachi   Kuala Lumpur   Madrid   Melbourne   Mexico City   Mumbai
Nairobi   Paris   São Paulo   Singapore   Taipei   Tokyo   Toronto   Warsaw

and associated companies in
Berlin   Ibadan

Published by Oxford University Press, Inc.
198 Madison Avenue, New York, New York 10016

Oxford is a registered trademark of Oxford University Press

Library of Congress Cataloging-in-Publication Data
A historical guide to Ernest Hemingway /
edited by Linda Wagner-Martin.
p.   cm. — (Historical guides to American authors)
Includes bibliographical references and index.
ISBN 0-19-512151-1; ISBN 0-19-512152-X (pbk.)
1. Hemingway, Ernest, 1899–1961—Criticism and interpretation.
2. Literature and history—United States—History—20th century.
I. Wagner-Martin, Linda.   II. Series.
PS3515.E37Z6325   1999
813'.52—dc21   99-10910
[B]

1 3 5 7 9 8 6 4 2

Printed in the United States of America
on acid-free paper

For Tom Wagner

Contents

A HISTORICAL GUIDE TO
Ernest Hemingway

Introduction

Linda Wagner-Martin

Here at the turn into the twenty-first century, *Ernest Hemingway* has become synonymous with *American writer*. Whenever students, readers, or the general public think of prominent authors, the name Hemingway surfaces. Not only in name, but also in a kind of iconic image—the seriously intent bearded and sweater-clad figure moves into our collective vision. His far-seeing eyes reassure us; his sweetly pursed lips lessen the steely impact of the almost somber visage. *Writing is serious business,* Hemingway reminds us, *the most important business anyone can undertake.*

Scarcely nineteen when he understood that time to live was a luxury, Hemingway made his pained way back to health after the 200-odd shrapnel leg wounds hospitalized him on the Italian front during World War I. He was only twenty-one when he married Hadley Richardson, his first wife, with all the conviction of the incurable romantic he was to show himself repeatedly to be. The talk of the international literary world before he was thirty, Hemingway was already living out his—and his readers'—American dream of early, dramatic, professional success. There is nothing the United States loves more than handsome, healthy, hard-driving youngsters, and Ernest Hemingway, disguising his inherent shyness under a commanding facade of eager friendliness, seemed typecast for the role.

3

Hemingway was only twenty-four when Robert McAlmon published *Three Stories & Ten Poems* in Paris and Gertrude Stein's "portrait" of him ("He and They, Hemingway") appeared in *Ex Libris*. (When Hemingway published poems in Harriet Monroe's *Poetry Magazine*, he was identified as a young Chicago poet.) At twenty-five, he saw his prose-poem collection, *in our time*, into print, praised by his then-mentor, Ezra Pound. At twenty-six, as an associate (and unpaid) editor of Ford Madox Ford's *transatlantic review*, he was first favorably reviewed when the stories and prose-poems of *In Our Time* appeared in the States (Edmund Wilson, among others, was impressed). The rest, as we cavalierly might say, was history—at least literary history. For in 1926, to a publishing world already thrilled by the work of F. Scott Fitzgerald, Jean Toomer, Sherwood Anderson, Sinclair Lewis, and countless other modernists, Hemingway added the novel that seemed to be the mark of the newest of American fiction—terse, tough, and shocking in its subject matter, *The Sun Also Rises*.

Most readers saw the book as a titillating scenario of expatriate life outside the Prohibition-restricted United States; it popularized both Paris and the centers of Spanish bullfighting. From the days in the early 1920s, when Gertrude Stein and Alice B. Toklas were among the very few Americans to go to Pamplona, through the later years of that decade, when hundreds of Americans came to the small Spanish town to run with the bulls, Hemingway's novel was the model for living life to the full, as well as living life with an eye for the new and the exotic—experiences, places, and moral and social codes. To a culture jaundiced after the "war to end all wars" had succeeded only in decimating humankind, the search for pleasure had credibility. To a United States where "only saps work" as the market built fortunes day after day, travel abroad, particularly at advantageous exchange rates, was easily possible. *The Sun Also Rises*—despite Hemingway's claims that it was the most moral of novels—became the handbook for social, and sexual, adventure.

While readers were still absorbing his 1926 novel, Scribner's brought out the second of his signature short story collections, *Men without Women*. The shock effect of the title, in the ages of both the New Woman and the Flapper, enhanced Hemingway's reputation: it announced that this writer was a man's man; a tough hunter, fisherman, war veteran; a man who could take women or leave them, on his own terms. "Hills Like White Elephants," a narrative in which an American man pushes his lover to abort their child, was only one of the unconventional stories that, for reasons both stylistic and thematic, excited readers.

The next year, *Scribner's Magazine* serialized the Hemingway novel that would be published in 1929, *A Farewell to Arms*. The bleak war story, based not on his experiences but on historical accounts of key events in World War I, used the familiar romance plot as an overlay to the war narrative, and while its real interest may have been the friendships among the men on the Italian front, readers were much more involved in the story of the doomed, unmarried lovers, Catherine and Frederic. While *The Sun Also Rises* as an entity remained etched in readers' minds, what was indelible about *A Farewell to Arms* was the desperately sad ending of the novel. Hemingway had given the world a contemporary version of Romeo and Juliet, Tristan and Isolde, but he had been wise enough to set that tale in the inherently tragic atmosphere of the war nobody won. In 1929 the world was just beginning to realize that truth.

It was enough. The film adaption of *A Farewell to Arms,* starring Gary Cooper and Helen Hayes, was released in 1932, along with Hemingway's third (and last) short story collection, *Winner Take Nothing.* Even though his other 1932 book, *Death in the Afternoon,* a treatise about the bullfights, was not important to the general reader, it was to its author: the Spanish ritual of bullfighting helped lead Hemingway to Catholicism, showing humankind as, finally, superior to the natural world. Humankind's dominance was to become his theme in much of his later writing, culminating with the brief fiction for which he won the Nobel Prize, *The Old Man and the Sea.* On the way to that late work, there was *For Whom the Bell Tolls,* another magnificent novel. And there were less successful books.

In point of fact, and in the popular mind, however, Hemingway could have coasted to the Nobel Prize on the back of the great writing in his first two novels and in the three short story collections that showed what "modern" writing could be. His stories took on lives of their own, of course, as they appeared in anthologies time after time, and American readers grew as familiar with "Big Two-Hearted River," "The Killers," "A Clean, Well-Lighted Place," "Fathers and Sons," "The Snows of Kilimanjaro," "The Short Happy Life of Francis Macomber," and "The Undefeated" as they were with the tales of Poe and Hawthorne. Eventually, many of Hemingway's short stories were also filmed.

The reason the work of one author lives and that of another does not depends, finally, on the writing itself. When readers can pick up a story or a novel and read it with understanding and empathy, regardless of the cultural context or the time in which it was written, the writing has some chance of lasting into another generation. In the best of literary worlds, the academic reputation of the work would enhance its staying power: what teachers like to teach in classrooms, whether at secondary or university levels, will probably endure for a time. But literary history is filled with works that were not taught, that never made it into fashionable academic circles, and that still have maintained their public readership.

What is interesting in many ways about the academic response to Hemingway's works is that it has been less than consistent. Taught as the hallmark of the new during the 1930s and 1940s, his writing then was eclipsed by academic interest in the works of both Thomas Wolfe and William Faulkner. Wolfe's novels were impressionistically powerful, a vivid contrast to Hemingway's laconic "tip-of-the-iceberg" style. They were also romantic in ways that made implicit the love of home, the rootedness of an America that feared it would never return to stable values. The tragedies of World War II had only intensified the cultural loss of direction after World War I; readers were in need of reassurance.

They did not find that reassurance in William Faulkner's many novels—at least not in the ones academic approval made classroom fodder, *The Sound and the Fury, As I Lay Dying, Light in August, Absalom, Absalom!*—but Faulkner's works were important for their undercurrent of existential probing, as well as for their immense contributions to the American modernist technique. Scholars and teachers loved to ponder Faulkner's writing. That both Wolfe and Faulkner were writers of the South, a region seemingly distant from the literary power centers of the United States, may also have increased their attraction. One could look intensely into their novels and yet feel safe from the authors' implied criticisms: their lands were not those of most critics or even of most readers.

During the 1950s and even into the 1960s, then, classrooms were devoted to helping students understand the greatness of American modernism through the study of both Faulkner and Wolfe. Hemingway made his way into the syllabus as well, but because the Wolfe, Faulkner, or sometimes John Dos Passos novels of pedagogic choice were likely to be long, the "simpler" writer—Ernest Hemingway—might be taught only through a short story or two. The brevity of classroom attention gave rise to an over-simplification of Hemingway. Surely if a writer's work was worth only a day or two of study, in contrast to a time period of two or three weeks, the assumption grew that it was inherently less demanding, and that criterion translated into the work's being somehow less "good."

Despite Hemingway's reputation in classrooms, his readers at large knew how central—and yet how unique—this American writer was. Not only had he given our literature a dozen of its recurring touchstones for moving, even stirring, portraits of human interaction in life, but his stylistic influence had helped to create an entire genre, the laconic, hard-boiled mystery and/or detective novel. And there are few writers who have been such important naturalists, with descriptions of lands and oceans— and the creatures therein—foreshadowing today's informed ecological concerns. As the writer of great, if tragic, love stories, Hemingway contributed his remarkable taut language to cartoons, greeting card legends, and borrowings in serious contemporary fiction. In that guise, Hemingway as icon of the world's great writers was to have a few of his post–World War I letters become the script for a commercially produced film, *In Love and War.*

There is little question of Hemingway's place among his readers and among the population entire, not only in the United States but throughout the world. But back in the academic classroom, since less time was likely to be spent reading Hemingway's work, critical perspectives were necessarily limited. Students probably learned about Hemingway's life or were taught close-reading techniques, even if other critical approaches might have been more useful. In contrast, the newest of critical and theoretical perspectives were enriching the greatness of a Faulkner work.

During the 1960s and the 1970s, then, it became more fashionable to work on the difficult Faulkner than on the easy-to-grasp Hemingway, and that attitude remained in place until about fifteen years ago. Jarred in part by the posthumous publication of several important Hemingway works, beginning with his memoir of the Paris years, *A Moveable Feast*, published in 1964, and continuing through his novel *The Garden of Eden*, in 1986, the complacency of teachers and scholars concerning what Hemingway was about as a writer started to change. Legitimate questions arose about the writer's themes; his characters; his concepts of morality, bravery, and appropriate sexuality; as well as what seemed to be the intrinsic values of his apparently economical style. Today, there is more varied and interesting criticism written about Hemingway than about any other modernist American novelist; the critical tide has come full circle. As Jane Tompkins so wisely noted, "Works of literature lead a life of their own, which they receive, in part, from each generation of readers that comes to them" (*College English* 174–5).

In fact, it might be said that Hemingway's work here at the turn into the twenty-first century lives as much through the secondary criticism devoted to it as through its valid existence as writing itself. The best criticism changes the lenses of the readers' view and thereby provides new ways of reading, seeing, and visualizing the art. It is in the interaction between the literature and its criticism that Hemingway's oeuvre remains most vital.

The aim of this collection is to add to the variety of those critical perspectives by placing Hemingway's work within reach of readers who may not be scholars. The emphasis on the "historical" is meant to suggest that for the development of the writer's career, certain themes and approaches were in place—even if criticism contemporary with the publication of one work or another was not aware of that particular pattern. Given that Hemingway was born in 1899, and that his writing continues through this hundred-year period with no diminishment of interest, such an approach is especially germane to the study of his work.

Beginning with Michael Reynolds's succinct yet authoritative biography of Hemingway, this collection attempts to re-script a number of key insights about the writer and his work for the modern reader. What is of interest to this targeted reader—the interested contemporary person—has provided the critical grid for the essays in this volume: all essays here are previously unpublished, written specifically for this collection. That an adaption of Michael Reynolds's earlier biographical essay opens the book is a reflection of the current interest in literary biography. So far as Hemingway himself is concerned, the attention biographers have given his life is unprecedented and extends from the first biography (Carlos Baker's *Ernest Hemingway: A Life Story,* 1969) to the five-volume biography by Michael Reynolds, the first book of which is *The Young Hemingway* (1986).

This compilation of biographical information has been useful; particularly as Hemingway aged, the stories he told in person seemed incredible. Had he been sent to find Nazi submarines off the shores of Cuba? Had he been the subject of intense FBI investigation through much of his career?[1] As Reynolds's biographical essay included here makes clear, many of the exploits Hemingway described in the late 1930s and during World War II were much less fiction than his friends and intimates had believed; Reynolds has found the valuable information that helps the reader sort necessarily secret war information from what later became the author's depressive paranoia.

Susan Beegel's informative essay about Hemingway's lifelong interest in matters ecological, beginning with his boyhood fascination with the Agassiz Club and his exploration of the Michigan forests and lakes during his first twenty summers, similarly brings a wealth of new material before readers. Beegel's work is the first of what will undoubtedly be many rich forays into the roles of nature, health, and vitality (including the principles of sexual vigor) important during the early years of the twentieth century. Much of the attraction of good health stemmed from middle-class conservation ethics, as well as from the luxury of a prosperous culture to have time and equipment to take care of itself. Much of this interest derived as well from the cultural prominence of Teddy Roosevelt. Dr. Beegel's interpretations are particularly valuable in underscoring one of Hemingway's own comments about the way a writer "trains" for his profession. As he told George Plimpton during an interview, "If a writer stops observing he is finished. But he does not have to observe consciously nor think how it will be useful. Perhaps that would be true at the beginning. But later everything he sees goes into the great reserve of things he knows or has seen" (*Ernest Hemingway: Five Decades of Criticism* 35).

Professor Elkins's essay, "The Fashion of *Machismo,*" approaches one of the myths about Hemingway and his life by concentrating on the author's use of his self-created fashions. As the illustrations and photographs here help to prove, Hemingway consistently defined himself through his attire—even if his choices of clothing might have seemed casual or negligible.[2] His early self-consciousness about the effect of clothing is clear in his column for the Toronto *Star*: "A good plan is to go to one of the stores handling secondhand army goods and purchase yourself a trench coat [or] . . . a pair of army shoes. . . . They will convince everyone you meet on a street car that you have seen service." The way this strategy figured into Hemingway's concept of masculine rapport becomes clear in his concluding sentence: "The trench coat and the army shoes will admit you at once into that camaraderie of returned men which is the main result we obtained from the war" (in Elkins). What Elkins draws from Hemingway's various models of appearance is a configuration of his ideas about masculinity. Hemingway's choices in clothing, Elkins shows, were never "anti-fashion." They were very consciously aimed at creating a macho style, which continues even today in J. Peterman catalogs.

Elkins's essay is linked in this collection with the historically based consideration of Ernest Hemingway's development in the midst of various turns within the women's movement. Dr. Jamie Barlowe provides consummate evidence that the roles of Hemingway's female relatives—from grandmothers through his mother, Grace Hall-Hemingway—impacted his development from a gender perspective. Professor Barlowe's argument in "Hemingway's Gender Training" is that throughout the writer's lifetime, "public discussions of gender issues were as commonplace as they are now in the last years of the twentieth century." She discusses the women relatives of Hadley Richardson Hemingway as well and the importance of women's education, suggesting that Hemingway's attraction for Hadley, his first wife, was both her similarity to the strong women he had been surrounded with as a youngster and an adolescent—and her difference from those women. In this essay, which is both biographical and cultural, Barlowe provides much previously uncorrelated information: readers learn more about the gender-linked riddles that marked both Hemingway's writing and his life.

That two of the six essays collected here deal with gender and sex roles accurately reflects the interest readers have evinced in this dimension of the Hemingway fiction during the past twenty years. Late in the 1960s critics began questioning the ready-to-hand interpretations of Hemingway's fictions, that the aesthetic was shaped around the "code hero" whose stoicism made him the brave, if dead, protagonist of modernism. Robert Jordan from *For Whom the Bell Tolls* did not survive the Spanish Civil War, but his image changed American writing from 1940 to the Vietnam conflict; vestiges of Jordan remain even in such antiwar works as *The Things They Carried* or *Dispatches*. *The Old Man and the Sea*'s Santiago was cut from the same mold, although he lived through his physical and psychological ordeal. Working backward from Jordan, however, what were readers to do with Frederic Henry, the deserter, or Jake Barnes, the lover of the bullfight who sold out the most promising young matador to his own aging lover, Brett Ashley?

Most criticism of Hemingway's works then focused on his male characters. During the 1980s critics both female and male began assessing his women characters, at first pointing to some artificially constructed "feminine" model that seemed less than realistic. Readers were increasingly fascinated by—and similarly skeptical of—Hemingway's female characters. More than a shift in focus from one sex to the other, readers found themselves interested in scenes, and entire themes, that they had not noticed in earlier readings.[3] Hemingway's fiction, for the modern reader, came to bear little resemblance to those same works that critics at mid-century had analyzed—differently—with such relentless thoroughness. Criticism then moved to the language used between men and women characters, then to the structural dynamics of relationships, and finally to outright considerations of gender. Mark Spilka's 1990 study, *Hemingway's Quarrel with Androgyny,* provided a point of departure for a number of subsequent readings, among them Nancy R. Comley and Robert Scholes's *Hemingway's Genders: Rereading the Hemingway Text.* The essays by Elkins and Barlowe serve as capstone comments to this important on-going discourse.

Whenever critics publish assessments of Hemingway's works, they hear echoing within their consciousness the author's famous statement about one of his early critics who, according to Hemingway, "think that literary history, or the secret of creative writing, lies in old laundry lists . . . . Please do not co-operate with him in any way" (*Ernest Hemingway: Selected Letters, 1917–1961* 805). Were Hemingway living today, his presence would affect the kinds of interpretations being made; but the point is moot: if he had lived to publish his own late works, criticism itself would be less speculative and more informed. Because so much recent Hemingway criticism has dealt with the posthumously published books, particularly with *A Moveable Feast* and *The Garden of Eden,* as well as with the results of intensive manuscript study, this collection does not include essays specifically about those matters.

It also does not include excerpts from two essential treatments of Hemingway's writing: Toni Morrison's 1992 *Playing in the Dark: Whiteness and the Literary Imagination* (in which Hemingway's use of black characters and Africanist tropes is studied) and John W. Crowley's *The White Logic, Alcoholism and Gender in American Modernist Fiction* (1994). In the latter book, Crowley defines new terms (for example, "the drunk narrative") for the work of all modernist writers, not only Hemingway, and brings into focus the ways in which alcohol impacted American modernism in substantive ways, not all of them biographical.

The other essays in this collection add a further chronological dimension to the reader's understanding of the Hemingway *oeuvre*. Frederic Svoboda approaches the core of Hemingway's thematic canon in his discussion of the author's uses of war and love, coupled with the omnipresent specter of loss and mitigated with the author's fascination for the wilderness. As Svoboda points out, nothing Hemingway ever wrote was simple. Judging from the comparative success of the 1996 Richard Attenborough film, *In Love and War*, Hemingway's combination of tragic elements still seduces viewers and readers. Linda Wagner-Martin explores the uses Henry James, Ford Madox Ford, and other early modernist writers made of these same themes, as she traces some possible parallels between the writing of Hemingway's contemporaries and his own work. Both essays provide quantities of new information—and new insight—about what time is showing to be that greatest of American modernist innovators.

NOTES

1. See Hemingway's letter of Dec. 4, 1960, written "To Whom It May Concern," exonerating his fourth wife Mary of any responsibility for Hemingway's finances or "illegal acts" (*Letters* 909). The letter was written from the Mayo Clinic, Rochester, Minnesota.

2. The most thorough assessment of the cultural impact of Hemingway (in many regards, although not in the sphere of fashion) is John Raeburn's *Fame Became of Him: Hemingway as Public Writer* (Bloomington: Indiana University Press, 1984).

3. For an ongoing assessment of critical issues, see the introductions to my previous collections of Hemingway criticism: Linda Welshimer Wagner, ed., *Ernest Hemingway: Five Decades of Criticism*, 1974; Linda W. Wagner, ed., *Ernest Hemingway: Six Decades of Criticism*, 1987; and Linda Wagner-Martin, ed., *Ernest Hemingway: Seven Decades of Criticism*, 1998 (all East Lansing: Michigan State University Press); and Linda Wagner-Martin, ed., *New Essays on "The Sun Also Rises"* (Cambridge: Cambridge University Press, 1987). One very interesting shift in the composition of the group of critics who write

on Hemingway is that in the 1974 collection, only a few essays included were by women scholars. By the 1998 collection, however, 40 percent of the essays included were by women. Hemingway had gone from being considered a macho writer that very few women scholars admired to being a writer with high visibility—and high interest—for the literary community at large.

WORKS CITED

Hemingway, Ernest. Quoted in George Plimpton's *Paris Review* interview with the author in *Ernest Hemingway: Five Decades of Criticism*. Ed. Linda Welshimer Wagner [Wagner-Martin]. East Lansing: Michigan State University Press, 1974. 35.

————. *Ernest Hemingway: Selected Letters, 1917–1961*. Ed. Carlos Baker. New York: Scribner's, 1981.

Tompkins, Jane P. "Criticism and Feeling," *College English* 39. 2 (Oct. 1977): 171–78.

Ernest Hemingway
1899–1961

A Brief Biography

Michael Reynolds

Born in a Chicago suburb on July 21, 1899, Ernest Hemingway was a child of the twentieth century, responding to its every pressure, recording its progress, and aging as it aged. His life seemed to embody the promise of America: with good fortune, hard work, talent, ambition, and a little ruthlessness a man can create himself in the image of his choosing. As a young man in Paris, Hemingway dedicated himself to his writing, and he let nothing interfere with his goal, not parents nor wives, not friends nor children. He created a public persona to match his prose, becoming the person he wanted to be. Like other self-made Americans, however, Hemingway's invented self was a mask that he wore with less and less ease as he grew older. Despite this public image, his raucous life and several wives, and the critics who turned on him, he left stories and novels so starkly moving that some have become a permanent part of our cultural inheritance.

Before he turned twenty-five Ernest Hemingway was already friends with James Joyce, Ezra Pound, and Gertrude Stein, and he had written most of the stories that were published as *In Our Time* (1925). Before he was thirty Hemingway had buried his father (a suicide) and written two of the best novels to come from his generation: *The Sun Also Rises* (1926) and *A Farewell to Arms* (1929). At thirty-six he reported the Spanish Civil War to neutral

Americans. At forty-four he reported on the Normandy invasion from a landing craft off Omaha Beach. At forty-six he married his fourth wife. At fifty-three he won the Pulitzer Prize for fiction and survived two plane crashes in Africa. At fifty-four the Nobel Prize was his. On the morning of July 2, 1961, Ernest Hemingway slipped two shells into his favorite shotgun and quite deliberately blew the top of his head away. He was survived by three wives, three sons, numerous rumors, five unpublished books, and a distinguished if frequently misunderstood body of work.

The Oak Park Years: 1899–1917

Hemingway's birthplace, Oak Park, Illinois, sits four square on the Illinois prairie, eight miles west of downtown Chicago, where it was developed to hold at bay the corruption of the city. With its insistence on constant vigil against corrupting forces, the Village of Oak Park, as it called itself, put tremendous pressures on its sons and daughters. In the village of his youth, Hemingway was theoretically protected by city ordinances from uncensored movies, boxing matches, any information on venereal disease or birth control, all forms of gambling and prostitution, and all consumption of alcohol. Until he turned eighteen, Hemingway could not legally buy cigarettes, play billiards, drive a car, or own a cap gun within the Village limits. Unless accompanied by a parent or responsible adult, young Hemingway, governed by the Village curfew, could not be out of the house after 8 P.M. in the fall and winter, and after 9 P.M. in spring and summer. That Hemingway rebelled against these pressures is not surprising; in fact, had that first generation of this century not rebelled, it would have been strange indeed.

Oak Park was a bastion of progressive Republicans, who voted overwhelmingly for Theodore Roosevelt when he ran on the Bull Moose ticket in 1912. Morally conservative, Oak Parkers were equally zealous to have the newest and the best—nothing was too modern for the Village except jazzy music and pool halls. They had the most advanced city water system available, an extraordinary school system, and well-lighted streets. The Scoville

Institute, which housed the large public library, was a continuous source of visiting lecturers from the University of Chicago. Each year the Chicago Symphony performed at least once in Oak Park. Numerous clubs and civic organizations provided a steady flow of ideas and entertainment. Hardly a week went by without its musical evening, play, public lecture, or amateur minstrel show. In those more innocent years before the Great European War, Oak Park was self-contained, a world to which its sons returned from the earth's far corners to give magic-lantern lectures on Africa, the Holy Land, and China. Its churches supported missionaries to Africa; no national disaster went without its Oak Park drive to help the needy. It was a hometown about which Hemingway, unlike most American writers, never wrote a single story.

Ernest Hemingway grew up in the bosom of a well-known, extended, and respected family, college educated at Wheaton, Oberlin, and Rush Medical School, a family whose sense of civic responsibility was strong and whose interests were divided among medicine, the Congregational Church, and real estate. Ernest's father, Clarence Edmonds Hemingway, was a physician. His grandfather Anson Hemingway helped develop the Chicago suburb; his uncle George Hemingway continued the practice, dealing in real estate, home insurance, and mortgages. Uncle Willoughby Hemingway was a medical missionary in China, returning periodically with amazing presents and even more amazing tales from Asia; Aunt Grace Hemingway was a storyteller on the Chautauqua circuit. Although Hemingway was sometimes embarrassed by his mother's free spirit and frightened by his father's retreat into depressions, his early years were not scarred by divorce or abuse; he grew up among his several sisters respecting his elders, submitting to discipline, and behaving like a good bad boy.

With plenty of parental and community rules, it was easy to be bad in Oak Park and just as easy to be forgiven, for the Hemingway name was a substantial one within the community. There were nothing shabby about the two-story Hemingway house on North Kenilworth, with its seven bedrooms, two full baths and two half baths, a large music studio, a living room of comparable size, dining room and kitchen, Dr. Hemingway's medical office, and a large screened porch. Ernest, along with his four sisters and one brother—Marcelline (1898), Ursula (1902), Madelaine (1904), Carol (1911), and Leicester (1915)—lived in a respectable neighborhood of businessmen, salesmen, doctors, and dentists who took the train each morning into Chicago proper, where they worked, returning each evening at supper.

In 1904 horses outnumbered automobiles 490 to 30 in Oak Park. Within a few years the Village was bragging that it housed more automobiles per capita than any other town in America. John Farson, the town's wealthy banker, owned a Franklin, a Packard, two Wintons, and a white Cadillac. In 1907 Dr. Hemingway's horse ran away down Oak Park Avenue, smashing his buggy against a tree. When Ernest was twelve, his father still made his rounds in a buggy. By 1914 the doctor was driving a black Ford that was stolen from in front of the Municipal Building and recovered the next day in South Side Chicago. By 1912 the Hemingway house on North Kenilworth was electrified and had a telephone. Soon villagers who had grown up on farms were complaining about smelly chickens and crowing roosters disturbing their lives. Times were changing.

In October 1913 Oak Parkers were horrified by the new, lascivious dances that had made their way into the country club dances and once sedate living rooms:

> The music of the bagnio finds its way to every piano, and our young people habitually sing songs, words and music produced by degenerates. . . . Now the dance has come from the brothel to take its place beside the nasty music and the sex gown. Ever since the group dance gave way to the waltz, the influence of the dissolute has been growing until now. . . . We must go to South America and bring to Oak Park the tango and the maxie. Everybody is "doing it, doing it" in the words of one of our most popular songs. (*Oak Leaves* paper)

When Grace Hall-Hemingway, as Ernest's mother hyphenated her last name, designed their Kenilworth house, she included a music studio and recital hall thirty-feet square with a vaulted ceiling and a narrow balcony. It was here that she gave music and voice lessons and scheduled her student recitals, and where she composed and practiced her own music, which was marketed by two different publishing houses. Today her lyrics, mostly written for contraltos like herself, are as dated as the long Victorian dresses that she wore until her death in 1951, but they are no more sentimental than most turn-of-the-century popular music. Incurably optimistic, she was the energy source in the Hemingway household, a woman always on stage, a personality that could not be ignored, a person, in fact, not unlike her eldest son, Ernest.

In a village filled with amateurs, Grace was a professional musician whose classically trained skills became her identity and her freedom. Wherever one went in Oak Park, Grace was singing by invitation. At the Third Congregational Church she was chairperson of the music committee and directed the fifty children in the vested choir and orchestra. After he left home, Hemingway obscured his mother's talents and personality by professing to hate her and to hold her responsible for his father's 1928 suicide. Ironically, it was from his mother that Hemingway's boundless energy and enthusiasm came. No one who met mother or son ever forgot either of them.

When young Hemingway was not hearing his mother practice her varied musical routines, or her students at her lessons, or himself on his cello, he was attending the annual high school student opera where he and Marcelline were in the orchestra together for two years. The impact of his musical training, both formal and casual, was long lasting. He continued to listen to classical music all of his life. During his courtship of his first wife, Hadley Richardson, piano concerts were part of their shared interests; after their marriage, Hadley replaced his mother at the piano that they rented in Paris. Out of this background came Hemingway's compulsion to public performance and his understanding of counterpoint, which he used to advantage in his writing.

Balanced against the propriety and culture of Oak Park were Hemingway's northern Michigan summers, where the family cottage was on one side of Walloon Lake and, later, his mother's farm on the other. Every July and August from his birth through the summer of 1917, Ernest explored the woods, streams, and the lake. For the first twelve years his father was with him, teaching him to hunt and fish, but after 1911, when Clarence Hemingway began to retreat into his deepening depressions, the boy was left to his own devices. Besides his several sisters for company, there were summer people in cottages like the Hemingway's all along the lake, summer friends from Horton Bay and Petoskey, and the last of the Ojibway Indians who lived in the woods close to Horton. Those summers of trout fishing, camping out, hiking, baseball games, and awakened sexuality were as important to the education of young Hemingway as were his school years in Oak Park.

Whatever else his culture taught him, young Hemingway learned early that perseverance and winning were Oak Park virtues. The Village expected its sons and daughters to bring home blue ribbons; a single loss made a football season mediocre. Like his boyhood hero, Theodore Roosevelt, Ernest was determined to excel in physical activities: twice he ran the high school cross-country race; twice he finished last. He played lightweight football until his late growth got him on the varsity team his senior year. Slow afoot and a little clumsy, he was a second-string interior lineman. He managed the swimming team, where his event was the "plunge," swimming underwater for distance. He captained the water polo team. When he got his height, he also got boxing gloves. Later in Europe he took up tennis, skiing, and the luge. He always admired professional boxers and baseball players and, later, bullfighters.

In high school Hemingway took the then-standard pre-college curriculum: six semesters of science, four of math, six of Latin, eight semesters of English literature and composition, four semesters of history, two semesters of applied music, and another two years of orchestra. In Latin, young Hemingway translated his Cicero; in history he wrote essays on Greek tyrants and the Marathon campaign and outlined the Punic Wars. In English courses, all of which required weekly writing and the study of composition, young Hemingway read the classic myths, Chaucer, Spenser, Shakespeare, Milton, Pope, the British Romantics, Walter Scott, Dickens, George Eliot, Tennyson, Browning, and Matthew Arnold. He spent ten weeks studying the history of the

English language, four weeks on formal rhetoric, and an entire semester of his senior year solely on prose composition. Along with his classmates, Hemingway memorized the opening lines of Chaucer's General Prologue to the *Canterbury Tales* and the then-standard ration of Shakespeare soliloquies (*Hemingway's Reading 1910–1940* 39–43). Whatever the course, humanities or science, there were always written assignments: weekly book reports, essays, and term papers. Hemingway outlined his reading of *Macbeth* and *Hamlet* and wrote reports on the anatomy of grasshoppers, the necessity of life insurance, the need for a standing army, and the causes of the American Revolution.

Hemingway also wrote humorous pieces for the school newspaper and the literary magazine. "Bill 3127 Introduced by Senator Hemingway" put the hunting of policemen under the game laws, making it a misdemeanor to kill them out of season. And like any Oak Parker, he could easily roll out his biblical parody:

> It is written that in the Library thou shalt not chew gum. Thou shalt not covet thy neighbor's magazine orally. Thou shalt not play tic tat-toe with Toots Johnson. Thou shalt not match pennies with Reed Milliken. Thou shalt not throw paper wads with Jim Adams. . . . Thou shalt not kid the Jane that sitteth upon thy right hand, nor kick the boob who sitteth across from thee, (Hemingway Collection, John F. Kennedy Library, Boston [Kennedy Library])

In his high school translation of Cicero, Hemingway emphasized three lines that might well have been his motto during those years: "I pray Cataline to what point will you try our patience. How long will you still mock our rage. To what limit will you display your ungoverned insolence" (Hemingway Collection, Kennedy Library).

Most of his courses required collateral reading in both the high school library and the Scoville Institute. Besides required texts, Hemingway also found time to read the books he enjoyed at age sixteen, the short stories of O. Henry, Rudyard Kipling's tales of empire, and Stewart Edward White's version of the strenuous life. From the Scoville's collection, Hemingway borrowed books, particularly during the summer, and frequently had late fees to pay. He may never have gone to college, but in Oak Park he acquired the cultural background he needed for the next step in his life (*The Young Hemingway*).

Early Journalism and the Great War: 1917–1921

In April 1917 President Woodrow Wilson, who had promised to keep America out of the European war that had begun three years earlier, asked Congress to make the world safe for democracy by saving those countries we now called our allies. That June, Hemingway graduated from high school and spent his last completely idyllic summer at Walloon Lake, where he turned eighteen, still too young to enlist in the army. In October of that year the Russian revolution overthrew Czar Nicholas and declared a separate peace with the Austro-Hungarian enemy. Late that month the Austrians broke through the Italian alpine lines at Caporetto, precipitating the greatest single defeat of the war. That same month Ernest Hemingway, with help from his Missouri relatives, signed on as a cub reporter for the Kansas City *Star*, where he said he "learned to write a simple, declarative sentence."

Hemingway also learned the *Star's* style sheet: short first paragraphs, vigorous language, no superfluous words, few adjectives, no trite phrases. For seven months young Hemingway covered the usual beats assigned to raw recruits: city council, train station, police station, and hospital emergency room. By March 1918 he wrote home that "we are having a laundry strike here and I am handling the police beat. The violence stories. [They are] wrecking trucks, running them over cliffs, and yesterday they murdered a non union guard. For over a month I have averaged a column a day" (Hemingway Collection, Kennedy Library). The romance of the newsman as crime fighter was part of what pulled young Hemingway into journalism. Three years later he would write nascent stories about a young reporter, Punk Alford, solving violent crimes.

As eager as most American males of his age to experience the

Great European War, Hemingway joined the Missouri Home Guard, which was eventually called to active duty. By that time Hemingway was already in Italy, a volunteer ambulance driver for the American Red Cross. After two weeks of limited action at Schio, he volunteered to man a rolling canteen on the Piave River front. There on the night of July 8, 1918, after barely a month in the war zone, young Hemingway was blown up by an Austrian trench mortar. He was not yet nineteen. All that summer and fall he recovered from his leg wounds in the Milan Red Cross hospital, where his nurse was Agnes von Kurowsky, an attractive young American woman eight years his senior. Although Agnes found Ernest handsome and entertaining, their relationship loomed larger in his mind than in hers. When he returned to America on January 21, 1919, he thought they were engaged to be married, but in March she wrote, breaking off whatever the relationship might have been, saying that she was far too old for him (*Hemingway's First War*).

In January 1920, still limping from his war wound and trading on his apprenticeship in Kansas City, Hemingway appeared at the Toronto *Star* desk looking for part-time work. The city editor agreed to buy Hemingway's stories on a piece by piece basis as they suited the needs of the paper. This arrangement produced Hemingway features on dental schools, prize fights, free shaves, and trout fishing. (*Dateline: Toronto—The Complete Toronto "Star" Dispatches, 1920–1924*). When Hemingway left Toronto in May 1920 to return to Chicago, his loose arrangement with the *Star* remained in place; over the next twenty months the paper regularly printed Hemingway features on rum-running and Chicago gangsters. During this same period, Hemingway was courting Hadley Richardson, a St. Louis woman eight years older than himself. They were married at Horton Bay on September 3, 1921, and immediately began planning to move to Italy.

In Chicago the new couple enjoyed the company and storytelling of Sherwood Anderson, who advised Ernest that a would-be writer should go to Paris, not Italy. At the time, Hemingway was churning out copy for the short lived *Cooperative Commonwealth* magazine for which he was editor, writer, and general factotum. The magazine soon went bankrupt in a scandal, leaving the Hemingways free to leave Chicago for Paris. Armed with Sherwood Anderson's letters of introduction to Gertrude Stein, Ezra Pound, and Sylvia Beach, Hemingway traveled as a special correspondent to the Toronto *Star*, which allowed him to submit features on a per piece basis and occasionally to work for weekly wages and expenses while covering major European news events (*Young Hemingway*). On January 9, 1922, he and Hadley moved into an inexpensive, fourth-floor walk-up apartment in the heart of Paris's Latin Quarter.

The Paris Years: 1922–1930

That first year in Paris, Hemingway had little time to work on his novel begun in Chicago. Not only were there the distractions of the city (galleries, cafés, racetracks, boxing matches) and the demands of newfound friends (Beach, Stein, Pound, Bill Bird), but there were also the demands of his newspaper work. During a twenty-month period in Europe, Hemingway filed more than eighty-eight stories with the Toronto *Star*, all but a few of which were printed. Between January 1922 and September 1923 the *Star* printed Hemingway's submissions, which ranged from local color ("American Bohemians in Paris a Weird Lot") to winter sports ("Try Bob-Sledding If You Want Thrills") and the Great War ("A Veteran Visits Old Front, Wishes He Had Stayed Away"). The *Star* also sent Hemingway to cover four important events: the Genoa Economic Conference (Apr. 6–27, 1922), the brief but intense Greco-Turkish War (Sept. 29–Oct. 21, 1922), the Lausanne Peace Conference (Nov. 21–Dec. 15, 1922), and the French military occupation of the German Ruhr (Mar. 30–Apr. 9, 1923) (*Dateline*).

At the Genoa conference, Hemingway was an early witness to the conflict between the fascist right and the Bolshevik left that would dominate his century. "The Fascisti," he wrote, "make no distinctions between socialists, communists, republicans or members of co-operative societies. They are all Reds and dangerous" (*By-Line: Ernest Hemingway, Selected Articles and Dispatches of Four Decades* 28). Less than a year later at Lausanne, Hemingway described the new fascist dictator of Italy, Benito

Mussolini, as "the biggest bluff in Europe" (*By-Line* 64). There was something permanently wrong, he said, with any man who would wear a black shirt and white spats.

In September 1922 the *Star* sent Hemingway on a five-day train trip to Constantinople, where he covered the short but violent Greco-Turkish War that culminated with the Turks burning Smyrna and the Greeks retreating hopelessly from Thrace. He wrote:

> It is a silent procession. Nobody even grunts. It is all they can do to keep moving. . . . A husband spreads a blanket over a woman in labor in one of the carts to keep off the driving rain. She is the only person making a sound. Her little daughter looks at her in horror and begins to cry. And the procession keeps moving. (*Dateline* 232)

These events began Hemingway's serious political education, giving him a privileged view of the postwar political leaders setting Europe's agenda: Clemenceau, Tchitcherin, Barthou, Lloyd George, and Mussolini. He wrote about anarchists, anti-Semitism, fascism, power politics, disarmament, German inflation, Paris nightlife, Spanish bullfights, and German trout fishing. And wherever he went, he always told his readers how to live well in another country: where to stay, what to eat, which wine to choose, how to get the most for their money. While covering the stories, Hemingway developed his admiration for the insider, the experienced man who knows the language, food, and customs of the country. As a foreign correspondent, such expert knowledge was expected of him; when he had it, he used it; when he lacked firsthand experience, he pretended to it with such ease that we later believed him to have written nothing that was not autobiographical. This bilingual insider, adapt at European travel, became the trademark of his later fiction, which was frequently set in a foreign country (Stephens 43–83).

Hemingway's short journalistic course in the sociopolitical aftermath of the Great War rubbed his Oak Park Republicanism up against European socialism. The impact added to his sense of being a man without a political home, a man more opposed to fascism than socialism but distrustful of all government. The experience also provided him with character types, themes, and images that would appear regularly in his fiction to the very end of his life. Jake Barnes's journalism (*The Sun Also Rises*), the socialist subtext in *A Farewell to Arms*, Harry's story of Constantinople in "The Snows of Kilimanjaro," Colonel Cantwell's return to the site of his first wound (*Across the River and Into the Trees*), and the Paris streets of *A Moveable Feast* are firmly rooted in Hemingway's Toronto journalism (Stevens 237–78, 362–77).

While covering the Lausanne Peace Conference in the early winter of 1922, Ernest asked Hadley to join him for a vacation at Chamby. Packing up most of her husband's Paris fiction, including the novel begun in Chicago, Hadley booked a seat on the night train to Switzerland. While buying mineral water at the station, she left her luggage unattended in her compartment. She returned to find that a thief had stolen the valise containing Ernest's writing. In tears, she arrived in Lausanne to face him with what he later reconstructed as one of his most painful experiences. Evidence now indicates that it was less traumatic than he remembered, for he apparently did not immediately return to Paris to check with the police or the station lost and found; nor did he post a meaningful reward (*Hemingway: The Paris Years* 84–104; Mellow). Shortly after he returned from Paris to Chamby, Hadley became pregnant, and reluctantly they began talking of moving back to a full-time newspaper job in Canada.

Despite the loss of his unfinished novel, Hemingway was not deeply discouraged about his creative future. Two of his best new stories—"My Old Man" and "Up in Michigan"—survived his loss, and Ernest was committed to be part of Bill Bird's inquest into the state of contemporary letters, edited by Ezra Pound. In January 1923 six of his poems appeared in *Poetry* magazine; in February Robert McAlmon agreed to publish a limited edition of Ernest's poems and stories. By March, Hemingway had produced six vignettes that he sent to Jane Heap's *Little Review* where, with another of his poems, they were published the following October. In August, two weeks before their ship sailed for Canada, McAlmon's edition of his *Three Stories & Ten Poems* appeared in the Shakespeare and Company bookstore, and Ernest finished the last short sketches that would complete the book that Bill Bird was to publish as *in our time* (1924). These "unwritten stories," as he called them, brought together what he had learned from Gertrude Stein, James Joyce, and his journalism. Some came from direct experience; some were based on the experience of others. Readers, then and later, were unable to tell the difference between the two types, which began the false notion that Hemingway first lived the experience and then wrote about it. All of his writing life, he insisted that his best writing was what he made up, but readers refused to believe it.

Returning to Toronto, Ernest expected to be welcomed as the *Star's* foreign correspondent. Instead, he found himself working with a new editor, who generally disliked primadonnas and particularly disliked Hemingway. No sooner did Ernest report for work than he was put on the night train to Kinston to cover the prison break of four convicts, including the bank robber Red Ryan (*Paris Years* 145–6). Two years later, while making notes for a novel, Hemingway vowed to write a picaresque novel about Ryan's escape from prison. "It will be the story of a tough kid," he said, "lucky for a long time and finally smashed by fate" (Hemingway Collection, Princeton University Library).

Although he never wrote the Red Ryan novel, his next fiction—the unpublished and unfinished "A New Slain Knight"— has a criminal breaking from custody and a central character who is a professional revolutionary with criminal tendencies (*Homecoming* 45–57). In *To Have and Have Not*, Hemingway gave us the fishing guide turned criminal in Harry Morgan who is gut-shot while killing three Cuban bank robbers. Many of his male characters live lives apart from the social norm, men without family, without homes, lonely, self-reliant men, men not so distantly related to Red Ryan.

Hemingway's first son, John Hadley Nicanor ("Bumby"), was born that October in Toronto while Ernest was returning from another out-of-town assignment. Furious with his editor, with Toronto, and with his inability to write for two masters—himself and the *Star*—Ernest quit his last full-time job in January 1924; he, Hadley, and their son returned to Paris that same month to live on her small trust fund and whatever money he could make writing.

They found an inexpensive, cold-water flat above a saw mill, close to Ezra Pound's apartment and near the heart of Montparnasse. Later he would mythologize his early Paris years in *A Moveable Feast*, insisting that he and Hadley were among the very poor on the Left Bank. The Hemingways lived and dressed cheaply by design, saving their money for summer excursions to Spain and winters in the Alps. With the exchange rate of twenty-five francs to the dollar, Hadley's reduced trust funds still produced enough for them to live with some comforts, including their son's regular nanny, who kept him during the Spanish summers.

With Ezra Pound as his mentor, Sylvia Beach as his friend, and Gertrude Stein as his surrogate mother and godmother to his son, Hemingway was as well connected as a young writer could be. Pound persuaded him to work as an unpaid assistant for Ford Madox Ford, who was then publishing the short-lived but important *transatlantic review*. From that vantage point, Ernest connected with every expatriate American writer in Paris. Through Gertrude Stein's salon, he fell in love with Cézanne's landscapes and met young painters on the rise—Juan Gris, Joan Miro, Pablo Picasso. At Sylvia Beach's bookshop and lending library, he extended his education and his circle of acquaintances: George Antheil, Adrienne Monnier, Archibald MacLeish, James Joyce.

Outwardly confidant, vibrant with energy, interested in everything and anyone, laughing and joking among his café friends, young Hemingway became a featured attraction along the Americanized Left Bank of Paris. Continuously moving with his curious, slow-footed gait, he was a man on his way somewhere else, always. He was six feet tall, broad shouldered, mustached, and handsome, a man who set his own style. Whatever the activity— hunting, fishing, walking, or writing—he was intense and competitive. Whether it was the bullfights at Pamplona, the ski slopes at Schruns, or an evening at a Paris dance hall, the Hemingway experience always demanded unexpected emotional resources. Few of his male friendships lasted longer than five years, but to whatever he touched in those days he added scale and a sense of importance. Gerald Murphy said, "The lives of some of us will seem, I suppose by comparison, piddling. . . . For me, he has the violence and excess of genius."[1]

In 1925 Hemingway's first collection of short stories was published in America by the avant garde publisher Horace Liveright, who published Sherwood Anderson and Harold Loeb, friends of Hemingway. The collection, called *In Our Time*, used the vignettes from *in our time* as counterpoints between stories, several of which became Hemingway classics. This collection, influenced by Joyce's *Dubliners*, staked out subject matter, perfected techniques, and crystallized structures that Hemingway would mine over the next ten years. Here he introduced his sometime alter ego, Nick Adams, a young boy coming of age in northern Michigan. In the last and anchor story in the collection, "Big Two-Hearted River," almost nothing happens on the surface but palpable subsurface tensions keep the reader riveted. These stories—"Indian Camp," "The Doctor and the Doctor's Wife," "The End of Something," and "Three Day Blow"—were all written during the wonder year of 1924 and would eventually remake the American short story, but not immediately. Liveright published only 1,100 copies of the book, which left Hemingway deeply unhappy but legally committed to the publisher by his contract, which specified that Liveright had first refusal on his next three books.

In the early summer of 1925 Hemingway met the inventor of the flapper and the high priest of the Jazz Age, F. Scott Fitzgerald, whose novel, *The Great Gatsby*, had been recently published. Fitzgerald, at the height of his powers, was already a great admirer of Hemingway's writing, having recommended him to his editor at Scribner's, Max Perkins, on the basis of the *in our time* vignettes. Delayed by wrong addresses and the transatlantic mails, Perkins's letter to Hemingway arrived after he had accepted the Liveright contract. Determined to move Hemingway to Scribner's, Fitzgerald probably planted the idea that if Hemingway wrote a book that Liveright could not accept, his contract would be broken. That summer of 1925, after a conflicted feria at Pamplona, Hemingway wrote the first draft of *The Sun Also Rises*, which he finished in Paris that fall, but did not submit to Liveright. Instead he quickly wrote *The Torrents of Spring*, a literary satire that made fun of Sherwood Anderson's *Dark Laughter*, recently published by Liveright. When Horace Liveright received

Torrents, he understood what Hemingway was trying to do; he also was aware of Fitzgerald's meddling and the novel Hemingway had not submitted. Early in 1926 Hemingway confronted Liveright in his New York office, insisting that *Torrents* was a serious book that Liveright must publish to get *The Sun Also Rises*. Unable to afford to offend Anderson, Liveright declined, freeing Hemingway to sign with Scribner's, who published *Torrents* that May, followed in October by *The Sun Also Rises*, which Hemingway called the pig Perkins bought in the poke.

Thus began Hemingway's lifelong relationship with Charles Scribner's Sons publishing house and his relationship with Max Perkins, whose tolerance and diplomacy Ernest would sorely test over the years until Max's death in 1947. The breakthrough novel, *The Sun Also Rises* (1926), was followed by a second collection of stories, *Men without Women* (1927), which contained two stories—"Hills Like White Elephants" and "The Killers"—that were soon anthologized in numerous collections and college textbooks, ever widening Hemingway's dedicated audience. The collection also pushed into taboo subject matter, which Hemingway explored obliquely, never naming the thing itself. "Hills Like White Elephants" was about abortion, although the word is never mentioned. His subject matter—a fixed championship boxing match, a homosexual proposition, contract killers, divorce, and a disturbed war veteran—challenged the mores of mainstream fiction and continued his lifelong insistence that there were no taboo words, no forbidden subjects. But it would not be until after his death in 1961 that the works of Henry Miller, for example, could be printed in the United States.

Between 1924 and 1927 Hemingway rose from an undiscovered writer known only to the expatriate Paris crowd to become one of the most promising young writers of his generation. This newfound success was not without its costs. In April 1927 Hadley divorced him, allowing him to marry Pauline Pfeiffer (May 10, 1927), with whom he had begun an affair more than a year earlier. In his divorce settlement, he gave Hadley rights to all of the income from *The Sun Also Rises*. Fortuitously, Pauline brought with her a substantial trust fund that for the next thirteen years provided Hemingway with the means to live beyond his means.

The first substantial return on this investment was Hemingway's first bestseller, *A Farewell to Arms* (1929), the story of an American ambulance driver and a British nurse brought together during the tumult of World War One. Destined to become the premier American war novel from that debacle, the story of Frederic Henry's wounding, Catherine Barkley's unwedded pregnancy, the Italian disaster at Caporetto, the lovers' desertion of duty, and Catherine's death in childbirth spoke to America's rejection of the war and its own political isolation during the 1920s. Because *The Sun Also Rises* was a roman à clef, readers assumed that *A Farewell to Arms* was another installment in Hemingway's thinly veiled autobiography. It would be almost half a century before anyone would notice that Hemingway was not in Italy during the Italian retreat from Caporetto (*Hemingway's First War*).

The Key West Years: 1930–1939

In 1928 Ernest and Pauline returned briefly to America for the caesarean birth of his second son, Patrick. During this visit, they discovered the then-isolated pleasures of Key West fishing and Wyoming dude ranches. After spending most of 1929 in and out of their Paris apartment, the Hemingways in 1930 moved back to Key West, where Ernest began writing his *vade mecum* and explanation of the bullfight, *Death in the Afternoon* (1932). On November 1, 1930, while driving John Dos Passos from their Wyoming hunting trip into Billings, Montana, to catch the eastbound train, Hemingway, confused by the lights of an approaching car, swerved sharply on a newly graveled road, ending up in the bar-ditch with his right arm badly broken. The surgeon repaired the compound spiral fracture, binding Hemingway's humerus together with kangaroo tendon. For the next seven weeks, he was hospitalized in a great deal of pain. When Pauline arrived, she brought him books, answered his mail, and slept in the room with him, keeping his spirits from sinking lower. It was almost a full year before Hemingway's right arm returned to something like normal and the damaged nerves in his writing hand repaired themselves.

During his seven-week hospital stay in Billings, the sale of the film rights to *A Farewell to Arms* brought him a $24,000 windfall. During the Great Depression, the Hemingways were supported by Pauline's trust fund, gifts from her wealthy uncle Augustus Pfeiffer, who paid for their home in Key West and their African safari, and by income from Hemingway's writing. For the last thirty years of his life, that income was richly supplemented first by Hollywood and later by television. During his lifetime, the film sales from five of his novels and numerous short stories gave him an independence enjoyed by few American writers.

While the American economy wallowed in the worst economic depression of modern times, Hemingway experimented freely with genre, voice, and subject matter, going ten years before writing anything like a traditional novel. *Death in the Afternoon,* with its multiple voices, its stories within the narrative, and its factual framework, was a book before its time; unclassifiable, it was and remains largely ignored as a text by Hemingway critics but is pilfered freely for its pithy quotes. This non-fictive, natural history of the bullfight was, in fact, the sort of book that Hemingway's early interests in the natural world had prepared him to write. Hemingway, like many another American writer, was troubled by the idea of writing fiction, whose very definition included the sense of telling lies. Despite his insistence that he invented stories that told truths, he was never completely comfortable as a fictionalist only and preferred to write in several different modes and genres, which he did despite Scribner's appetite for his novels.

In 1933 Hemingway published his third collection of short stories, *Winner Take Nothing,* which was even more abrasive to the prevailing American moral view of itself. When two young boys walk into the train station in "Light of the World," they are confronted by five whores and a homosexual cook, with whom anyone can "interfere." In "God Rest You Merry, Gentlemen," we read a Christmas Day story in which a young boy emasculates himself with a razor to avoid sins against purity. Other stories involved homosexuality, insanity, suicide, nihilism, and veneral disease. In the anchor story, "Fathers and Sons," Nick Adams, now a father, finds he is no more capable of speaking truthfully to his son than was his own father a generation earlier. To a reading public mired in the economic woes of the Depression, this collection of stories offered no significant hope and no exit.

Winner Take Nothing was followed two years later by Hemingway's semi-nonfictional account of his 1933 African safari, *Green Hills of Africa* (1935). Mixing humor, flashbacks, literary pontification, and self-exposure with his fable on aesthetics, Hemingway once again wrote outside the reception range of the critics. In 1936 he published his most experimental short story, "The Snows of Kilimanjaro," which contained a collection of vignettes similar to those of *in our time* embedded in a larger story. Written in tandem with what was to become his most popular short story— "The Short Happy Life of Francis Macomber"—Hemingway presented, among other things, two contrasting views of American men and women.

During this period (1933–1936) Hemingway was also writing a series of personal essays, called "Letters," for the newly founded *Esquire* magazine. This forum allowed him to create a public persona that became as well known as that of many movie stars. His subject matter was himself in situ: Africa, the Gulf Stream, Paris, Spain, Cuba, Key West, wherever his interests took him. The voice was personal and frequently humorous, combative, or prophetic. In September 1935 he warned his audience about the next war, which he said would begin within two years. In September 1937 he was in Madrid reporting on the Spanish Civil War.

That October, Hemingway was on the cover of *Time* magazine, and his last experimental work from the Key West years, *To Have and Have Not*, was published to tepid reviews. What had begun as two stories about Harry Morgan, a Key West fishing guide and rum runner, expanded in the planning stage to be a complex novel comparing a Cuban revolution with a parallel revolution in Spain. The book he intended to write was abandoned, the revolutions reduced to a whisper, and the remainder cobbled together as well as he could.

The author was under self-imposed pressure to reach the newly begun Spanish Civil War, as well as pressure to find a safe haven for his recently begun affair with the twenty-nine-year-old Martha Gellhorn. With Pauline confined to Key West with their two sons, Patrick and Gregory, what safer place to conduct a love affair than Madrid under seige. The immediate results were his journalistic coverage of the war for the North American News Alliance and the short-lived *Ken* magazine; a film, *The Spanish Earth,* to which he contributed narrative; and his only play, *The Fifth Column* (1938), in which the counterintelligence agent Philip Rawlings says that the world is in for fifty years of undeclared wars and that he has signed up for the duration.

In February 1939, with his marriage to Pauline over in all but name, Hemingway took his fishing boat, the *Pilar,* to Havana, Cuba, where he took his favorite room in the Hotel Ambos Mundos and began writing what would be received as his finest novel, *For Whom the Bell Tolls.* In April, Martha Gellhorn rented and made habitable property outside of Havana, La Finca Vigía, where she and Ernest set up their writers' workshop. Ernest worked steadily on his Spanish Civil War story of the American dynamiter Robert Jordan and his epic task of destroying the bridge behind Republican lines, a story he earlier intended to use in *To Have and Have Not.* Martha, who had seen almost as much of Spain as Ernest, wisely chose to write instead about her recent stay in Prague as it prepared to face the approaching Nazi invasion.

On December 24, 1939, Hemingway left his empty Key West house for the last time as Pauline's husband. Taking with him eight hundred books and his personal belongings, including several paintings by Miro, Léger, and Juan Gris, he moved permanently into La Finca, his penultimate residence. In Europe, Hitler's blitzkrieg had overrun Poland; the war Hemingway had predicted had begun, but America was not yet a part of it. That March, Martha's new novel, dedicated to Ernest, was published as *A Stricken Field,* the title taken from a pseudo-medieval quote written for her by Hemingway. That same month, *The Fifth Column,* rewritten for the stage, opened in New York with mixed reviews.

By the end of July 1940 Hemingway delivered his completed typescript of *For Whom the Bell Tolls* to Max Perkins. On October 21 the novel appeared to ecstatic reviews; four days later Paramount Pictures offered Ernest $100,000 for the film rights. On November 4 Pauline's divorce suit against her husband on grounds of desertion was granted, leaving Ernest free to marry Martha Gellhorn on November 21. By the end of 1940 German troops occupied a fallen Paris; Japanese troops were in Hong Kong. The Battle for Britain had begun, and German submarines were turning the North Atlantic into a shooting gallery. On the homefront, Roosevelt had been reelected to an unprecedented third presidential term, and Scott Fitzgerald was dead from a heart attack. Just as the roar of the 1920s was put out by the Great Depression, the economic moaning of the 1930s was silenced by what we would call the Second World War.

The Cuban Years: 1940–1959

While the last two decades of Hemingway's life produced seven volumes of fiction and nonfiction, these years remain the murkiest and the least understood by his literary biographers. The first five years of this period were subsumed by Hemingway's various war efforts. Cuba, ruled by the dictator Batista, was a haven for spies and intelligence agencies of every stripe. When Germany declared war on the United States following the Japanese attack on Pearl Harbor in December 1941, German submarines operated freely up and down the Atlantic coast and throughout the Caribbean, sinking freighters and oil tankers at will.

All that summer of 1942, while Ernest was rearranging the contents and writing the introduction for *Men at War*, the war was close at hand, but he had no way to go to it. Too old for the draft, too controversial for the government, and too far from Key West, he had few options. In April the U.S. Marines at Bataan surrendered to the Japanese army, the worst U.S. military humiliation since the Sioux destroyed Custer. In May the German plan of Admiral Doennitz, Operation Drumbeat, began its attack on the American pipeline of war matériel flowing to England and Russia. Knowing how crucial oil, gasoline, and aviation fuel were to fighting a war, the German U-boat commanders focused on three refining centers: Aruba in the Caribbean and New Orleans and Houston in the Gulf of Mexico. Knowing that without bauxite, there was no aluminum, and without aluminum, no airplanes, the German raiders also centered on the British and Dutch Guianas, which then produced most of the ore in the western hemisphere.

The evening of February 16 was calm and warm at the entrance to Lake Maracaibo, where Venezuelan crude oil came across the bar in shallow draft tankers to be refined at Aruba. At the Lago refinery on Aruba, the graveyard shift came to work with the nightlights fully lit and flare gas burning. Each month this refinery, the world's largest, was producing 7 million barrels of gasoline, aviation fuel, and lubricants, most of which was going to support the British war effort. At 1:30 A.M., in a coordinated attack, German U-boats turned seven tankers into burning hulks, shelled the refinery with surface guns, and left without a scratch on their gray hulls. Observing the smoking ruins the next morning, the Chinese crews refused to sail without protection, forcing the refinery to shut down and Lake Maracaibo oil production to stop, having no more storage space. Nineteen ships went down that month in the Caribbean; nineteen more the next month; eleven in April; thirty-eight in May. Between February and November 1942, almost twice as many ships were sunk in this confined area than were sunk on the North Atlantic convoy routes. By the end of November 1942, 263 were on the bottom of the Caribbean Sea.[2]

While tankers were going down all around the island of Cuba, the new American ambassador, Spruille Braden, became worried about the loyalties of the 300,000 Spanish residents of Cuba, as many as 10 percent of whom were thought to be dedicated Falangists and therefore potential sources of aid to the Nazi cause. Until the FBI could find the right men for the Havana station, Braden recruited Hemingway to organize a makeshift intelligence service, an assignment that Ernest accepted enthusiastically. As Braden remembered it, Hemingway

> enlisted a bizarre combination of Spaniards: some bar tenders; a few wharf rats; some down-at-heel pelota players and former bullfighters; two Basque priests; assorted exiled counts and dukes; several Loyalists and Francistas. He built up an excellent organization and did an A-One job.[3]

Although Martha and others thought the "Crook Factory" something of a joke, Ambassador Braden thought Ernest's reports on the activities of Spanish Falangists in Cuba significant enough to include them almost verbatim in several long reports to the State Department.[4] The crucial diplomatic question was what would Cuba do if Franco's Spain joined the Axis in the war, a very real possibility given the German-Italian support of Franco's successful rebellion. In October 1942 Spruille Braden's cogent review of the Cuban situation documented the Spanish Embassy's clandestine support of the Falange, which was generating Axis rumors and propaganda. There was also the strong possibility that the Falangists were gathering information on military installations, communicating with and refueling German U-boats, and planning and executing "attempts at sabotage." Despite being outlawed by the Cuban government, the pro-Nazi Falange was both active and dangerous to American interests.[5]

Ernest's long-standing fascination with spies and counterspies was, for this brief period, completely in synch with prevalent American war fears. We were a nation on edge, expecting the worst. When crude sound detection gear picked up what seemed to be two flights of unidentified aircraft, the entire San Francisco Bay area was blacked out all the way to Sacramento for almost an hour. When Jacob Steinberg's lights failed on the Williamsburg Bridge, he made the mistake of stopping his truck. Unable to fix them, he continued on toward his Brooklyn home, never hearing the warning whistle from the soldier on guard duty at the bridge. Jacob did hear the five warning slots, however, one of which flattened a tire, another almost hitting him. In Indiana the Civilian Defense Headquarters was asked by a county official, "Would it be possible to have a bomb dropped in our county to have the people realize this country is at war?" He was told, "We're saving all bombs for Tokyo."[6] On June 13 the fears became a reality when a Nazi U-boat landed four saboteurs on the south shore of Long Island. Four days later another group of German agents was put ashore close to Jacksonville, Florida. On June 27 J. Edgar Hoover, head of the FBI, called a late evening news conference to announce that all eight agents were under arrest, their caches of explosives recovered, and the safety of the nation for the moment assured. Their objectives, he said, were the bridges leading into Manhattan, three major aluminum plants, the New York City water supply, the hydroelectric plant at Niagara Falls, and key rail centers. Shortly after noon on August 7, six of the eighth German agents were executed in a portable electric chair installed at the District of Columbia jail.[7] By the time the saboteurs were dead, 250 enemy aliens, many of them naturalized American citizens, were in jail, charged with various subversive goals, most particularly blowing up the Pennsylvania Railroad's horseshoe curve outside of Altoona.[8] And the British-Honduran businessman suspected of refueling German U-boats in the Caribbean and smuggling spies into the Panama Canal Zone was arrested by the U.S. Navy at sea.[9]

With its large international population, its critical location, and its long history of revolutionary activity, Cuba was not immune to the war fears on the mainland. In April the *Havana Post* reported that "almost fifty German, Italians and Japanese were rounded up and arrested in a swift and simultaneous action by agents of the Enemy Activities Section of the Cuban Bureau of Investigation . . . [charged with] espionage and other illicit activities on behalf of the Axis powers . . . most of those arrested are on the U.S. blacklist." Among those arrested were several associated with the German spy ring at Nuevitas, "from which port several freighters have departed during recent weeks and been later sunk by enemy subs off the Cuban coast.[10] On July 14, as Hemingway's "Crook Factory" was being formed, the FBI sent Raymond Leddy to the Havana embassy as an attaché to replace the FBI agent who could not "tell fact from rumor."[11]

By the first of May the submarine threat was so intense in the Gulf of Mexico that all shipping was stopped along the north coast of Cuba until convoys could be established.[12] Seventeen days later, a further order came down: "Movements are stopped between Gulf or Caribbean ports and U.S. Atlantic Coast . . . and from Gulf and Caribbean ports to east coast of South America."[13] In those first eight months of 1942, when attack ships and planes were few and their crews inexperienced with new electronic gear, U-boat commanders were earning Iron Crosses on every trip west. Although Havana and other Cuban ports did not contribute to the tanker traffic, the island, which barricaded a major section of the Gulf, had primary shipping lanes on all sides. In June and July of 1942, more than thirty ships were torpedoed within easy reach of the Cuban coast. Cuba was no longer an American protectorate, and the coming of war put its neutrality in a precarious position, which quickly resolved in its own best interests by declaring war against the Axis powers and cooperating with the U.S. anti-submarine efforts. Small tent outposts were established quickly on remote islands and keys off the north coast to support Sykorzky seaplanes and to act as supply bases when Anti-Submarine Warfare cutters were in the area. By mid-April Army Air Force planes using bases in Cuba were patrolling the Yucatan and Old Bahama Channels by day and later by night.

Initially undermanned and out-planned, the United States did what Americans have always done best: it improvised solutions with whatever materials were at hand. Less than a month into the war, the Coast Guard began organizing East Coast yachtsmen and small boat owners into auxiliary units. Larger private sail and motor driven ships were "rented" at a dollar a year for submarine patrols in coastal waters.[14] In late June, with shipping being sunk at unsustainable rates, the navy took desperate measures:

> Washington, June 27 (AP)—In a move to put a great fleet of small boats into the war against submarines off the Atlantic and Gulf coasts, the navy called today for all owners of seagoing craft to volunteer their services of themselves and their vessels. . . . Approximately 1,200 small boats are in such service now . . . [and] it is hoped that upward of 1,000 additional small boats for offshore navigation may be added to the auxiliary. . . . Boats found to be qualified will be equipped with radio, armament and suitable anti-submarine devices as rapidly as possible.[15]

In July the recruitment for the auxiliary patrol was intensified. Secretary of the Navy Frank Knox issued a call for "patriotic yachtsmen and small-boat owners" to come to the aid of their country, offering them the opportunity which they have been so earnestly seeking: to serve their country and combat its enemies in the sea-going manner for which their experience fits them. . . . These boats are needed right now—not only for . . . Harbor Patrol duties but for actual offensive operations against enemy submarines.[16]

By the time Secretary Knox issued his plea, Ernest Hemingway's private war against the U-boats was well under way.

From his reading about Q-Ships, as they were called in World War One, Ernest saw immediately the possibilities for the auxiliary force the U.S. Navy was recruiting. If a small and secretly armed ship could lure a German submarine to the surface, it might be able to get in the first shot, crippling the raider.[17] Early in the war, German submarines operating in the Caribbean and the Gulf of Mexico were, in fact, liable to attack on the surface, using their deck guns to conserve torpedoes. The long range Type-XY U-boat common in the Gulf was formidably armed for surface combat: a primary 105-mm. deck gun, a 37-mm. auxiliary gun, and two 20-mm. machine guns.[18] On May 2 Ernest read in the local paper of a running battle between a lightly armed tanker and a U-boat off the north coast of Cuba. Attacking on the surface with its deck gun, the submarine sank the tanker after a two-hour exchange of fire.[19]

While his "Crook Factory" continued to collect counterintelligence on Falangists and German nationals in Cuba, Hemingway was busy outfitting the *Pilar* as an armed patrol boat. On November 2, 1942, Hemingway reported to Colonel Boyden at the U.S. Embassy that he and his crew were prepared to leave for a shakedown cruise no later than November 11, providing all the "materials" required arrived in time. The pirate-black hull and newly painted dark green deck of the *Pilar* were being taken out of the water for anti-fouling paint and a new stern bearing, but in four days it would be ready for outfitting. It was vital, Hemingway said, that the training exercises with guns, grenades, and satchel charges be conducted in an area to the east of Havana if their first armed patrol was going to be along the West Coast.[20] On November 20 Hemingway; Winston Guest; Gregorio Fuentes, the cook and most experienced sailor; Pachi, the jai alai bomb thrower; and two other Cubans passed under the battlements guarding Havana harbor, moved out into the Gulf Stream, and turned eastward on their first patrol. For the next twelve months, the *Pilar* conducted several patrols, mostly in the Old Bahama Channel on Cuba's eastern edge. Although never able to attack a sub, Hemingway's crew performed needed patrol duties, including checking inlets, bays, and unhabited islands for signs of German activity.

Drinking heavily and arguing with Martha whenever he was in port, Hemingway was suffering through the longest hiatus he had ever experienced in his writing career. Since finishing *For Whom the Bell Tolls* thirty months earlier, he had written nothing but an introduction for *Men at War* (1942). During this same period, Martha had published a short story collection, *The Heart of Another* (1941), and begun her next novel, *Liana* (1944), which she finished in June 1943. All that year and into 1944, Hemingway stayed in Cuba, where he returned to his self-appointed submarine patrols and wrote nothing. At the end of 1943 Martha left the Finca to cover the European war for *Collier's* magazine; she urged her husband to come with her. He brooded alone at the Finca, where his typewriter continued to gather dust until 1945. At the peak of his career, the foremost American male novelist went six years without writing any new fiction. Only later would he recognize this hiatus as the onset of the severe depression that would eventually destroy Hemingway just as it destroyed his father before him. By this point, the Hemingway-Gellhorn marriage was finished in all but name. In April 1944 Ernest signed on as a war correspondent for *Collier's,* displacing Martha; by the end of May, he had met Mary Welsh Monks, his fourth wife to be, and Martha had closed the door behind her.

Between June and December 1944 Hemingway covered the European war with manic energy, deliberately putting himself in dangerous situations. On D-Day, June 6, rather than observe the Normandy landing from the relative safety of the correspondents' ship, Hemingway went aboard a landing craft to get a closer view. The result was his essay, "Voyage to Victory," which remains vintage Hemingway:

I saw a ragged shell hole through the steel plates forward of
her pilothouse where an 88-mm. German shell had punched
through. Blood was dripping from the shiny edges of the hole
into the sea with each roll of the LCI. Her rails and hull had
been befouled by seasick men, and her dead were laid forward
of her pilothouse. (*By-Line* 351)

At the end of that month, he flew twice on Royal Air Force mis-
sions intercepting German rockets headed for England. In July he
was attached briefly to George Patton's Third Army before trans-
ferring to Colonel Charles "Buck" Lanham's Twenty-Second Division of the Fourth Army. By August, when *Collier's* published
"London Fights the Robots," Hemingway was leading a small
group of French irregulars and unattached GIs toward the liberation of Paris and the Ritz Bar.

In and out of Paris all that fall, Hemingway alternated between the battlefields of France and the bedroom of the Ritz
Hotel, where his affair with Mary Welsh Monks was proceeding
as well as the war effort. When he was not sick with colds and
sore throats or suffering with recurring headaches from a severe
concussion he sustained in London, Hemingway was by turns
brave, gentle, obsessive, foolhardy, loving, and brutal: a man surf-
ing along the edge of his manic drive. That fall *Collier's* published
his two essays, "Battle for Paris" and "How We Came to Paris."
On October 8 a U.S. Army court-martial cleared Hemingway of
conduct forbidden to correspondents as non-combatants, conduct like carrying weapons, shooting Germans, and behaving
like a field officer. Under oath, Hemingway lied about his field activities prior to the liberation of Paris, lies for which he suffered
deep remorse (Hemingway Collection, Kennedy Library).

On November 15, 1944, Hemingway rejoined Lanham's
Twenty-Second Division for nineteen days of the bloodiest fighting he or anyone else saw during the war. On the German-
Belgium border, in rolling, thickly forested hills cut by muddy
logging roads, the German defense had prepared thick bunkers,
thousands of mines, and heavy artillery zeroed in on all crossroads. In snow and winter mud, both sides suffered incredible ca-
sualties under the worst conditions. It was here that Hemingway

verifiably killed a German soldier who was charging across the clearing toward Lanham's command post. Attack and counterattack finally left 33,000 American troops killed, wounded, or missing in the action they called Hurtgenwald. That Hemingway survived this battle was more a matter of chance than of caution on his part (Hemingway Collection Kennedy Library).

Sick, weary, his speech slurred from concussion, and his memory temporarily damaged, Hemingway had seen enough of the war. He returned to New York and then to Cuba, where Mary Welsh Monks joined him in May. The following month Hemingway wrecked his car, cutting Mary's face while breaking four of his ribs and reinjuring his head. That summer of 1945, as the war on both fronts came to an end, Hemingway began putting his writing life back together, working on what he said would be his "trilogy." In September he filed an uncontested suit for divorce from Martha on the grounds of her desertion. In November a $112,000 sale of movie rights to two short stories provided him the financial freedom to write without pressure to publish. Through the remainder of his life, sales to Hollywood and to the fledgling television industry kept him financially secure.

On March 14, 1946, Ernest and Mary Welsh, both recently divorced from other mates, were married in Havana. By mid-June he claimed to have finished 1,000 pages on a new novel; by December he said it was 1,200 pages but would not be finished for several months. For the first seven months of 1947 Hemingway remained in Cuba, writing steadily through March. On June 17 Max Perkins died suddenly in New York; in August, Hemingway, morose, overweight, and ears buzzing, was diagnosed with high blood pressure. From this point to his death, he was to fight a holding action against hypertension, diabetes, depression, paranoia, and perhaps hemochromatosis—many of the same problems that led to his father's suicide and would, years later, lead to his younger brother's suicide.

The Hemingways spent that fall and winter of 1947, as they frequently would, hunting game birds in and around Ketchum, Idaho. Returning to Cuba in February, Hemingway continued writing on what may have become *Islands in the Stream*. Because the bulk of his work during these later years was unpublished by the author, and because he seems to have been working simultaneously on what we later received as discrete texts that he saw as a trilogy (*Islands, Garden of Eden, A Moveable Feast*), nothing definitive can yet be said about this period's texts. It is, however, becoming increasingly evident that these three posthumous texts, mixing fact and fiction, engage thematically the role of the artist in modern times and have at their core, for good or ill, the experience of Paris in the 1920s. It was to be a trilogy unlike any other, bringing to closure the experiments begun in Paris twenty-five years earlier. Because these posthumous publications were edited by three different editors, one of whom's credentials included knowing nothing about Hemingway, neither the general reader nor most scholars yet have access to the texts as Hemingway wrote them.

From September 1948 through April 1949 Ernest and Mary lived in northern Italy, principally Venice and Cortina, and visited sites from Hemingway's first war. Nostalgic returns to previously good places became a feature of Hemingway's later years—Italy, Pamplona, Africa, Paris—and each return was less than happy. In Italy, between duck hunting in the Venetian marshes and skiing in the Dolomites, Hemingway met and became infatuated with an eighteen-year-old Venetian beauty, Adriana Ivancich. Mary tolerated her husband's behavior with what grace she could manage. In January, Mary broke her leg skiing, and in March, Hemingway's eye, infected with erysipelas, put him in the Padua hospital. Before they returned to Cuba at the end of April, Hemingway had begun the story of a Venetian duck hunt.

For six months at the Finca, Hemingway, having put aside his trilogy, used the duck-hunt story as a framing device for a novel—*Across the River and Into the Trees*. Aaron Hotchner, acting as Hemingway's sounding board and agent, negotiated an $85,000 price for the novel's serial rights. Hemingway took Mary, Hotchner, and the manuscript back to Paris, where he finished the story in a hotel room at the Ritz. Just before Christmas 1949, the group drove through the south of France, revisiting, among other places, Aigues Morte and Grau-du-Roi, where Ernest and Pauline once honeymooned. The Hemingways spent two months in Venice before returning to Paris and eventually to

Cuba early in April. There Hemingway revised the book galleys for *Across the River;* in September the courtly love story of the dying American colonel and the teenage Venetian beauty received overwhelmingly negative reviews. By the end of 1950 Adriana and her mother were visiting at the Finca, where Hemingway finished *Islands in the Stream* and may have begun *The Old Man and the Sea.* Mary, reduced to household drudge and the object of her husband's ridicule, wanted out of her marriage but did not act on her feelings.

Fifty-one years old, sicker than most knew, and eleven years without a successful novel, Ernest Hemingway seemed to have reached the end of his career. Would-be biographers and scholars were in general agreement that this was the end of the line. Meanwhile, in a two-month burst of writing, Hemingway completed the first draft of *The Old Man and the Sea* and returned to add Thomas Hudson's last sub chase to the *Islands* manuscript, which he declared finished in May 1951. What was looking like a banner year turned to sorrow when Grace Hall-Hemingway died at the end of June and Pauline Hemingway, after a violent phone argument with Ernest, died unexpectedly in October. These two losses were followed by Charles Scribner's mortal heart attack in February 1952.

Each of these deaths diminished Hemingway's reserves but contributed to his art in ways that a writer can feel but not explain, refueling what seemed to be exhausted supplies. No matter how much he claimed to have hated his mother, he was ever the dutiful son, caring for her financially, writing occasionally, and telephoning her regularly. At the heart of him, he could not avoid seeing her face in his mirror. In March, he began a story, "The Last Good Country," in which the mother stoutly stands up in authority in defense of her son. Pauline's death, coming on the heels of his Grau-du-Roi revisit, took him back to the *The Garden of Eden* manuscript. Charles Scribner's death may have been the hardest of all to bear, for without him Ernest lost his last father surrogate to whom he could take his work seeking approval. At fifty-two and about to receive his greatest public adulation, Ernest Hemingway was more alone than he had ever been in his life.

Life magazine, having paid $40,000 for the serial rights, published and sold five million copies of its September 1, 1952, issue containing *The Old Man and the Sea* in its entirety. The Book of the Month Club bought the novella, and Scribner's sold out its 50,000-copy first run. Critics and readers delighted in the simple, moving story of an old fisherman's losing battle with sharks over the carcass of his giant marlin. In early April 1953 the film crew arrived in Havana to begin filming Hemingway's pocket-sized epic. In May, Hemingway was awarded the Pulitzer Prize for fiction, which had been denied his *For Whom the Bell Tolls.*

In June, with a sizable advance from *Look* magazine to do a series of articles on a return safari to the Serengeti, Ernest and Mary left Havana for Europe and eventually Africa. Beginning with the Pamplona feria, Hemingway returned for the first time since 1931 to the Spanish bullfight circuit, which he and Mary followed for a month. By September they were in Kenya on safari that did not end until January 21, when Ernest treated Mary to a small-plane trip to see Africa from the air. Two days later at Murchison Falls, the plane struck a telegraph wire and crash-landed. Newspapers worldwide banner headlined Hemingway's death. Soon afterward, the Hemingway party, bruised but alive, boarded another small plane, which crashed in flames on takeoff. More death notices appeared, but Hemingway again survived, badly injured internally and with serious burns. The couple returned to Venice to recuperate until Ernest was ready to drive back to Spain in May. On June 6, 1954, they departed Europe for Havana, where on October 28 Ernest received news that he had been awarded the Nobel Price for Literature, but he could not make the trip to Stockholm because of poor health.

Between 1955 and 1961 Hemingway's life alternated between ever-shortening cycles of euphoric writing and paranoia-ridden depression. His weight rose and fell alarmingly; his hypertension worsened. Medication for his blood pressure exacerbated his depressions. The public did not see his vulnerability, but close friends became increasingly concerned. Yet, when his health did not prevent him, Hemingway wrote steadily on his trilogy. *The Garden of Eden* expanded in several drafts, and he was now working alternately on *A Moveable Feast.* This pattern continued well into 1958. In January 1959, when the Batista government was brought down by the Castro revolution, Hemingway bought a house in Ketchum, Idaho, where he could safely watch the revolution for which he had a good deal of sympathy.

During the summer of 1959 Hemingway returned to Spain to cover for *Life* magazine the mano-a-mano bullfights of the young Ordonez and the veteran Dominguin. All that summer and into the fall, Hemingway's behavior became more erratic, unpredictable, and uncontrollable. His mood shifts frightened Mary and bewildered his male friends. That winter and into the next year, Hemingway worked on his contracted 10,000-word feature for *Life* magazine. By May 1960 he had written 120,000 words, which he asked Hotchner to edit. *Life* paid $90,000 for the shortened version but printed only part of it.

When Hemingway insisted on returning to Spain during the summer of 1960, Mary remained in New York. From Spain he wrote her plaintive letters about his fear of cracking up. That November, under the care of his Ketchum doctor, Hemingway entered the Mayo Clinic to be treated for hypertension, an enlarged liver, paranoia, and severe depression. He received extended treatments of electroshock therapy before being released on January 22, 1961. By the end of April, after two suicide attempts, he was back at Mayo for more electroshock. Discharged on June 26, he was driven back to Ketchum, where on July 2, 1961, he brought his story to its seemingly inevitable, sad conclusion. In *Death in the Afternoon*, Hemingway's Old Lady is told that all stories, if followed far enough, end sadly, and that he is no true writer who would tell you otherwise. The words could have been put on Hemingway's tombstone.

Envoi

Ernest Hemingway took us with him to Africa, whose dark heart beats deep within his writing in ways not always obvious. He studied trout streams in several countries, studied Gulf Stream marlin, studied Spanish bulls and African game. He studied the flight of birds, the bends of rivers, and the flow of country. But what he studied first, last, and always was that strange animal, his fellow man, rampant in his natural setting. Like his mother, Ernest was an artist; like his father, he was a natural historian. Like both, he found his calling in Oak Park. But like neither parent, he was a child of the twentieth century, born too late for the frontier and too soon for outer space, leaving only that dark country within himself to explore. Despite wives, children, wars, injuries, mental and physical illness, and his strenuous life, Hemingway left, permanently embedded in our literary history, several of the finest short stories written in the twentieth century, at least three—possibly four—major novels, and a writer's life carried out on an epic scale. His influential style has, at some point, influenced most American writers of his time. That he self-destructed affirmed his humanity. That he wrote as well as he did promises his permanence.

NOTES

This essay has been adapted from the entry "Hemingway, Ernest" by Michael Reynolds that appears in the *American National Biography,* 10: 545–53, published by Oxford University Press © 1999 American Council of Learned Societies, use of portions of the text of the entry by permission of the ACLS.

1. Gerald Murphy to Sara Murphy, 4–9 Sept. 1937, in *Letters from the Lost Generation,* ed. Linda P. Miller (New Brunswick, N.J.: Rutgers University Press, 1991), pp. 199–200.

2. Cdr. C. Alphonso Smith, USNR. "Battle of the Caribbean," *United States Naval Institute Proceedings* (Sept. 1954), 976–82.

3. Spruille Braden, *Diplomats and Demagogues.* (New Rochelle, N.Y.: Arlington House, 1971), pp. 282–84.

4. National Archives and Records Administration (College Park, Md.) Record Group 84, E-2359, Confidential Letter File, American Embassy, Havana, 1942–43.

5. "The United States and Cuban-Spanish Relations," October 28, 1942, copy in the Hemingway Collection at the John F. Kennedy Library, Boston.

6. *New York Times,* Jan. 4, 1942, p. 1; *New York Times* Jan. 2, 1942, p. 11; *New York Times,* Feb. 1, 1942, p. 6.

7. "The Invaders," *Newsweek* (July 6, 1942), p. 304; *Newsweek* (Aug. 17, 1942), pp. 29–31.

8. *New York Times*, July 2, 1942, pp. 1, 8.

9. *Newsweek* (July 13, 1942), pp. 27–28. Leicester Hemingway's feature stories proved more accurate than Ernest once thought.

10. *Havana Post*, Apr. 14, 1942.

11. National Archives and Records Administration (College Park, Md.). Record Group-84: Foreign Service Posts, Havana Embassy Confidential File 1Comejen: a 942–43 Part 2: 711–815.6

12. National Archives and Record Administration (College Park, Md.). Record Group 313 Records of Naval Operating Forces, Subset Record Group 313.7 Records of Naval Sea Frontiers 1940–1950, War Diary, Commander, Gulf Sea Frontier, May 1, 1942.

13. War Diary, May 18, 1942, Navy Operating Procedures update.

14. See *New York Times*, Jan. 4, 1942, p. 4; *New York Times*, Jan. 11, 1942, V, 7:1; *New York Times*, Jan. 25, 1942, p.20; *New York Times*, Apr. 19, 1942, p. III, 7.

15. *New York Times*, June 28, 1942, p. 21.

16. *New York Times*, July 26, 1942, p. 22.

17. See *Hemingway's Reading* (Princeton, N.J.: Princeton University Press, 1981) item 1357, Felix Luckner, *The Last Privateer*, misidentified in *Hemingway, Selected Letters*, ed. Carlos Baker (New York: Scribner's 1981).

18. Office of Naval Intelligence publications ONI 220-M and ONI 220-G. Hemingway's copy of ONI 220-M is in the Hemingway Collection, John F. Kennedy Library, Boston.

19. *Havana Post*, May 2, 1942.

20. Hayne D. Boyden, letter to Ernest Hemingway, Nov. 2, 1942, Hemingway Collection, John F. Kennedy Library. Since the Carlos Baker biography, it has been commonly held that the *Pilar* patrols began in June of 1942. Letters and documents at the Kennedy Library make it clear that the first armed cruise did not take place until mid-November.

WORKS CITED

Hemingway, Ernest. *By-Line: Ernest Hemingway, Selected Articles and Dispatches of Four Decades.* Ed. William White. New York: Scribner's, 1967.

Hemingway, Ernest. *Dateline: Toronto—The Complete Toronto "Star" Dispatches, 1920–1924.* Ed. William White. New York: Scribner's, 1985.

Hemingway Collection. John F. Kennedy Library, Boston.

Hemingway Collection. Princeton University Library, Princeton, N.J.

Hemingway Museum. Oak Park, Ill.

Mellow, James R. *Hemingway: A Life without Consequences.* Boston: Houghton Mifflin, 1992.

Miller, Linda P. *Letters from the Lost Generation.* New Brunswick, N.J.: Rutgers University Press, 1991.

Reynolds, Michael. *Hemingway's First War: The Making of "A Farewell to Arms."* Princeton: Princeton University Press, 1976.

———. *Hemingway's Reading, 1910–1940: An Inventory.* Princeton: Princeton University Press, 1981.

———. *Hemingway: The American Homecoming.* Cambridge, U.K.: Blackwell, 1992.

———. *Hemingway: The Paris Years.* New York: Blackwell, 1989.

———. *The Young Hemingway.* New York: Blackwell, 1986.

Stephens, Robert O. *Hemingway's Non-Fiction: The Public Voice.* Chapel Hill: University of North Carolina Press, 1968.

HEMINGWAY IN
HIS TIME

Eye and Heart

Hemingway's Education as a Naturalist

Susan F. Beegel

> It does not matter much what children
> play, so they play in the sun: and I sub-
> mit that all this is good. For if it does
> not serve science, it serves art, a service
> by no means less.
>
> Joseph Russell Taylor,
> "Nature Study," 1903

Introduction: "A Field for the Observations of the Naturalist"

In 1835 Ralph Waldo Emerson defined "Nature" as "all that is separate from us," and, with few exceptions, criticism and biography of Ernest Hemingway to date exemplifies our separation of nature and culture (22). We believe that Hemingway's most significant milieu was Paris in the 1920s and forget that he grew up in the midst of an environmental awakening as extreme as any America has experienced, in a town where other manifestations of the "back to nature" movement included the prairie architecture of Frank Lloyd Wright, the urban parkscapes of Frederick Law Olmstead, and the Tarzan stories of Edgar Rice Burroughs. We attribute his elegiac stance to the trauma of World War I and not to the disappearance beneath the gargantuan growth of Chicago of the tall grass prairie where he played as a child or to the removal of 4,000 million board feet of timber per year from his beloved Michigan woods (Williams 1989, 197–98; Beegel 1998, 83–86). We study his indebtedness to sophisticated and esoteric writers such as Ezra Pound, Gertrude Stein, James Joyce, and T. S. Eliot and largely ignore his indebtedness to popular nature writers such as Rudyard Kipling, Jack London, and Ernest Seton Thompson. We attribute his famous spare style to the influence of Imagist poetry and not to his object-oriented scientific training in the Agassiz method. We worry about his evangelical Protestantism and conversion to Catholicism without discussing his upbringing as a creation scientist.

I want to give a "natural history" of Hemingway's formative years from infancy to young manhood, the years when he received the education as a naturalist that would make him the writer that he became. That education molded him not only as a man but as an artist. Taken into the field for nature study from earliest childhood, Hemingway learned to describe the natural world with a scientist's unwavering gaze, respect for truth, interest in detail, and objective language. Witnessing a baby's birth by Caesarean section in "Indian Camp" or a matador's death from pneumonia in "Banal Story," he adopts the scientific stance of affective neutrality. As a naturalist, he describes with equal detachment both the "visible tar-like iridescence" of human corpses decaying on a summer battlefield and "the purple, formalized, iridescent, gelatinous bladder of a Portuguese man-of-war" ("A Natural History of the Dead," *The Short Stories of Ernest Hemingway* [*Short Stories*] 443; *The Old Man and the Sea* [*Old Man*] 35). Even his minimalist style conforms to the scientific ideal of "originating the maximum amount of information with the minimum expenditure of energy. Beauty is the cleanness of line in such formulations, along with symmetry, surprise, and congruence with other prevailing beliefs" (Wilson 60).

"I go to Nature to be soothed and healed, and to have my

senses put in tune once more," wrote John Burroughs ("Gospel" 245), America's most popular and prolific nature writer during Hemingway's childhood. Taken by his parents every summer from the perimeter of unwholesome Chicago to the fresh air of Michigan woods, Hemingway learned to regard nature as a source of refreshment and healing, like the snowbound mountain fastnesses of Switzerland, where Frederic and Catherine seek refuge from war in *A Farewell to Arms;* or the beech forests and trout streams of Spain, where Jake Barnes finds relief from the pathology of postwar Paris in *The Sun Also Rises.* After his father's suicide, Robert Jordan of *For Whom The Bell Tolls* rides his horse to the top of Montana's Bear Tooth Plateau, "where the air was thin and there was snow all summer on the hills," and drops his father's gun into the still water of a glacial tarn (337).

For the nature writer, "the enemy is civilization, progress, and society; and the friend is wilderness, primitiveness, and anarchical individualism" (Stephenson 178). Hemingway rejected the civilized values of home and hearth, of job and office, of "settling down" and "being really a credit to the community" ("Soldier's Home," *Short Stories* 151), in favor of the primitive values of freedom and self-reliance. His Frederic Henry deserts the politically sanctioned, mechanized slaughter of World War I by plunging into the Tagliamento River, finding that "anger was washed away in the river along with any obligation" (*A Farewell to Arms* [*Farewell*] 232). His Robert Jordan exchanges a life teaching "undergraduates who take Spanish IV" for a few doomed days making love and war in Spain's Sierra de Guadarrama (*For Whom the Bell Tolls* [*For Whom*] 164–65).

Hemingway repudiated the organized piety of the straitlaced suburb where he was raised in favor of spirituality imbibed direct from nature. "Let no man be ashamed to kneel here in the great out-of-doors," Bill Gorton adjures us in *The Sun Also Rises* (122). In the shade of great trees, of virgin pine rising sixty feet before beginning to branch, Nick and Littless in "The Last Good Country" feel "strange" and "solemn" and "awfully religious," like they "ought to feel in church" (*The Nick Adams Stories* 89–90). The dying Harry, in "The Snows of Kilimanjaro," *knows* that he is going to the "great, high, and unbelievably white top" of the mountain called "Ngàje Ngài, the House of God," by the Masai (*Short Stories* 76, 52).

Hemingway also rejected middle-class America's repressive sexual morality—"His father had summed up the whole matter by stating that . . . the thing to do was to keep your hands off people"—in favor of the unalloyed, innocent joy of unfallen sex in Eden, of lovemaking beneath a hemlock tree with an Ojibway girl—"plump brown legs, flat belly, hard little breasts, well hold-ing arms, quick searching tongue, the flat eyes, the good taste of mouth, then uncomfortably, tightly, sweetly, moistly, lovely, tightly, achingly, fully, finally, unendingly, never-endingly, never-to-endingly, suddenly ended, the great bird flown like an owl in the twilight, only it daylight in the woods and hemlock needles stuck against your belly" ("Fathers and Sons," *Short Stories* 491, 497).

Some Hemingway characters remain imprisoned in a "moral chastity belt" (Fitzgerald 195), and one, a teenaged boy in the short story "God Rest You Merry, Gentlemen," is so traumatized by re-ligious prohibitions against desire that he amputates his own penis. In *The Garden of Eden,* sexual experimentation turns into a nightmare reminiscent of sixteenth-century artist Hieronymus Bosch's triptych, "The Garden of Earthly Delights," whose bi-zarre combinations of flora, fauna, and deviant human sexuality Hemingway studied at Madrid's Prado Museum. But most of his characters seek a return to the Garden's prelapsarian sexuality with women who break the "pattern" set by the parentally favored "nice girls" of "Soldier's Home" with their "sweaters and shirt-waists with round Dutch collars" (*Short Stories* 147–48).

Instead, Hemingway's heroines are women "without shame," who flee civilization and its discontents with their lovers—actual sisters like Littless in "The Last Good Country," who accompa-nies Nick on his escape into the forest, or spiritual sisters like Catherine Barkley in *A Farewell to Arms,* who deserts with Fred-eric in a rowboat across Lago Maggiore. Hemingway women do not share suburban kitchens and bedrooms with their men, but campfires and safari cots and bedrolls under the stars. Like Helen in "The Snows of Kilimanjaro" or Marge in "The End of Some-thing," they are sometimes hunters and fisherwomen.

The loveliest of Hemingway's women partake of the erotic and regenerative principles of earth: "Maria lay close against him and he felt the long smoothness of her thighs against his and her breasts like two small hills that rise out of the long plain where there is a well, and the far country beyond the hills was the valley of her throat where his lips were" (*For Whom* 341). The loveliest of Hemingway's wildscapes partake of the erotic and regenerative principles of women: "I loved the country so that I was happy as you are after you have been with a woman that you really love, when, empty, you feel it welling up again and there it is and you can never have it all and yet what there is, now, you can have" (*Green Hills of Africa* [*Green Hills*] 72). "Biologists, geologists, writers," notes Terry Tempest Williams, are "lovers, engaged in an erotics of place. Loving the land. Honoring its mysteries. Acknowledging, embracing the spirit of place" (84). Hemingway is just such a naturalist-scientist-writer-lover, everywhere embracing what Tempest Williams calls the wild "Feminine" (53).

To love the land as Hemingway loved it, perhaps especially to love the land *when* Hemingway loved it, in the early years of the twentieth century, when the coming of the automobile and urban sprawl driven by a fully mature Industrial Revolution rapidly transformed the rural and wilderness areas of the United States into a web of highways and destroyed landscapes, was to live in a state of continual bereavement. "Our people went to America because that was the place to go then," he would write in *Green Hills of Africa*. "It had been a good country and we had made a bloody mess of it" (285). Virtually all of Hemingway's writing is elegiac in tone, continually confronting loss and probing its pain, but perhaps no elegy is more beautiful than his short story "Fathers and Sons," combining grief for his father with mourning for the Michigan land: "His father came back to him in the fall of the year, or in the early spring when there had been jacksnipe on the prairie, or when he saw shocks of corn, or when he saw a lake, or if he ever saw a horse and buggy, or when he saw, or heard, wild geese, or in a duck blind" (*Short Stories* 496).

Commenting on the anguish of loving the land in a period of rapid change, Robert Michael Pyle writes in "Editorial: Receding from Grief" that there is no "clear distinction between the extension of love and the reconciliation of loss, whether for places or people. . . . As long as we live on the land, and among others, we shall know a state of permanent grief, for loss is continual, and always with us. . . . Yet there is a balm, and it comes from the same source" (3). Like his troubled Nick Adams in "Big Two-Hearted River," finding a small and fragile island of refuge in a burned-over landscape, pitching his tent near a too-brief stretch of unspoiled river, Hemingway would spend a lifetime seeking that balm. Over and over again, he extended his love to "other new country and other new country"—to Illinois tall grass prairie; to Michigan hemlock and white pine forests; to Spanish trout streams and mountains; to East African savannahs; to the islands and Gulf Stream waters of Key West, Bimini, and Cuba; and to the Yellowstone Plateau and Rocky Mountains of the American West—despite knowing that "the same things happen to it all" (quoted in Beegel 1988, 55).

Seeking both a title and an epigraph for *The Sun Also Rises*, Hemingway turned to a passage in the biblical book of Ecclesiastes expressing the ultimate consolation of nature: "One generation passeth away, and another generation cometh; but the earth abideth forever. . . . The sun also ariseth, and the sun goeth down, and hasteth to the place where he arose" (1.4–10). Change and mortality are tragic for the individual, but in nature, as Rachel Carson expressed it: "Nothing is lost. One dies, another lives, as the precious elements of life are passed on and on in endless chains" (105). Hemingway's Robert Jordan seeks this biblical and natural consolation in *For Whom the Bell Tolls*. Confronting his imminent death, a death undertaken on behalf of the group, and perhaps on behalf of his unborn child, Jordan does not pray or call on God for courage and solace, but instead looks up at the "big white clouds" in the sky and carefully touches "the palm of his hand against the pine needles where he lay . . . and the bark of the tree trunk that he lay behind" (471). He is "completely integrated." He feels "his heart beating against the pine needle floor of the forest" (471).

Yet Hemingway's love for nature is not unvexed by cruelty and guilt. Taught to fish and hunt as a very small boy, he paradoxically learned, while killing, to be at one with wildlife, to enter into the courage and agony of the wounded lion in "The Short Happy Life of Francis Macomber," to experience "how a bull elk must feel if you break a shoulder and he gets away" (*Green Hills* 55). His vision of man's own predicament as biological drove his empathy. "Most men die like animals, not men," he observes in "A Natural History of the Dead" (*Short Stories* 444). "It doesn't hurt any worse than things hurt that you and I have shot together," Thomas Hudson comments on his shrapnel wounds in *Islands in the Stream* (462). Again, Hemingway evokes Ecclesiastes: "As the fishes that are taken in an evil net, and as the birds that are caught in the snare; so are the sons of men snared in an evil time, when [death] falleth suddenly upon them" (9.12). The brutality and tenderness of predator to prey suffuses his works, whether it's young David Bourne experiencing the suffering of the dying elephant in *The Garden of Eden* or Claude kissing the brow of a dying German soldier in "Black Ass at the Crossroads" (*The Complete Short Stories of Ernest Hemingway: The Finca Vigía Edition* [*Complete Short Stories*] 588).

Hemingway crafted *The Sun Also Rises* to be "a damn tragedy with the earth abiding for ever as the hero" (*Ernest Hemingway: Selected Letters, 1917–1961* [*Selected Letters*] 229). Throughout the Hemingway canon, nature preceded man and will outlast him:

> [T]his Gulf Stream you are living with, knowing, learning about, and loving has moved, as it moves, since before man, and . . . the things that you find out about it, and those that have always lived in it are permanent and of value because that stream will flow, as it has flowed, after the Indians, after the Spaniards, after the British, after the Americans and after all the Cubans and all the systems of governments, the richness, the poverty, the martyrdom, the sacrifice and the venality and the cruelty are all gone. (*Green Hills* 149)

Hemingway takes the long view of a scientist who understands geologic time. Human history is insignificant when juxtaposed with nature: "The worn light bulbs of our discoveries and the empty condoms of our great loves float with no significance against one single lasting thing—the stream" (*Green Hills* 150).

And yet, ironically, we need history to help us understand how nature became the central subject of this great American writer, how culture became for him "a field for the observations of the naturalist" ("A Natural History of the Dead," *Short Stories* 440), how his ideas about nature were shaped by culture, and how training as a natural historian affected both the style and substance of his art.

"The Fruit of His Home Tree": Mother and Nature

On July 21, 1899, Dr. Clarence Edmonds Hemingway stepped onto the porch of his Oak Park, Illinois, home to announce—with a joyous blast on a cornet—that his wife, Grace Hall-Hemingway, had given birth to a son. The new baby, Ernest Hemingway, was about to become the hero of five scrapbooks kept by his mother from his infancy through his graduation from high school. In these meticulously kept volumes, Grace recorded the sayings and doings of the growing boy and collected family photos, school papers and reports, greeting cards, theater programs, newspaper clippings, invitations, and letters sent to the child. As Ernest grew, his mother preserved his earliest creative and scientific writing. Beautifully arranged exercises in the art of collage, Grace's scrapbooks construct the idealized childhood this mother envisioned for her son and show the pivotal role she expected nature study— then a national rage—to play in his education.

A talented musician, Grace composed a lullaby for Ernest, "The Oriole Song" (Scrapbook I, 94),[1] treating the woven, pendant nests of the Baltimore oriole swinging from the branches of blossoming apple trees. "Swing low, swing low / Gentle Southland breeze," Grace wrote, "Softly rock the cradles / Swinging on the trees." The "grateful" father oriole guards "the fruit of his home tree" from "insects rife," and the blue heavens "bend low" to "Breathe into the firebird's song / Notes of mother love." The song is sentimental, but its natural history is accurate. Apple orchards are the oriole's preferred nesting site, and Grace understands the unique architecture of their nests, the unusual fact that oriole females may sing on the nest, and the bird's role in pest control. (Forbush and May 468–71). Obviously derived from the gospel classic "Swing Low, Sweet Chariot," Grace's "Oriole Song" embraces what John Burroughs called "the gospel of nature."

In 1901, the year that the Audubon Society, founded for the protection of birds and their eggs, became a national organization, (Fox 153), Grace Hall-Hemingway proudly recorded that her nineteen-month-old son knew "40 birds by name when he [saw] their pictures" (I, 88–89). Duck, pheasant, robin, kingfisher, tern, chickadee, hawk, plover, wild turkey, and woodpecker were among the toddler's repertoire. When Ernest was nearly four years old, she would write, "He is a natural scientist loving everything in the way of bugs, stones, shells, birds, animals, insects, and blossoms" (II, 52).

Grace valued her son's identification with animals: "He loves all animals, especially wild ones" (II, 24). "At about 21 months old . . . he saw performing elephants, and is never tired of having you tell about them. Early, oh so early in the morning, you hear 'Tell Ernie bout dat big elephant, Da-Bear,'" she noted (I, 99). Grace, who trained chipmunks to eat from her hand, saw her son's love of wildlife as connected to kindness—"He is very tender-hearted, crying bitterly over the death of a fly he had tried to revive on sugar and water" (II, 24).

Yet Grace saw no inconsistency in celebrating his delight "in shooting imaginary wolves, bears, lions, buffalo, etc." (II, 23), nor in the sensitive child's actually learning to hunt at a very early age—"Ernest Miller at almost 4 years of age is able to go hunting with Daddy many miles through the dense wood and carry his own gun" (II, 52). Noting that the little boy walked over seven miles, she admired his "nerve and endurance" (II, 53).

Hemingway biographers and critics have made much of Grace's concurrent valuing of her son's "tough and tender ways" (Spilka 57). Kenneth Lynn argues that she confused Ernest's gender identity by dressing him and his sisters in identical outfits— either frilly dresses worn by early twentieth-century toddlers for special occasions in town, or sturdy denim overalls worn for rough-and-tumble days at the lake (41). He criticizes Grace for encouraging her children of both sexes to play with dolls and tea sets or to fish and hike together, rather than separating them for gender-restricted play (41). Mark Spilka determines that a genteel Victorian feminine tradition exemplified by Frances Hodgson Burnett's popular children's novel, *Little Lord Fauntleroy*, dictated Grace's "feminization" of Ernest. Spilka believes her actions conflict with the masculine tradition of wilderness independence exemplified by an equally popular children's novel, Mark Twain's *Huckleberry Finn* (43–64). Yet Grace's scrapbooks show that she valued *both* traditions for children of *both* sexes.

Spilka and Lynn overlook the child-rearing values of the back-to-nature movement reaching national proportions by the year 1900. Nature study was supposed not only to bring boys and girls the benefits of wholesome outdoor exercise and science education, but also to emancipate them by breaking down gender stereotypes. Feminists such as Grace Gellatin Seton Thompson, author of *A Woman Tenderfoot* (1900) and wife of Ernest Seton Thompson, began founding the first summer camps for girls in the early 1900s, hoping to create a New Woman who would be far closer to the Hemingway heroine than the 1920s flapper (Lutts 17, 19). According to a 1903 account:

> [She] paddles like an Indian through the chain of lakes. She sends a bullet into the heart of a deer without a touch of "buck fever." She can construct a lean-to, and build and light a smudge in front of it with the best of men; and withal she is so charmingly feminine that the best of men flock around her as devoted slaves. ("Appropriate Costumes for Girls to Wear When Camping Out")

New Women require New Men, and children's nature study was expected to produce them as well. Edward F. Bigelow, who edited the "Nature and Science for Young Folks" feature in *St. Nicholas* children's magazine, a favorite in the Hemingway household, discourses on the subject in his 1907 book, *The Spirit of Nature Study*. In a chapter titled "Sissies and Tomboys," Bigelow advocates a world of "manly little men and womanly little women . . . all climbing the same fences, listening to the same bird songs, watching the same squirrels, picking and examining the same flowers" (24). Nature study, he argues, will not only endow girls with "hardiness and strength," but boys with "gentleness, refinement, and purity" (20, 22):

> How much bravery it requires on the part of a boy to be what his own conscience tells him he should be in gentleness, truthfulness, and kindness; what he should be in purity, and in a love of the true and beautiful because he fears to be called "sissy," or "Miss Nancy." Is there any reason why a boy should not pick flowers and give a bouquet to a boy? If the girls do it why should he not, if he wants to do it? Any reason why he shouldn't see and exclaim over the beauties of a landscape as enthusiastically as a girl? Any reason why he shouldn't be as gentle as the girl should be and as free from cruelty or a desire to be cruel? (25)

Bigelow recommends that parents "strive to bring boys to be one hundred per cent. boys, and girls to be one hundred per cent. girls. Then for full measure . . . add to the boys twenty-five per cent. of girlishness, and to the girls twenty-five per cent. of boyishness" (25–26). Grace Hall-Hemingway's scrapbooks suggest that she subscribed not only to *St. Nicholas* magazine for her children, but to Bigelow's concept of nature study as training for gender egalitarianism.

A performance artist, Grace took pleasure in her children's games of make-believe and reinforced young Ernest's interest in Native Americans by admiring his play and providing props such as fringed buckskins. "He shoots his bow and arrow and dances like a young Bear Cub," she wrote (I, 101). "He and Marcelline [Ernest's older sister] dramatize 'Hyawatha' [*sic*] and play Indian in various ways" (II, 24). Grace recorded Ernest's attendance at events such as Pawnee Bill's Wild West Show and an annual summer pageant of Longfellow's narrative poem "Hiawatha," enacted by Michigan Indians (Miller 26).

These entries chronicle the Hemingway family's participation in the period vogue for things Native American. Frank Stewart explains the national craze: "Now that these peoples had been nearly eradicated and the survivors removed to reservations, they were thought of as having lived an idyllic existence in an American Eden. Sentimental portraits represented them as what America should have been" (78). Ernest's first spelling test, preserved by his mother, shows that Oak Park schools participated in this nostalgic vision. Miss Pumphrey asked the children to spell "forest," "wigwam," "owlet," "dark," "pine-tree," "moon," and "Nokomis" (III, 52), and the six-year-old future author of "Indian Camp" received a perfect score.

Small wonder, because what was a fad for most Americans resonated for Ernest in special ways. The little boy from the suburbs of "Chigagou"—Potawatomie for "the wild-garlic place," a major Indian trading post in the 1800s because of easy portage between the Great Lakes and Mississippi watersheds—would, like his father before him, play among Indian ghosts and hunt arrowheads at burial mounds near his Oak Park home (Cronon 23–4). Near the family's summer cottage in Michigan, he would visit the camps of Ojibway bark-peelers and play with their children and learn the art of paddling a birch bark canoe from Albert Wabanosa, who claimed to be the grandson of Longfellow's Indian guide (Miller 25–27). Hemingway's fiction would be deeply informed not only by the era's sentimental vision of the Native American tragedy, but also by early intimacy with its reality.

The summer cottage where the Hemingway children became acquainted with Indian ways was, during the years of Ernest's childhood, considered an important responsibility of middle-class parents. The Hemingways purchased property on Michigan's Walloon Lake shortly after their first child was born (Sanford 69). In an era without reliable refrigeration or rapid transportation, the fresh vegetables, meat, eggs, and dairy products essential for child nutrition were available in summer only near farms. Before widespread pasteurization, warm weather could mean spoiled raw milk carrying baby-killing bacterial infections. Congested urban and suburban areas experienced summer epidemics of childhood diseases, including polio, whooping cough, measles, diphtheria, and scarlet fever—often lethal in a time without vaccines and antibiotics. "Fresh Air" charities sprang up nationwide to remove children from cities during summer's atmospheric inversions of air almost unimaginably polluted by today's standards

(Stewart 80). The claustrophobic, choking black pall of Chicago, the product of businesses and homes burning 10,000 tons of soft coal per day, was visible for miles (Cronon 11). The period association of nature with health was not whimsical.

Summering in the country, however, was far more than a mere flight from cities and towns. Grace's scrapbooks show how she envisioned summers at Walloon Lake, where the family lived by the beach in a white-clapboarded cottage she designed (Sanford 69). The photos she pasted in Ernest's scrapbooks show spotted cows drinking from the lake in the early morning and a great blue heron posing in the water. They show her naked children (Marcelline aged three and Ernest at two) splashing in the lake by their handsome clinker-built rowboat—a picture Grace had made into a postcard to send to friends (Sanford 74). Most telling is a photo of Ernest's baby sister Carol, sitting in a wild-flower-studded fallow pasture by the edge of the woods, a picture Grace labeled "In the Garden of Eden" (Scrapbook IV, 84).

"Eden is a home from which we have been evicted," writes Evan Eisenberg, a place that murmurs "of childhood," the "wild place at the heart of the world where all life bubbles up" (xv, xviii). The annual experience of eviction from a home in nature was almost universal for middle-class American children of Hemingway's generation. "Just now," Hildegarde Hawthorne would write in an October 1912 column for *St. Nicholas,* "most of you are coming home from . . . all sorts of spots by sea and lake and river, mountain camp or country farm-house, coming back to your city and town homes" (1,148). Echoing her young readers' sentiments, she writes, "I could look forward quite calmly to the finish of cities" (1,148). For Ernest too, childhood meant seasonal expulsion from Eden, from "the freedom of the woods and hills, the secret wild places of summer" for return to "the clangor and dust of town" (Hawthorne 1,148).

Eden is not Eden without sensuality, and at the lake Grace allowed her children to swim naked, to wear nothing but overalls, and to go barefoot. Her logic was practical—at a cottage without plumbing, swimming substituted for bathing, and simple clothing kept laundry to a minimum. Even in their teens, Ernest and his sisters swam naked in the evening, a practice they called their

"Secret Society" (Sanford 75). Nick Adams's ability to "feel" all of the trail to the Indian camp with bare feet ("Fathers and Sons," *Short Stories* 492) and the delicious swimming scenes of "Summer People" and *The Garden of Eden* owe much to early freedoms at the lake.

Grace would eventually exile her twenty-one-year-old son from the family cottage for keeping young neighboring girls out all night at a campfire sing-along, accusing Ernest of "general lawlessness" (quoted in Reynolds 1986, 136). Yet her scrapbooks suggest that she originally valued such freedoms, for she included a letter to Ernest in Michigan from his friend "Sam," reporting from non-Edenic Oak Park: "A bunch of kids got pinched yesterday for swimming in the [Des Plaines] river without bathing suits. I suppose Evans is responsible for this" (Scrapbook II, 82). "These are a few of the things that you see along the river," Sam continued, including pictures of a sign reading "Keep Out No Trespassing W. Evans" and a bridge with a sign saying "No Fishing Allowed" (II, 82). No skinny-dipping, no trespassing, no fishing, no Eden. Evans would become the villain of Hemingway's final and unfinished Nick Adams story, "The Last Good Country."

Singer, composer, musician, performer, and landscape painter, Grace—who would build herself a studio on the lake—viewed nature as a wellspring for art. The mother who named the family cottage "Windemere," evoking the shades of English Lake Poets Wordsworth, Coleridge, and Southey, nurtured a love of literature in her children. The journey to Eden meant packing trunks with books taken from the Oak Park Library and bound volumes of *St. Nicholas* to last the summer (Sanford 19). "Ernie took the most books," his sister Sunny remembered, and "these vacation books became treasures" (Sanford 19). At the lake, he relished such boyhood favorites of the back-to-nature movement as Kipling's *The Jungle Books* and Edgar Rice Burroughs's *Tarzan of the Apes* (see Spilka 92; Davison 35, 37).

Then, when the inevitable return to town became reality, Ernest would seek, as *St. Nicholas* recommended, books "that will continue your summer memories, will take you out on the long trail of adventure, under the open sky, seat you by campfires in forest nights, and keep you a while longer in the company of nature" (Hawthorne 1,148). Books such as Ernest Seton Thompson's *Wild Animals I Have Known* and Stewart Edward White's *The Forest* were among his favorites. For Hemingway, literature would become the return trail to Eden, a way to revisit in fiction a paradise lost in reality.

Although her literary models differed from her son's, Grace was naturally proud of the Lake Poet she was raising, pasting into teenaged Ernest's scrapbook a Kiplingesque venture he called "The Day": "When you started before daybreak / Mist a rising from the water; / When your oar strokes sped the row boat past the Reeds . . . Tell me brother / Was not that the Day?" (Scrapbook V, 44). The memory was to be hoarded as a charm against winter, when "we're living in the city, trying to earn three squares a day." The scrapbooks Grace kept for Ernest not only provide us with a detailed record of his upbringing but would, more importantly, provide him with a trove of memories to draw on when revisioning his childhood and young manhood in the Nick Adams stories.

"The Manuscripts of God": Dr. Hemingway and the Agassiz Method

"Nature writers," according to William Stephenson, "operate in middle ground between scientific information and artistic expression. Scientists reach toward poetry and humanists reach toward fact, producing the tradition's hallmark—a blend of objective and subjective, factual and experiential knowledge" (172–73). If Hemingway's artistic mother encouraged her son to reach toward poetry, his scientific father encouraged him to reach toward fact.

A family physician with a specialty in obstetrics, "Ed" Hemingway received his medical degree from Rush Medical College in Chicago. Earlier, he had taken a heavy load of science courses at Oberlin and participated in a scientific expedition to the Great Smoky Mountains (Sanford 23–24). Some botanical specimens he collected and identified on that trip are in the herbarium of the

Moreton Arboretum. But Ed's interest in nature dated from his own childhood, nurtured by his mother, Adelaide Edmonds Hemingway, a college-educated and enthusiastic amateur botanist and astronomer (Sanford 19).

At Oberlin, Ed Hemingway became a member of the Agassiz Association (Scrapbook III, 32–33), an organization honoring the memory of the great Swiss-American scientist Louis Agassiz (1807–1873), founder of Harvard University's Museum of Comparative Zoology, of our National Academy of Science, and of a prototype field station that would become the Marine Biological Laboratory at Woods Hole. The Agassiz Association was devoted to amateur nature study through fieldwork out-of-doors, a concept Agassiz pioneered with Swiss schoolchildren and helped to popularize in America.

One of several national organizations devoted to children's nature study during the back-to-nature movement, the Agassiz Association in the United States consisted of close to 1,000 neighborhood, family, and school chapters largely comprised of children, with some clubs of adult "graduates" involved in advanced fieldwork. Chapters conducted their own courses of nature study in subjects including botany, entomology, zoology, and mineralogy but took as their guiding principle: "Nature must be studied from her own book." Harlan H. Ballard, an early proponent, defined the Agassiz Association's goals:

> While we ever recognize in printed books and papers necessary and cherished guides, yet we believe that our first business is to meet Nature face to face. Therefore we leave the confines of the library and the school, and go out under the open sky,—into the forest, and along the stream. (6)

The organization was so important to Ed Hemingway that he founded a chapter for young men in Oak Park even prior to marrying and having children of his own. Into one of Ernest's scrapbooks Grace pasted a newspaper clipping of a 1895 letter from "Clarence E. Hemingway, President of the Oak Park Agassiz Chapter" to "My Dear Agassiz Boys" (III, 32–33). Traveling in the

Isle of Man, Ed wrote to the boys in his club about the island's flora, fauna, mineralogy, and geomorphology:

> The island is nicely wooded and there are many glens in which are running streams of clear cold water, in which there are plenty of speckled trout. . . . Were you to look at the flora here you would at once notice the great number of ferns and fine wild honeysuckles, and the ivy, winding over the banks and up the trees. . . . The trees are principally the birch, much stunted, beech, large and branching, and fruit trees. . . . There are a plenty of large black and white magpies, large crows, jackdaws, swallows, titlarks, starlings, and cuckoos. The rocks are mostly hard limestone, with occasional veins of quartz and galena. . . . There are a great many glacial boulders on the island and shore . . . they were brought by the ice during the Glacial epoch from their mother rock away off to the north west in Scotland. (III, 32–33)

"Ernest," according to his mother, "at 4 years 8 months. . . . Goes to the Agassiz of which he is a member and makes observations with the big boys" (II, 76). His father directed him in home nature study as well. Grace writes, "At five years old . . . he is delighted to look at specimens of rocks and insects by the hour through his microscope" (II, 87). When Ernest and Marcelline began school, their father organized an Agassiz Club for the boys and girls of the Holmes Elementary School and stayed involved until 1911, when Ernest turned twelve (Reynolds 1986, 112). Photos of the Agassiz Club in the field show children with their hands full of leaves and wildflowers, abandoned bird nests, collecting baskets, jars of insects and pond scum, and notebooks. Ernest glows with enjoyment.

"'Train your pupils to be observers, and have them provided with the specimens about which you speak,'" Agassiz urged science teachers. "'Teach your children to bring them in themselves. Take your text from the brooks, not from the booksellers'" (Cooper 82). The Agassiz method of instructing children involved sending them into the field to learn from the accompanying adult leader about an area's geology and geography and to collect specimens of stones, fossils, flowers, fruits, and other natural objects. Students gathered to share their specimens, and the leader explained them both to the group and to each child separately. Children pointed out and described aspects of their specimens and took their collections home for preservation, classification, and study. Agassiz Clubs also held indoor meetings, where the children gave formal presentations of their findings (Cooper 6–7). Dr. Hemingway's Agassiz chapter maintained a small natural history collection of unusual specimens gathered by the young members (Reynolds 1986, 112).

The Agassiz method of science education was profoundly object-oriented, with a specimen organism to be examined and dissected until the student discovered "the relation between form or structure and function or essential effect" (Cooper 4). Agassiz himself was notorious for giving graduate students a small pickled fish in a tin pan and asking them to study it without consulting anyone or reading any related work. In the course of an hour the student (and Agassiz's students included such illustrious scientists as William James, David Starr Jordan, and Nathaniel Shaler) would naturally feel that he had "compassed" the fish, but Agassiz would leave the student to work for more than 100 hours, and then reward his discourse on "how the scales went in series, their shape, the form and placement of the teeth" with a terse "That is not right" (Cooper 41–42). Only after another hundred or more hours of work on the student's part would Agassiz declare himself satisfied by rewarding his charge with another specimen. Asked to name his greatest accomplishment, Agassiz replied, "I have taught men to observe" (Cooper 1).

Ernest's early training in the Agassiz method by his father was powerfully reinforced by the Oak Park school system, which also emphasized object-oriented science education. Agassiz's institutes for science teachers had such a profound effect on American education that in 1896 William James could write, "There is probably no public school teacher . . . who will not tell you how Agassiz used to lock a student up in a room full of turtle-shells, or lobster-shells, or oyster-shells, without a book or a word to help him, and not let him out until he had discovered all the truths which the objects contained" (quoted in Cooper 78).

Hemingway's high school notebooks tells us that this situation obtained in science classes at Oak Park High School. Every day students were given specimens such as box elder twigs and corn stems for "Experiment 43." Every day Hemingway dissected specimens, examined them under the microscope, and prepared scientific drawings. Every day he labeled parts such as pith and epidermis, medullary rays and fibrovascular bundles.

Lane Cooper notes that the Agassiz "method of teaching cannot fail to be illuminating to the teacher of literature" because "the fundamental operations of observation and comparison in the study of living forms . . . [develop] the original powers of the student" (3). Hemingway's high school classes were also exercises in writing. Every day he recorded his observations and described what he saw, always using the words "look," "notice," and "examine." "We *looked* at the laurel leaf and *noticed* that it had no stipules," he would write. "We *examined* a twig of the box elder and *noticed* the terminal bud" (Experiments 39 and 43, Oak Park High School Notebooks). The quality of his written observations mattered to the science teacher. When Hemingway wrote, "In some of the different plants the openings of the stoma are not able to be closed such as the willow and other swampy plants which take up the water they use thru their roots," the science teacher responded, "English poor. A minus" (Experiment 42, Oak Park High School Notebooks).

The beautifully observed and poetically resonant grasshoppers of "Big Two-Hearted River" demonstrate how the Agassiz method of object-oriented science education developed Hemingway's "original powers." Agassiz was renowned for using grasshoppers—a common and available insect—to train public school science teachers (Cooper 82). At Oak Park High, Hemingway wrote an extended biology test paper on the insects that his mother preserved (IV, 94). If, in "Big Two-Hearted River," a grasshopper nibbles at the wool of Nick's sock with a "fourway lip" (*Short Stories* 211), it is because young Hemingway noticed that "the mouth parts . . . consist of the labium, first and second maxillae [and the] mandabils" (Scrapbook IV, 94). Nick holds the grasshopper carefully by the wings and notices his "jointed belly" (*Short Stories* 212); young Hemingway noticed the grasshopper's "pro, meso, and meta thoraxes" (Scrapbook IV, 94). Nick speculates that the grasshoppers have turned black from living in the burned-over land; Hemingway wrote about protective coloration in his biology test paper.

Science education in the Agassiz tradition also had a strong religious basis that appealed to Dr. Hemingway, raised in the stern tradition of evangelical Calvinism and a deacon of Oak Park's Third Congregational Church from 1906 to 1909. (Grimes 45). Louis Agassiz was Charles Darwin's principal American opponent, despite the fact that Agassiz's own detailed paleontological work on fossil fishes and his theory of an Ice Age helped make Darwin's theory of evolution possible. An idealistic romantic who "saw the power of the Creator exemplified in all flora and fauna," Agassiz accounted for similarities and differences between ancient and modern species by postulating as many as twenty separate creations (Lurie 72–73).

Although Larry Grimes views Dr. Hemingway's position as a "Protestant naturalist" as a kind of "double bind" (48), Agassiz pointed the way out of that contradiction for devout men of science like Ed Hemingway. Agassiz insisted that *because* man is "made in the spiritual image of God," he alone among animals is "competent to rise to the conception of His plan and purpose in the works of Creation" (Agassiz and Gould 1–2). This philosophy made it possible for Ed to teach his children, when contemplating dinosaur remains at Chicago's Field Museum, "that the men who wrote the Bible explained natural history the best they could, but that now through research we knew much more about how things must have been made thousands of years ago. He told us that our new knowledge only added to the truths we learned in Sunday school" (Sanford 39).

Hemingway's education as a naturalist, then, was almost entirely devoid of instruction in the scientific basis of evolutionary theory. The Agassiz method paradoxically asks students to observe the effects of evolution without inquiring any further into their causes than "the genius of the Creator." "Darwin's theory," wrote Agassiz, is "merely conjectural. . . . I regret that the young and ardent spirits of our day give themselves to speculation rather than to close and accurate investigation" (quoted in Cooper 84–85). Under Agassiz's spell, a science writer for *St. Nicholas* could describe the breeding plumage of male birds in exquisite detail and still dismiss the concept of sexual selection: "As for the purpose of the fancy colors and patterns, the learned Darwin supposed that the birds themselves appreciate and admire their own beauty . . . [but] it is not at all clear that they have any other 'excuse for being' than that they really are beautiful" (Sawyer 1,131). Hemingway's high school biology test paper discusses protective coloration and seasonal dimorphism in insects but does not mention the evolutionary mechanism of selection that acts on individual variations to create these adaptations (IV, 84).

Such gentle acknowledgement-but-censorship of Darwin, made possible by Agassiz, was common in educated-but-pious communities like Oak Park at the beginning of the twentieth century. Not until 1925, when the clash of attorney Clarence Darrow and fundamentalist William Jennings Bryan in *Scopes v. the State of Tennessee* electrified the nation, would progressive middle-class parents begin to perceive a creationist stance as allied with anti-intellectualism and demagoguery. Darrow, defending the constitutional right of high school teacher John Scopes to teach evolution in defiance of state law, placed Bryan on the stand and subjected him to national ridicule by exposing his scientific and theological ignorance. Bryan, in poor health, collapsed and died within hours of the trial's conclusion (see de Camp). The most widely covered and sensational trial of its time, the Scopes trial plays a key role in the comedy and allusive structure of the trout fishing idyll at the heart of Hemingway's 1926 novel, *The Sun Also Rises*. But during the crucial years for the author's education as a naturalist, Darrow had not yet arisen to defend the right to study evolution and to collapse the religious foundation of the Agassiz method.

Agassiz's first principle of zoology—that "the Animal Kingdom . . . is the exhibition of the divine thought, as it is carried out in one department of that grand whole which we call Nature" (Agassiz and Gould 1)—affected Hemingway's literary as well as his scientific education in the pre-Scopes era. A traditional literary curriculum consisted of nineteenth-century poets such as Henry Wadsworth Longfellow, James Russell Lowell, Oliver Wendell Holmes, and John Greenleaf Whittier—all not coincidentally under the sway of Agassiz at Boston's famous symposium, the Saturday Club. Of this generation, William Cullen Bryant would become America's principal poet of natural theology. Oak Park High School required Hemingway to memorize both Bryant's "Ode to a Waterfowl" ("There is a Power whose care / Teaches thy way along that pathless coast" [26]) and "Thanatopsis" ("Go forth, under the open sky, and list to Nature's teachings, while from all around. . . . Comes a still voice" [10]) (Reynolds 1981, 104).

Hemingway's Agassiz-dominated education left him to derive his knowledge of evolution from popular culture, not science. When his seventh grade English teacher, Edith Stryker, assigned Jack London's bestselling *Call of the Wild,* both of Hemingway's parents disapproved, and his mother went to visit Miss Stryker and complain that *Call of the Wild* was a book "no Christian gentleman" should read (Buske; Sanford 107; Reynolds 1986, 109). Yet like all teenagers, Ernest actively sought the forbidden, imitating London in early short stories of his own, "Sepi Jingan" and "The Judgment of Manitou." London, a self-styled literary naturalist, ignored the many complex factors involved in the adaptive fitness of individuals and the success of a species, omitting principles such as cooperation and interdependence, making Darwin's theory exclusively a matter of individualistic struggle and primitive violence. London called it "the law of club and fang": "[M]aster or be mastered . . . Kill or be killed, eat or be eaten" (*Call of the Wild* 110).

Such "modern" ideas of nature's godless brutality contrasted sharply with an earlier century's vision of its divine beneficence. For Hemingway, as for others of the "Lost Generation," the fundamental rupture would occur on the battlefields of World War I. After encountering the grim biological realities of human death and decomposition as a Red Cross ambulance driver on the Italian front, he would write a "A Natural History of the Dead," viciously satirizing the Christian naturalist's belief in the immanence of a benevolent God in nature. In "A Way You'll Never

Be," shell-shocked Nick Adams babbles like an Agassiz naturalist about the American locust—they make "a very dry sound, have vivid colored wings, some are bright red, others barred with black." But as Nick discusses trapping the locusts for bait and becomes increasingly manic, his discourse shifts to the underlying, brutal fact of nature all this detail obscures, repeating over and over—"Gentlemen, either you must govern, or you must be governed" (*Short Stories* 411–12). Nick is quoting military commander Sir Henry Wilson, but his dictum sounds suspiciously like London's "law of club and fang."

Yet Hemingway remained throughout his life first and foremost an Agassiz-trained naturalist, keenly observant of detail, seeking the relationship between form and function, always in pursuit of inspiration from nature. Children in the Agassiz Club were adjured to study "with the eye not only, but with the heart" (Ballard 5), and Hemingway never stopped looking at nature with heart as well as eye. Longfellow imagined that Nature spoke to Agassiz:

> "Come, wander with me," she said,
> "Into regions yet untrod;
> And read what is still unread
> In the manuscripts of God." (59)

Nature spoke to Hemingway as well, but his reading of God's manuscripts would be revisionary.

"Relic of an Instinctive Passion": The Hunter-Naturalist Tradition

Charles Darwin, writing in his 1836 *Journal of Researches by H.M.S. Beagle,* associated his "extreme delight" in scientific collecting with man's atavistic urge to hunt: "The love of the chase is an inherent delight in man—a relic of an instinctive passion. . . . It is the savage returning to his wild and native habits" (quoted in Finch and Elder 165). For many male naturalists and field biologists, Darwin's association continues to ring true. In *Biophilia*

(1984), Edward O. Wilson makes an identical connection between scientific collecting and a primitive joy in the hunt: "On a chill morning when the clouds lifted and the sun shone brightly, my Papuan guides stopped hunting alpine wallabies with dogs and arrows, I stopped putting beetles and frogs in bottles of alcohol, and together we scanned the rare panoramic view" (52).

Dr. Hemingway introduced his son both to hunting and to Agassiz Club field trips at age four. Some of the boy's earliest hunting took the form of scientific collecting, as father and son shot animals to prepare as study skins or to taxiderm for the club's natural history "museum." The extent and nature of their collection remain something of a mystery. When the Agassiz Club disbanded, Dr. Hemingway donated their stuffed birds, mammals, and other specimens to the Oak Park High School, where the collection has since been lost or destroyed. Two muskrats, a loon, and a "small warbler-like bird" taxidermed by Dr. Hemingway survive at the Ernest Hemingway Birthplace Museum in Oak Park, along with a pair of owls he shot on his Michigan honeymoon (Wheeler). Ernest, at age ten, was "assistant curator" of the Agassiz Club and brought seaweeds, horseshoe crabs, shells, and a large swordfish bill home from a Nantucket vacation (Beegel 1985, 26–27). At age fourteen he was fined for shooting a protected great blue heron "for the school museum" (Sanford 100).

High-powered binoculars, spotting scopes, cameras, and video and audio recorders have made obsolete the need of earlier naturalists to kill animals for study. But during the years of Hemingway's childhood, "even birdwatching was done with a shotgun. The poor quality of field glasses and bird guidebooks . . . often required that the nature lover blast the bird out of the sky in order to identify it and, perhaps, to preserve it as a study skin or taxidermy mount" (Lutts 25). Countless children and adults pursued scientific collecting as a healthful open air hobby analogous to birdwatching today, and such was the national passion for this kind of nature study that "the first issue of *Audubon Magazine* promoted . . . a guide to egg and nest collecting and five taxidermy manuals" (Lutts 24).

From Darwin in Patagonia to Edward O. Wilson in New Guinea, the hunter-naturalist tradition is also one of adventure travel. Hemingway's childhood coincided with the years of hunter-naturalist Theodore Roosevelt's presidency (1901–1909) and of his expeditions to Africa for the Smithsonian Institution (1909) and to South America for the American Museum of Natural History (1914). Collecting expeditions and their scientist heroes were constantly in the public eye. As a young boy, Hemingway was nourished not only by his father's accounts of encounters with bear and mountain lion on his college expedition to the Smoky Mountains, but also by such Roosevelt-era features of *St. Nicholas* children's magazine as Ariadne Gilbert's "Torch-Bearer of the Dark Continent" and A. W. Rolker's "The Wild Animal Trapper and His Captives." Grown older, he enjoyed both popular magazine accounts of Roosevelt's expeditions and the now former president's own books, such as *African Game Trails* (1910) and *Through the Brazilian Wilderness* (1914).

However, there was a famous hunter-naturalist closer to home—Carl Akeley of Chicago's Field Museum of Natural History, a weekend haunt of the Hemingway children and their father. Akeley worked for the Field Museum from 1895 until 1909, making expeditions to Africa for specimens and using them to create large habitat groups showing African mammals in their natural surroundings. A gifted sculptor, he devised new techniques for laying skins on highly modeled forms, giving his taxidermy unrivaled realism. In 1905, the year Ernest turned six, Akeley collected the elephants for the Field Museum's famous "Fighting Bulls" group. The boy continued to follow Akeley's adventures after he moved to the American Museum of Natural History in 1909, making three more collecting expeditions to Africa—trips that included adventures such as killing an attacking leopard with his bare hands and filming gorillas in the wild with a motion picture camera of his own design. Akeley's memoir, *In Brightest Africa,* was part of Hemingway's adult library.

Collecting specimens of local flora and fauna for the Agassiz Club, young Hemingway imagined himself working in the tradition of Roosevelt and Akeley. At age sixteen, he wrote:

I desire to do pioneering or exploring work in the 3 last great frontiers Africa southern central South America or the coun-

try around and north of Hudson Bay. . . . I believe that any
training I get by hiking in the spring or farm work in the summer or any work in the woods which tends to develop resourcefulness and self reliance is of inestimable value in the
work I intend to pursue. (Pocket Account Book)

Hemingway's childhood training most obviously inspired his
adult safaris to Africa and some of his finest fiction ("Snows of
Kilimanjaro," "The Short Happy Life of Francis Macomber," and
the "elephant story" in *The Garden of Eden*) and non-fiction (*Green
Hills of Africa* and the posthumously published "African Journal").

But the hunter-naturalist tradition, with its emphasis on *"last
great frontiers,"* would contribute to the elegiac tone of Hemingway's nature writing as surely as the disappearance of the Illinois prairies and Michigan woods of his childhood. The world
was shrinking faster than a boy could grow, and science was
turning its attention away from exploration and nature study to
technology. In his January 1910 "Nature and Science" feature for
St. Nicholas, Edward F. Bigelow reviewed the past year's scientific
achievements—the discovery of the North Pole, boats called to
the assistance of a sinking ship by wireless telegraphy, new
records for ocean speed (four days from Ireland to Sandy Hook,
N.J.), successful flights by the Wright Brothers and Count Zep-
pelin, advances in the use of the telephone. "We are all born too
late," Hemingway would mourn (quoted in Beegel 1988, 55).

The hunter-naturalist tradition also stresses that the scientist
has obligations to the kill transcending those of men who hunt
for meat or trophies. He handles the animal, studies and preserves it; looks, notices, and examines; records his observations
in drawing or in writing. If trained in the Agassiz method, with
its basis in natural theology, the hunter-naturalist may approach
the kill with "disposition to wonder and adore," in quest of "the
spirit of the whole," searching for inspiration in Nature ("A Natural History of the Dead," *Short Stories* 441; Agassiz 2).

The Old Man and the Sea exemplifies this aspect of Hemingway's hunter-naturalist education. His primitive Cuban fisherman Santiago is analogous to Darwin's scientist-as-savage, or
Wilson's field biologist as cloud forest Papuan tribesman. With

knowledge derived from Hemingway's years of fishing the Gulf Stream and collecting specimens of marlin and tuna for the Academy of Natural Sciences of Philadelphia, (see Fowler and Cadwalader), Santiago looks, notices, and examines: "He *saw* a man-of-war bird with his long black wings circling in the sky"; "He *watched* the flying fish burst out again and again"; "He *looked* down into it and he saw the red shifting of the plankton in the dark water" (my italics; *Old Man* 34–35). Santiago is "not religious" (64) but approaches nature as manifested in the marlin with wonder ("I wonder why he jumped" [64]; "I wonder how much he sees at that depth" [67]) and with adoration ("Never have I seen a greater or more beautiful, or a calmer or more noble thing than you, brother" [92]). Santiago seeks answers to questions about the "spirit of the whole" from nature: "Why did they make birds so delicate and fine as those sea swallows when the ocean can be so cruel?" (29). He does not record his observations, but Santiago does bring back his specimen, the marlin's great skeleton, for measurement by experts and misinterpretation by tourists.

During the years of Hemingway's childhood, hunter-naturalist President Theodore Roosevelt became embroiled in a public controversy called the "Nature Faker Debate," an imbroglio that made an artist's obligation to uphold scientific standards of accuracy in nature writing a matter of national concern. At this time, "nature books were bought in astonishing quantities and published in astounding varieties" (Stewart 83). Many of them, including nature study guides used in classrooms, animal tales for children, and wilderness novels for adults, featured anthropomorphized wild animals as their protagonists and were more idealized than factual, more sentimental than scientific. The trouble began when, in a 1903 article titled "Real and Sham Natural History," aging naturalist John Burroughs launched an attack on writers who sought to "float into public favor and into pecuniary profit with a nature-book," exploiting the "popular love for the sentimental and improbable" (298).

Burroughs's targets (the Reverend William Long, Jack London, and Ernest Seton Thompson among them) responded, and a controversy began that raged in the popular press for four years and involved the nation's most distinguished nature writers and scientists. Roosevelt, a friend of Burroughs, considered it his duty, both as a natural historian and as president, to send frequent broadsides from the White House condemning the "Nature Fakers," and the "outrage" of giving their books to "children for the purpose of teaching them the facts of natural history" (quoted in Lutts 107). The debate was rich and complex, centering not only on the distortion and fabrication of facts by so-called yellow journalists of the woods but also on the capacity of animals to reason and feel emotion, as well as on the morality of hunting them. At least one of Roosevelt's opponents, May Estelle Cook, thought she heard "the steel-cold click of the hunter's gun" in the president's professed respect for facts untinged by emotion (quoted in Lutts 120).

Although Hemingway would draw strength from writers on both sides of the "Nature Faker Debate," he and his father, as hunter-naturalists, belonged most obviously to the Roosevelt-Burroughs camp, favoring science over sentiment. Dr. Hemingway would warn his son about the dubious authenticity of a specimen albatross foot with the words "don't get faked," and throughout his life Ernest would use the term "faking" to mean falsifying facts to manipulate readers' emotions. He would also use the nouns "naturalist" and "writer" interchangeably to refer to his profession (*Green Hills* 21). Clearly Hemingway absorbed the Roosevelt-era nature writing credo promulgated by John Burroughs:

> The poet and the artist see nature through the imagination, but the natural history observer sees through his eyes, or else his observations have no value as natural history. With him, it is not a question of temperament, but a question of accurate seeing and of honest reporting. (quoted in Lutts 122)

Yet the hunter-naturalist tradition, for all its lack of sentiment, still led to ambivalence about killing. Even the redoubtable Roosevelt, after shooting a yellow-throated warbler and sending its skin to the American Museum of Natural History, would write to Burroughs: "The breeding season was past and no damage can come to the species from shooting the specimen; but I must say that I care less and less for the mere 'collecting' as I grow older" (quoted in Lutts 124). For Roosevelt, as for other hunter-naturalists, to study or wonder about an animal was sometimes to identify painfully with the kill. Young David Bourne's question about the elephant—"How long do you suppose he and his friend had been together?" (*Garden of Eden* [*Garden*] 180)—prompts his sudden agonizing identification with the animal—"Thinking of Juma killing the elephant's friend . . . had made the elephant his brother" (197). So too Santiago's wondering connects him to his brother fish and prompts his most difficult and unanswerable question: "If you love him, it is not a sin to kill him. Or is it more?" (*Old Man* 105).

"Look to the Future and Kill Accordingly": Hunting, Fishing, and the Conservation Ethic

Scientific collecting, however, was the least part of the hunting and fishing Hemingway pursued as a child with his father. At home in Oak Park, they hunted for sport on the nearby prairies and in the mixed hardwood forests along the Des Plains River, also a favorite spot for fishing. During summers in Michigan, they fished for trout, pike, and perch in Walloon Lake and hunted squirrels in the woods. Ernest took to "the chase" with an "instinctive passion" lasting a lifetime:

> You can remember the first snipe you ever hit walking on the prairie with your father. How the jacksnipe rose with a jump and you hit him on the second swerve and had to wade out into a slough after him and brought him in wet, holding him by the bill, as proud as a bird dog, and you can remember all the snipe since in many places. ("Remembering Shooting-Flying," *By-Line: Ernest Hemingway, Selected Articles and Dispatches of Four Decades* 187)

The hunting ethics he learned from his father would affect Hemingway's stance toward nature throughout his life. Dr. Hemingway believed that a sportsman should not take more game than he and his family could use for food, and his children were raised on venison, fried squirrel, turtle meat and turtle eggs, frogs' legs, opossum baked with sweet potatoes, and "all kinds of fish cooked in every conceivable way" (Sanford 36). He endeavored to keep his children from hunting and fishing indiscriminately by insisting that they eat everything they killed, even forcing a teenaged Ernest and his friend Harold Sampson to cook and eat a porcupine they shot on a 1913 hunting trip (Sanford 81).

For Hemingway, the hunt was not ethically complete without the sacrament of taking meat. Santiago—who lives on turtle eggs, shark liver oil, flying fish, and dolphin meat—feels his sin of pride when the marlin, a fish to feed "many people," is instead reduced to "garbage waiting to go out with the tide" (*Old Man* 75, 126). We feel David Bourne's father's sin of greed when he chops the ivory tusks from the elephant and leaves "the grey wrinkled swelling dead body" to rot (*Garden* 201). Although Hemingway did engage in trophy-hunting in Africa, in a 1951 article titled "The Shot," he would write: "The author of this article . . . admitting his guilt on all counts, believes that it is a sin to kill any non-dangerous game animal except for food" (*By-Line* 419). The taste of porcupine lingers in Hemingway's characterizations of trophy-hunters—the self-indulgent Macombers and the corrupt and softened Harry Walden—in his African stories.

In addition to "eat what you kill," Dr. Hemingway taught his children never to close their eyes when firing a gun because "A marksman can be a murderer in a split second if he's not in control of his weapon" (Sanford 81). This tenet of the sportsman's code perhaps explains why Hemingway does not reveal whether Francis Macomber's death is murder or an accident, a point much argued by critics. In terms of hunter safety, there is no difference. Whether Margot deliberately took aim or handled her weapon carelessly, the result is homicide. Dr. Hemingway taught his son that "it takes kindness to kill cleanly" (Sanford 81), and the agonizing deaths of the gut-shot lion in "The Short Happy Life of Francis Macomber" and the lung-shot elephant in *The Garden of Eden* show how seriously Ernest took this injunction. His father also taught him to leave nesting birds, breeding animals, and spawning fish alone to reproduce, and that hunting was about self-reliance and resourcefulness.

While teaching his son to hunt, Dr. Hemingway instilled in him some attitudes that may seem shocking in these more ecologically enlightened times but were quite common in the early years of the twentieth century. The first was an almost total contempt for game laws. Although Dr. Hemingway was "a great believer in conservation and an exponent of decency in sport," he fished out of season, hid illegally caught brook trout in his bedroom slippers for smuggling out-of-state, shot protected grouse and woodcock for the table, and responded to his son's brush with the game warden over the blue heron with the fatherly advice of "Don't get caught" (Sanford 42, 82, 102). Ernest entered into the spirit of civil disobedience, parodying game laws in his high school notebook:

> Bill 3127 Introduced by Senator Hemingway. An act making policemen come under the Game Laws. An act making it a misdemeanor to kill a policeman out of season. An act providing that no one person shall kill any more policemen in one day than his family can dispose of. An act providing that a special license be issued to Taxidermists.

Dr. Hemingway's objection to regulation of hunting and fishing stemmed from what John F. Reiger calls the American "heritage of opposition to any restraint on 'freedom,' particularly that vestige of Old World tyranny, the game law" (59). When his wife chided him, Ed would rail belligerently, "I pay taxes for this land all year round. Too bad a man can't fire a shot at a moving object on his own property once a year without permission" (Sanford 81). Like many other sportsmen of his day, Dr. Hemingway embraced most of the conservation practices and ethical principles upon which game laws were based while resenting the laws themselves as "encroachments upon the liberties of the people" (Reiger 61).

For father and son alike, game laws seemed to spell the death, not the perpetuation, of wilderness freedoms and hunting. Aldo Leopold tells us that "in America until about 1905 the dominant idea . . . was that the restriction of hunting could 'string out' the remnants of the virgin supply and make them last a longer time. Hunting was thought of and written about as *something which must eventually disappear"* (Leopold's italics, 17). Hunters expected American wildlife to follow the buffalo, whose original herds numbering between 20 and 60 million animals dwindled to just 541 individuals before the species was protected in 1904 (Cronon 214; Quammen 130). Passenger pigeons, whose mass migrations once took hours and even days to pass and darkened the sky, (Forbush and May 255), also haunted American sportsmen. The last passenger pigeon died in a Cincinnati zoo the year Ernest turned fifteen. Game laws were considered "a device for *dividing up* a dwindling treasure" (Leopold's italics, 17), and hunters like Dr. Hemingway wanted their share.

Ernest never lost his fear that one day the hunt would be gone. In *Green Hills of Africa,* he writes: "The way to hunt is for as long as you live against as long as there is such and such an animal" (12). In "Wine of Wyoming," he predicts the death of hunting in the next generation (*Short Stories* 467). His unfinished Nick Adams story "The Last Good Country" is a late, bleak view of American nature's future—armed game wardens hunt children fleeing through a clearcut to a final stand of virgin forest.

President Theodore Roosevelt attempted to reverse this picture, introducing the nation to conservation through "wise use," the idea that "wild life, forests, ranges, and waterpower were . . . *renewable organic resources,* which might last forever if they were *harvested scientifically, and not faster than they reproduced"* (Leopold's italics, 17). His achievement cannot be underestimated; Roosevelt "doubled the number of national parks, created the first federal bird and game preserves, increased the national forest reserves by about 300%, and set aside eighteen natural wonders, including the Grand Canyon in Arizona, Devil's Tower in Wyoming, and Muir Woods in California" (Gable 2).

Yet Roosevelt-era conservation has its philosophical roots in the biblical notion that God gave man "dominion . . . over all the earth" (Genesis 1.26), that nature exists for man's exploitation. Roosevelt would, for instance, write that the destruction of the buffalo "was the condition precedent upon the advance of white civilization in the West" and therefore "a blessing" (1910, 269–70). The conservation biology used to pursue such exploitation "wisely," thanks to the long creationist shadow Agassiz cast on American science, had only a weak basis in evolutionary theory, and none in the still embryonic science of ecology, the study of interrelationships between organisms and their environments.

For today's readers, some of the most disturbing passages in Hemingway's nature writing involve brutality to predators and scavengers. These attitudes belong to the Roosevelt conservation ethic of Hemingway's childhood. Santiago, for instance, knows that the shark is "no accident" and that "everything kills everything else in some way" (Old Man 100, 106) but nevertheless stabs, hacks, and clubs with "complete malignancy" at makos and galanos, labeling the latter "hateful sharks, bad smelling, killers as well as scavengers" (102, 106–7). Their crime: "cut[ting] the turtles' legs and flippers off when the turtles were asleep on the surface . . . hit[ting] a man in the water, if they were hungry" (108). In Green Hills of Africa, Hemingway writes about the gut-shot hyena who "hit too far back while running, would circle madly, snapping and tearing at himself until he pulled his own intestines out, and then stood there, jerking them out and then eating them with relish" (37–38). His crime: being an "awful beast. . . . Fisi, the hyena, hermaphroditic, self-eating devourer of the dead, trailer of calving cows, ham-stringer, potential biter-off of your face at night while you sleep, sad yowler, camp-follower, stinking, foul, with jaws that crack the bones the lion leaves" (38).

During the Roosevelt era, before the importance of balanced predatory-prey relationships to healthy ecosystems was recognized, all species were assigned to "an absolute ethical category: good or bad" (Worster 260). Animals perceived as good (game animals and song birds) were accorded protection by laws such as the Lacey Act of 1900, prohibiting interstate commerce in game, and the Migratory Bird Act of 1913, an agreement with Canada and Mexico establishing international protection for some species of birds. Animals perceived as bad (predators on livestock and game) were actively persecuted in the name of "conservation." Roosevelt, the "Conservation President," could vilify a mountain lion he shot on the rim of the Grand Canyon as "the big horse-killing cat, the destroyer of the deer, the lord of stealthy murder, facing his doom with a heart both craven and cruel" (quoted in Worster 260). Under his administration, the Bureau of the Biological Survey, a forerunner of the Fish and Wildlife Service, set up a bounty system that in 1907 alone supervised the killing of 1,800 wolves and 23,000 coyotes on federal land (Worster 263).

Learning to hunt and fish during this period, young Hemingway necessarily imbibed the conservation ethic of his day. Even children's stories in *St. Nicholas* saw killing predators as synonymous with "protecting" game. In Frank Lillie Pollock's "The Peacemaker," forest ranger Scott Caldwell perceives his duty as "kill[ing] wolves whenever he got a chance" (963). The hero of Dewey Austin Cobb's "Adrift on the Amazon" learns that he "needn't waste sympathy" on pumas because they kill "colts and cattle" (1,067). Despite growing scientific evidence that eradication of predators leads to overpopulation, starvation, and disease among prey species, many state fish and game departments pursued Roosevelt-era "conservation" strategies throughout Hemingway's lifetime, as the author's hunting and fishing licenses attest. In 1928 Florida State Game Commissioner J. B. Royall was enjoining hunters to "look to the future and kill accordingly," asking them to "kill vermin and other enemies of game" (Report of Game Killed). Mary Hemingway's 1946 Idaho non-resident bird license reminds hunters to shoot and destroy the nests and eggs of "English sparrows, crows, owls, ravens, hawks, kingfishers, blackbirds, magpies, or pelicans" (State of Idaho Non-Resident Bird License).

And so Santiago envisions nature as comprised of "friends and enemies": migrating warblers and the hawks who fly out from the land to meet them, sea turtles and the stinging jellyfish they feed on, giant marlin and the sharks who destroy them. This tradition of placing animals in absolute ethical categories, possible only for those whose knowledge of evolution is confined to Jack London, poses a special problem for the Agassiz-trained scientist. If the naturalist is to seek God's "plan and purpose in Creation" and study out "the spirit of the whole," then how to explain the apparent existence of evil in nature, explain creatures like the self-devouring hyena and the voracious shark? "What god made him shark?" Queequeg inquires in Herman Melville's *Moby-Dick*, asking one of natural theology's oldest questions (310). Hemingway's answer, both in *The Old Man and the Sea* and elsewhere, seems to echo that given by John Burroughs in 1912:

> If the ways of the Eternal as revealed in his works are past finding out, we must still unflinchingly face what our reason reveals to us. "Red in tooth and claw." Nature does not preach; she enforces, she executes. . . . Of the virtues and beatitudes of which the gospel of Christ makes so much—meekness, forgiveness, self-denial, charity, love, holiness—she knows nothing. ("Gospel" 262)

Conclusion: "Outsong"

Ernest Hemingway's parents hoped that their gifted son would attend college. But in the summer of 1916, with his high school graduation only a year away, Ernest found Kipling's "Outsong"—"what the animals say to Mowgli when he leaves the jungle"—running through his head together with a listless comparison of Illinois and Cornell universities (Letter to Emily Goetsmann). Although he knew "how pleased my family would be if they would civilize me and inculcate a taste for Math and a distaste for Fishing," he could not imagine himself, in Kipling's words, "prisoned from our mother sky" or "heartsick for the jungle's sake" (Letter to Emily Goetsmann). Hemingway had truly absorbed the credo of the Agassiz Club. He deliberately chose not to attend college but "to leave the confines of the library and the school" and "meet Nature face to face" (Ballard 6).

That same summer, in a casually spelled letter to his sister Marcelline written from a Michigan fishing trip, Hemingway thought of older friends graduating from high school back in Oak Park and imagined some graduation exercises of his own. His graduation took place not in a stuffy high school auditorium, but "on a pool of the Rapid River 50 miles from no where. Murmuring pines and hemlock, black still pool, roar of rapids around bend of river, devilish solemn still, dammed poetic." He wore "the costume of Adam" and delivered a "masterly oration" in "English French and Ojibway." His "alumni banquet" was a "sacred can of apricots" he had packed to the river, and his senior prom "a rain dance . . . enveloped by a cloud of mosquitoes." A "big rainbow [trout] out of the pool" served as his diploma, and, having received that diploma, Hemingway wrote to Marcelline, "I shook hands with all the balsams, bowed to my trout-basket [and] kissed my flyrod."

We call such a ceremony "commencement." There would be no end to Hemingway's education as a naturalist—like all true education, his was always only the beginning of things to come.

NOTES

My thanks to Wes Tiffney and Terry Tempest Williams for helping me connect "scientific information and artistic expression," and to Sharon Carlee of the Nantucket Atheneum, Stephen Plotkin of the John F. Kennedy Library, and Morris Buske and Jennifer Wheeler of the Ernest Hemingway Foundation of Oak Park for research support.

1. The scrapbooks of Grace Hall-Hemingway, part of the Hemingway Collection at the John F. Kennedy Library in Boston, are in extremely fragile condition. To preserve the scrapbooks from unnecessary handling, researchers work from a transcript. Quotations from the scrapbooks in this essay, and the volume and page numbers given in parenthetical citations, are as given in the transcript.

WORKS CITED

Agassiz, Louis, and Augustus A. Gould. *Principles of Zoology.* Part 1. Boston: Gould, Kendall, and Lincoln, 1848.

Akeley, Carl. *In Brightest Africa.* New York: Doubleday, 1923.

"Appropriate Costumes for Girls to Wear When Camping Out." *Boston Sunday Herald,* 19 July 1903.

Ballard, Harlan H. "History of the Agassiz Association." *Swiss Cross* I Jan. 1887: 4–7,.

Beegel, Susan F. *Hemingway's Craft of Omission: Four Manuscript Examples.* Ann Arbor, Mich.: UMI, 1988.

————. "Second Growth: The Ecology of Loss in 'Fathers and Sons.'" *New Essays on Hemingway's Short Fiction*. Ed. Paul Smith. New York: Cambridge University Press, 1998. 74–110.

————. "The Young Boy and the Sea: Ernest Hemingway's Visit to Nantucket Island." *Historic Nantucket* 32.3 (Jan. 1985): 18–30.

Bigelow, Edward F. *The Spirit of Nature Study: A Book of Social Suggestion and Sympathy for All Who Love or Teach Nature*. New York: Barnes, 1907.

————. "The Year 1909 Doubly Famous." Nature and Science for Young Folks. *St. Nicholas*, Jan. 1910: 266–71.

Bryant, William Cullen. *The Poems of William Cullen Bryant*. Ed. Louis Untermeyer. New York: Heritage, 1947.

Burroughs, John. "The Gospel of Nature." *Time and Change*. Boston: Houghton, 1912. 243–73.

Buske, Morris. Letter to the author. 22 July 1998.

Cadwalader, Charles M. B. Letter to Ernest Hemingway. 16 Apr. 1935. Hemingway Collection. John F. Kennedy Library, Boston.

Carson, Rachel. *Under the Sea Wind*. 1941. New York: Penguin, 1991.

Cobb, Dewey Austin. "Adrift on the Amazon." *St. Nicholas*, Oct. 1912: 1066–67.

Cooper, Lane. *Louis Agassiz as a Teacher*. Ithaca, N.Y.: Comstock, 1945.

Cronon, William. *Nature's Metropolis: Chicago and the Great West*. New York: Norton, 1991.

Davison, Richard Allan. "Edgar Rice Burroughs, Tarzan, and Hemingway." *North Dakota Quarterly* 63.3 (Summer 1996): 34–39.

de Camp, Lyon Sprague. *The Great Monkey Trial*. New York: Doubleday, 1968.

Eisenberg, Evan. *The Ecology of Eden*. New York: Knopf, 1998.

Emerson, Ralph Waldo. "Nature." *Selections from Ralph Waldo Emerson*. Ed. Stephen E. Whicher. Boston: Houghton, 1957. 22–56.

Finch, Robert, and John Elder. *The Norton Book of Nature Writing*. New York: Norton, 1990.

Fitzgerald, F. Scott. "To Ernest Hemingway." June 1926. *Correspondence of F. Scott Fitzgerald*. Ed. Matthew J. Bruccoli and Margaret M. Duggan. New York: Random, 1980. 193–96.

Forbush, Edward Howe, and John Richard May. *Natural History of the Birds of Eastern and Central North America*. Boston: Houghton, 1939.

Fowler, Henry W. Letter to Ernest Hemingway. 8 Aug. 1935. Hemingway Collection. John F. Kennedy Library, Boston.

Fox, Stephen. *The American Conservation Movement: John Muir and His Legacy.* Madison: University of Wisconsin Press, 1981.

Gable, John A. "Theodore Roosevelt and the American Museum of Natural History." *Theodore Roosevelt Association Journal* 8.3 (Summer 1982): n. pag.

Gilbert, Ariadne. "The Torch-Bearer of the Dark Continent." More Than Conquerors. *St. Nicholas,* June 1913: 678–84.

Grimes, Larry E. "Hemingway's Religious Odyssey: The Oak Park Years." *Ernest Hemingway: The Oak Park Legacy.* Ed. James Nagel. Tuscaloosa: University of Alabama Press, 1996. 37–58.

Hawthorne, Hildegarde. "Wild Places of America." Books and Reading. *St. Nicholas,* Oct. 1912: 1148–49.

Hemingway, Ernest." African Journal." *Sports Illustrated* 35 (20 Dec. 1971), 5, 40–52, 57–66; 36 (3 Jan. 1972), 26–46; 36 (10 Jan. 1972), 22–30, 43–50.

———. *By-Line: Ernest Hemingway, Selected Articles and Dispatches of Four Decades.* Ed. William White. New York: Scribner's, 1967.

———. *The Complete Short Stories of Ernest Hemingway: The Finca Vigia Edition.* New York: Scribner's, 1987.

———. *Ernest Hemingway: Selected Letters, 1917–1961.* Ed. Carlos Baker. New York: Scribner's, 1981.

———. *A Farewell to Arms.* New York: Scribner's, 1929.

———. *For Whom the Bell Tolls.* New York: Scribner's, 1940.

———. *The Garden of Eden.* New York: Scribner's, 1986.

———. *Green Hills of Africa.* New York: Scribner's, 1935.

———. *Islands in the Stream.* New York: Scribner's, 1970.

———. Letter to Emily Goetsmann. 13 July 1916. Hemingway Collection. John F. Kennedy Library, Boston.

———. Letter to Marcelline Hemingway. 24 June 1916. Private collection.

———. *The Nick Adams Stories.* New York: Scribner's, 1972.

———. Oak Park High School Notebook. Hemingway Collection. John F. Kennedy Library, Boston.

———. *The Old Man and the Sea.* New York: Scribner's, 1952.

———. Pocket Account Book. C. 1915. Hemingway Collection, John F. Kennedy Library. Boston.

————. *The Short Stories of Ernest Hemingway.* New York: Scribner's, 1938.

————. *The Sun Also Rises.* New York: Scribner's, 1926.

Hemingway, Grace Hall. Scrapbooks. Volumes I–V. Hemingway Collection. John F. Kennedy Library, Boston.

Indian Boundary Division Picnic Areas and Trail Map. Chicago: Forest Preserve District, n.d.

Kipling, Rudyard. "Outsong." *The Jungle Books.* 1895. Ed. Daniel Karlin. New York: Penguin, 1989, 343–44.

Leopold, Aldo. *Game Management.* 1933. Madison: University of Wisconsin Press, 1986.

London, Jack. *The Call of the Wild, White Fang, and Other Stories.* Ed. Andrew Sinclair. New York: Viking-Penguin, 1981.

Longfellow, Henry Wadsworth. "The Fiftieth Birthday of Agassiz." *The Poetical Works of Henry Wadsworth Longfellow.* Vol. 3. Boston: Houghton, 1886. 59–60.

Lurie, Edward. "Jean Louis Rodolphe Agassiz." *Dictionary of Scientific Biography.* ed. Charles Coulston Gillespie. Vol. 1. New York: Scribner's, [1981]. 72–74.

Lutts, Ralph H. *The Nature Fakers: Wildlife, Science, and Sentiment.* Golden, Colo: Fulcrum, 1990.

Lynn, Kenneth. *Hemingway.* New York: Simon, 1987.

Melville, Herman. *Moby-Dick; or, The Whale.* 1851. Berkeley: University of California Press, 1979.

Miller, Madelaine Hemingway. *Ernie: Hemingway's Sister "Sunny" Remembers.* New York: Crown, 1975.

Pollock, Frank Lillie. "The Peacemaker." *St. Nicholas,* Sept. 1908: 963–66.

Pyle, Robert Michael. "Editorial: Receding from Grief." *Orion* 13.1 (Winter 1994): 2–3.

Quammen, David. "The Last Bison." *Natural Acts: A Sidelong View of Science and Nature.* New York: Avon, 1985. 130–34.

Reiger, John F. *American Sportsmen and the Origins of Conservation.* Rev. ed. Norman: University of Oklahoma Press, 1986.

Report of Game Killed. Florida 1928–1929. Hemingway Collection. John F. Kennedy Library, Boston.

Reynolds, Michael. *Hemingway's Reading, 1910–1940: An Inventory.* Princeton: Princeton University Press, 1981.

————. *The Young Hemingway.* Oxford: Blackwell, 1986.

Rolker, A. W. "The Wild Animal Trapper and His Captives." *St. Nicholas*, Dec. 1909: 156–63.

Roosevelt, Theodore. *Hunting Trips on the Prairie and in the Mountains.* Homeward Bound ed. New York: Review of Reviews, 1910.

———. "Nature Fakers." *Everybody's Magazine* 17 (Sept. 1907): 427–30.

Sanford, Marcelline Hemingway. *At the Hemingways: A Family Portrait.* London: Putnam, 1962.

Sawyer, Edmund J. "Some Remarkable Head-dresses and Tails of Birds." Nature and Science for Young Folks. *St. Nicholas*, Oct. 1912: 1129–31.

Spilka, Mark. *Hemingway's Quarrel with Androgyny.* Lincoln: University of Nebraska Press, 1990.

State of Idaho Non-Resident Bird License. 26 Sept. 1946. Hemingway Collection. John F. Kennedy Library, Boston.

Stephenson, William C. "A New Type of Nature Writing?" *Midwest Quarterly* 36 (1995): 170–90.

Stewart, Frank. *A Natural History of Nature Writing.* Washington, D.C.: Island, 1995.

Taylor, Joseph Russell. "Nature Study." *Atlantic Monthly* 92 (Dec. 1903): 763–66.

Wheeler, Jennifer. "Re: Stuffed Animals." E-mail to the author. 15 June 1998.

Williams, Michael. *Americans and Their Forests: A Historical Geography.* Cambridge: Cambridge University Press, 1989.

Williams, Terry Tempest. *An Unspoken Hunger: Stories from the Field.* New York: Pantheon, 1994.

Wilson, Edward O. *Biophilia.* Cambridge, Mass.: Harvard University Press, 1984.

Worster, Donald. *Nature's Economy: A History of Ecological Ideas.* 2nd ed. New York: Cambridge University Press, 1995.

The Fashion of *Machismo*

Marilyn Elkins

> The man who consciously pays no
> heed to fashion accepts its form just as
> much as the dude does, only he em-
> bodies it in another category, the for-
> mer in that of exaggeration, the latter
> in that of negation. Indeed, it occasion-
> ally happens that it becomes fashion-
> able in whole bodies of a large class to
> depart altogether from the standards
> set by fashion.
>
> Georg Simmel

The title of this chapter may appear an oxymoron. And perhaps it is. For the very nature of *machismo* would seem to
preclude any consideration of that which is trendy or fashionable. Yet attire, fashionable or otherwise, is always already a sig-
nifier, subtly encoding and transmitting its wearers' attempts at
self-definition. The clothing and accouterments of the macho
man—whether he is the subject of lyrics being sung by the Village People or a Hemingwayesque image used as a selling device
in J. Peterman catalogs—signal an anti-fashion stance that is decidedly about fashion even as it appears to disdain both its practice and practitioners. As such, its studied ambivalence reflects

the philosophy underlying many other major movements of the twentieth century. Early modernist philosophers, such as Nietzsche in *The Will to Power*, argued that the human condition is itself inherently ambivalent, claiming ambivalence as the essential psychic grounding on which modernity's social and cultural contradictions are built. Pushing Nietzsche's notion even further, Freud suggests in a number of texts that ambivalence is virtually a biologically determined condition of man.

Whether or not ambivalence is an essential component of all human nature, it is clearly manifest in men's fashion of the twentieth century in an uneasy combination of conformity and individualism. Nowhere is the tension of this ostensible binary more apparent than in the fashion of *machismo*. While not initiated by Ernest Hemingway, his Abercrombie and Fitch/J. Peterman (or, at a less expensive level, L. L. Bean/Eddie Bauer/Banana Republic) style has gained international recognition and popularity partly through its public connection with the preeminent sportsman-writer-cosmopolite of the twentieth century. Through Hemingway's self-fashioned public persona, American *machismo* became culturally linked with his personal style of dress.

As Ruth P. Rubinstein has pointed out, "The self is also an audience, and clothing allows individuals to view themselves as social objects" (3); for most of his career, Hemingway was able to regard himself as such an object and extricate himself from a setting or situation, scrutinize the image he was presenting with regard to the desired social response, and correct or change that representation of self when necessary to obtain the desired response. By his death in 1961, Hemingway was a cultural icon: the man who had set standards for both minimalist prose and attire and had become the quintessential American novelist. He possessed a discerning ability to embody the cultural moment. As the most celebrated American public writer of the twentieth century, Hemingway achieved such popularity partly through his ability to read and translate meaning via the language of clothes, reflected in his personal dress as well as in his writing.[1]

Certainly, America's greatest public writer has always had to be male, a man's man who was easily recognizable as a fearless sportsman and bon vivant, for Americans have a well-established idea that culture is not useful and that artists and writers are ineffectual. Therefore, Americans view culture as feminine and the men who deal in it as effeminate and unimportant to the "real world." From Walt Whitman to Norman Mailer, American crossover writers—those who have appealed to consumers of both low and high culture—have displayed the guises of masculinity, regardless of their private practices.

One of the stances of *machismo* is its adherence to the code of "cool"—in Hemingway's own terms "grace under pressure," which, ironically, requires a calculated approach to nonchalance—both in action and attire. Hence, its mask of seeming inattention to clothing and fashion becomes its own camouflage and fashion statement, a stance that is clearly evident in the life and writing of Ernest Hemingway. Both the man and his prose occupy a position of derision toward fashion and those who bother with such insignificant details as they simultaneously reinforce the importance of apparel and appearances through the manner in which they execute their critique.

Roland Barthes points out that "in order to blunt the buyer's calculating consciousness, a veil must be drawn around the object—a veil of images, of reasons, of meanings; a mediate substance of an aperitive order must be elaborated" (xi–xii). Looking at the historical reality of the clothing Hemingway wore offers fruitful ground for inquiry, for the code inherent in his choice of real objects is also relevant to his textual discourse about clothing and helps to offer an explanation for his cult-like status among non-academic Americans. The fashion of *machismo* as it was inscribed and practiced by Hemingway constitutes an image system calculated with desire as its goal but expressed through a feigned lack of desire. This pretense of disinterest becomes its practitioners' essential costume.

Hemingway's personal style of dress and writing rely heavily on codes that call for restraint or apparent insouciance as they demonstrate the necessity of hiding desire (i.e., the tip of the iceberg is all that should show in writing or in dress). Such a code fit the primary mood of twentieth-century America until the more open attitude of the late 1960s, which insisted that disguise and restraint were unnecessary and decidedly old-fashioned.[2]

After the nineteenth century, standardized dress offered a protective camouflage when the distinction between private and public space merged. Clothing became a practical buffer between the public and private selves as well. Thorstein Veblen argues that by the end of the nineteenth century, clothing had also become useful for covering up one's social origins, suggesting that it had a number of uses for hiding ulterior motives while publicly proclaiming others.

Specific items of clothing connected with a particular zeitgeist, a cultural moment, or a public figure become a part of our collective memory, and such images become signifiers that connote specific values and meaning. As Rubinstein argues, the ideas of strong and active presidents help determine the fashions of their terms, and these styles vary somewhat during presidencies that are considered weak and passive; she insists that "a president's personal preferences in dress, like those of the monarchs of the past, are often emulated" (237).

The first American president whom the press photographed frequently wearing informal and sportsman's clothing, Teddy Roosevelt and his "public" attire validated the American public's belief that sports activities equal the functions of the intellect in importance. Roosevelt's emphasis on physicality and sport were an important part of his public appeal—an effect that was not lost on the young Hemingway. Like many Americans, Hemingway saw frequent photographs demonstrating the vigorous style of Teddy Roosevelt, whose "walk softly and carry a big stick" policy has analogous ideology in Hemingway's comments about writing. Like many Americans of the period, Hemingway emulated the president whom he so admired—both in his boyish exploits in the great outdoors and in his preference for casual clothing.[3] Years later, he too would don safari gear and journey to Africa, emphasizing his mettle as a man of action. These highly publicized and photographed journeys in which Hemingway and Roosevelt always appear wearing rugged, outdoor clothing publicly signify that they could alternate successfully between civilization and nature. Their public dress advertised their manly vitality and placed them in a heroic status far above more ordinary men. The fashion training he received from watching the president of his boyhood remained with Hemingway and helped him publicly signal his later rejection of the role of Oak Park Christian Gentlemen and the public clothing recommended by his mother, Grace.

Often described as strong and active during his presidency from 1913 to 1921, Woodrow Wilson presented a somewhat more formal image. He also initiated public policies that empowered women, and this empowerment would eventually call for the man who had admired Teddy Roosevelt's style to find ways to reclaim its masculine stance as a means of reestablishing what increasingly seemed to be a collapsed sexual binary. Because of the war effort, women had been asked to abandon the steel corset and to don the uniforms of the army, navy and Marine Corps; many also joined the workforce and began to acquire independent means. By 1919 women were wearing loose fitting garments with short skirts—clothing that obscured breasts, waistlines, and hips. Short hairstyles were also a necessary part of the newly liberated woman's dress. In 1920 these already-"masculinized" or "adrogynized" women also received the vote—making their "masculine" power official. In response, men of the period began to wear mustaches and military-like clothing to reestablish or reconfirm their power and control; their emphasis on masculine dress was only part of their efforts to reclaim the territory they had lost at home by participating in the Great War. Intensifying the masculine aspects of their appearance and refusing to dress as the nice young men their mothers had reared in dark suits, starched collars, and ties, men, by dressing in more relaxed attire, publicly declared that the power of the patriarchy still existed despite women's apparent gains.

Looking at chronologically-arranged photographs of Hemingway, one is struck by the way in which he exemplifies this pattern, moving farther and farther away from being photographed in clothing that Grace Hemingway would have approved.[4] Grace had inherited her family's feeling for propriety—readily apparent in the way in which she dressed her children. Setting a proper example for the young Ernest, Hemingway's maternal grandfather,

Ernest Hall, always came to visit—even at the family's summer home in Windemere—wearing a starched collar, tie, and a suit coat. This properly dressed namesake was the model Grace held up for her son throughout his life (Mellow 15, 17). Kenneth Lynn and others have discussed in some detail the way in which Grace followed the correct style of the time by clothing the young Ernest in dresses, so that he and his older sister were often attired as twins, causing him to wear pink dresses and bonnets much longer than the average male of the period.⁵ In family pictures taken after Grace allows him to adopt long pants, the young Hemingway usually wears a dark suit and tie and a starched white shirt—he even dons a spiffy version of this conventional attire in the photo of *The Trapeze* staff taken for his high school yearbook. The solemn expression he wears in such photos contrasts sharply with the smiling face he offers in shots showing him in more casual clothing or engaged in sporting activities.

Hemingway makes his first move toward less traditional public raiment with the black Italian cape with the silver clasp that he sports upon his return from war, and he follows up in what seems to be a brief flirtation with dandyism by wearing white flannel trousers, as do the males in the wedding party, at his marriage to Hadley in 1921. Hemingway made this decision because the light-colored pants were becoming increasingly popular for summer weddings, but Ernest is the only Hemingway male who sports this new fashion in the wedding photos. Their selection was a matter he openly discussed with Hadley and may have served as an unconscious public signal of the independence he hoped to gain through his marriage to Hadley (Mellow 139).

It certainly seems to be a calculated image that the eighteen-year-old Hemingway offered when he returned to his hometown after his participation in World War I. In addition to the dashing cape, the young Hemingway sported a *Spagnoli* uniform that he had had specially tailored and that was rightfully reserved for officers of the Italian army—not for Red Cross volunteers. Whether or not it was mere coincidence, the adopted uniform afforded Hemingway the appearance, at least, of one who had seen active duty.⁶ His arrival in this uniform is all the more startling when we realize that the full extent of his actual military service was as a Red Cross volunteer for the Italian army during four weeks in July and August 1918.

Hemingway's self-assured claim to his right as *the* World War I writer matches the bravado with which he donned this full-regalia dress uniform. He had had no literal war experience that entitled him to either his role as its chronicler or as wearer of its Italian soldiers' uniform. After having spent three weeks picking up the wounded and the dead and then being wounded himself shortly after he requested a transfer to canteen duty near the front, Hemingway was soon boasting that he had seen prolonged active duty as an Italian soldier. Writing in Toronto's *Star*, he gave those who had been slackers but who wanted to appear as though they had seen military service some telling advice:

> A good plan is to go to one of the stores handling secondhand army goods and purchase yourself a trench coat. A trench coat worn in winter time is a better advertisement of military service than an M.C. If you cannot get a trench coat buy a pair of army shoes. They will convince everyone you meet on a street car that you have seen service. . . . The trench coat and the army shoes will admit you at once into that camaraderie of returned men which is the main result we obtained from the war. (*Dateline: Toronto—The Complete Toronto "Star" Dispatches, 1920–1924* 10–11)

Hemingway followed his own advice rather assiduously, for his *Spagnoli* uniform soon gave way to trench coats and khakis, clothing that reflected a military kinship and suggested that he had seen active duty. When he spoke to groups in Oak Park about being wounded, however, he showed up in his "field uniform" and often passed around the blood-stained and bullet-riddled trousers he had been wearing when he was wounded, so that the crowd could see how extensively he had been hit by shrapnel. He was already using clothing to substantiate his exaggerated claims of personal bravery. In doing so, he failed to follow the rest of his advice to his readers who had not seen active duty: when they were asked about their war service Hemingway recommended they reply that they did "not care to advertise" their military service (*Dateline* 11). Hemingway not only advertised; he exaggerated.

In another dispatch, one of Hemingway's imaginary veterans discusses the war and says he "didn't get nothing good out of the war except the lieutenant's mustaches" (*Dateline* 21)—a prop that Hemingway would soon adopt. It helped emphasize its wearer's masculinity and served as an ideal cosmetic for reinscribing his masculinity. Facial hair provided a safe marker for maleness because women would find adopting the style rather more difficult than bobbing their hair or wearing the new pantsuits that gained popularity following the war and reflected their contribution to the war effort.

Hemingway assumed that seeming to have genuine war experience was essential for war chroniclers, as is apparent in his response to Willa Cather's front line scene in *One of Ours*. Writing to Edmund Wilson, he dismisses this episode as a "Catherized" version of the battle scene in *Birth of a Nation*. He says that "the poor woman had to get her war experience somewhere," implying that actual experience is a prerequisite for imaginative creation (Wilson 118). Because Hemingway had so little actual experience of his own, in addition to dressing the part, he cultivated the advice of two good men, gaining necessary military information about World War I experiences from E. E. "Chink" Dorman-Smith and about World War II from Charles T. "Buck" Lanham. His association with these real life army officers and heroes helped provide him with authentic war stories and tactical theories. What he could not recall from his brief sojourn as a shell-shocked volunteer or glean from history books, Hemingway was soon busily collecting in late-night drinking sessions with those who had had the experience but, to borrow words from his fellow modernist T. S. Eliot, had "missed the meaning," one that Hemingway was happy to provide in his fiction. Hemingway listened to their tales, adapting and recycling the information he gained—just as he would continue to adapt and recycle their military dress into a streamlined version of civilian garb. In fact, Hemingway's stripped prose style soon paralleled his practical-

but-dashing clothing: a military uniform with no epaulets or
brass buttons but still clearly displaying the basic outlines of a
soldier's uniform—one that Hemingway had never earned the
right to wear—which served as a testament of its wearer's manliness. It successfully qualified Hemingway, both the man and the
writer, as an authorized possessor of the basic ingredients of
machismo.

This approach to style is also evident in Hemingway's reaction
to, and treatment of, the standard warrior's stock-and-trade of
hollowed abstract words. While Frederic Henry attacks the ob-
scenity of such words and their poverty to express the horrors of
the war that he and his fellow soldiers have experienced, he nevertheless is forced to rely upon words. And so he turns to the
concrete—the names of places, certain numbers, and certain
dates—as the only repository of meaning.

In much the same way, the man who had suffered the Great
War must refuse to talk about his experience, but he could allow his experience to constitute a subtext through his choice of
soldier-like clothing. If the young Hemingway could return wearing the uniform of an Italian officer and later in life continue to
wear military-like clothing, he could subtly remind others of his
firsthand experience of the great abstractions of "glory, honor,
courage" under fire without seeming to be obscenely masculine—
not to mention downright dishonest. The clothing became a real
object that could present a recognizable persona for Hemingway—a highly invented visual bravado that became an integral
part of his carefully constructed costume of *machismo*.

By the time Hemingway and Hadley were living in Paris, Hemingway began to appear in rumpled tweeds, often tieless, and
usually sporting a vest that would later be replaced by a hunting
vest—even when not on safari. He often wears a beret in photos
from this time, as though he can somehow become less American by adopting the French and/or Spanish headgear—even
when the other American men in the group are hatless or wearing the gentleman's mandatory slouch felt hat of the period. In
the photos taken during his visit to Pamplona with the Murphys,

he alone wears the Basque beret, and though, like Gerald Murphy, he sports a tie, his unbuttoned jacket (Murphy has buttoned the obligatory bottom button) and beret make him look considerably less formal and more sportif than the other men in the group. Hemingway also "wears" the women who sit on either side of him—both Pauline, who is to become his second wife, and Hadley seem to be Hemingway appendages and appear distant from the Murphys.

In his *Star* articles of the period, Hemingway pays "as much attention to dress codes as to political dialectics," noting that "Stambouliski had taken to wearing silk socks" and that Chicherin now sported "fancy uniforms, even though he had never been a soldier" and informing his readers that Chicherin's mother had kept him in dresses until he was twelve (Mellow 203).[7] In the 1928 photos that record the Hemingway family's first meeting with Pauline, Clarence is wearing a suit, tie, and hat, while Hemingway appears tieless and hatless, wearing only a vest over his open-necked shirt.

Photos of the 1930s show Hemingway moving toward a preference for big-white-hunter clothing: safari hats, khakis, and vests and coats that provide storage for shells and hunting and/or fishing equipment. In the photo taken with his big marlin in Havana in 1934, he appears in light, casual clothing, even though others are wearing suits and ties. By this decade Hemingway's attire has become continuant; it now fully reflects his personal self. Informal in formal situations and often unkempt when neatness was the norm, his appearance communicated the power of the artist and his ability to withstand the pressure to conform. While it followed the code of the outdoorsman, when it appears in more formal settings the clothing also indicates its wearer's rebellious nature and his resistance to the norms of society. Hemingway's public attire reflects the private nature he hoped to project: strong, self-reliant, realistic, and capable of handling the challenges of nature or man: clothes developed for hunting and fishing are practical, and a vest keeps the body warm and yet it also accommodates additional layers of clothing—both over and under—and can be removed and stored more readily than a suit coat should the weather change. When such items are worn out-

side the realm for which they were designed, they suggest that
the wearer is a man of pragmatism and efficiency (W. Wilson
188). The casualness of his open shirts also indicates an attitude
of openness and friendliness (W. Wilson 147), implying that he is
not an effete artist. All of these elements of dress combine to signal to Hemingway's growing public that he is a man's man who
also happens to be a writer—one who can be trusted to provide
real men and the real women who admire them with real truths
about their existence in a world that is undergoing tremendous
economic and gender upheaval.

By 1934 Hemingway's personal style had made such an im-
print on the American public that *Vanity Fair* published an article
that offered costumes representing various aspects of his public
persona; readers could cut them out and place them on a Hemingway paper doll. They included "Ernie, the Neanderthal Man"
(a loincloth and a rabbit for one hand and a club for the other);
"Ernie as the Lost Generation" (turtleneck, beret, and a café
table covered with empty bottles as a prop); "Ernie as Isaac Walton" (fisherman's attire and gear and a boat loaded with fish as
background); "Ernie as Don Jose, the Toreador" (a matador's
outfit and a dead bull as a prop); and "Ernie the Unknown Soldier" (a military uniform, crutches, and a bloody battle scene as
backdrop).

Attaching any of these costumes to the Hemingway doll
would attest to its all-American maleness, for the American masculine ideal stems from two sources. One is simple physical
strength and the other is agility; both are connected with the idea
that the male role entails competition and physical strength in
the service of some higher ideal (Rubinstein 91). And, as usual,
Hemingway was in tune with the public zeitgeist; Ann Douglas
insists that the "new masculine ideal" that first came into prominence in the 1920s and was "as attractive to Freud as to Hemingway, was that, in D. H. Lawrence's words, of a 'hard, isolate,
stoic' 'killer' who dared to come up *mano a mano* against the father and was now suffering the consequences" (244). Stressing
that American history has been marked by action and reaction
with regard to gender—eras of masculinization followed by eras
of feminization in an apparently endless cycle—Douglas points

out that the title of Hemingway's first, still unpublished, short story about Nick Adams is entitled "Did You Ever Kill Anyone?" If Hemingway did not actually have the credentials for the new definition of masculinity—if he had indeed never killed anyone—then he could fake them through his pretense of extensive military service by adopting a uniform-like dress that confirmed his manliness.[8]

The style Hemingway helped establish became the primary American visual image for rejecting aristocratic notions of elegance, opulence, leisure, or the overt seeking of amatory adventure or approval. It also signaled the end of two prominent Victorian styles for writers: the fop, replete in Wildean splendor; and the gentleman, austere in Jamesian comportment. Through Hemingway's personal fashion, one that he increasingly gave to his heroes as well, he announced his continued adherence to the values of the 1920s and 1930s—a man who could go *mano a mano* with the father or whomever he was required to do battle against. Such a man became sensitive and squeamish about wearing any item of clothing that suggested femininity or passivity. Such a man might well opt, as Hemingway did, for a sartorial dialectic of status through underplaying status symbols. For the fashion of *machismo,* for which he began to serve as public standard-bearer, demanded that its followers wear clothing that celebrated burliness, honesty, naturalness, and integrity—manifest by military khakis, hunting vests, flannel shirts, sweaters, and trench coats (originally designed to keep soldiers dry in the trenches). Such calculated underdressing—a conventionalized indifferent posture, an anticonformist conformity—offered a symbolic nuance: it paralleled one-upmanship by subtly claiming elevated status through refusing to make that claim. Such an act trumped the hierarchical principle of the expensive well-tailored man's business suit or tuxedo by appearing to reject their claims of class and propriety altogether.

By the 1940s Hemingway had added his signature white curly beard to his mustache, thus enlarging his announcement that he was entitled to all that is rightfully the purview of the male, and by the mid-1950s this beard would become such a recognizable symbol for Hemingway that a *Look* photoquiz edition, which asked readers to identify celebrities by an identifying characteristic, would use it as Hemingway's trademark (Raeburn 1). In 1944 his attempt to retain his claim to masculine fitness and readiness to do battle—and perhaps to exaggerate his masculinity against the independence, physical courage, and youthfulness exhibited by his wife Martha, who would divorce him within the year—led Hemingway to pose for the photographers of *PM* in the most masculine of dress: boxing shorts and gloves and a bare, muscled, hairy chest. Throughout the 1940s he appears in print wearing shorts, often appearing shirtless as well—almost as though the fitness publicly reclaims his waning youth. Half-dressed with his pants on, he offers an attractive image of being stripped for action, of still possessing the necessary strength and virility to compete with the younger men whom he consistently seems to be shadow-boxing in this decade. His public photographs fully embody his well-honored dictum about writing that "less is more." He also reinforces his public image as tough guy with printed photographs in which he rides in jeeps wearing a soldier's field coat and steel helmet, reassuring the American public that he is no slacker and is making a real man's contribution to the war effort.

With the advent of the 1950s, Hemingway's more casual public appearance began to give way to the disheveled and unkempt look that his mother had so disliked in his great-uncle Tyley Hancock—the alcoholic, favorite male relative of the young Hemingway—whose baggy pants and jacket pockets were stuffed with tobacco pouches and fishing gear. Uncle Tyley's influence on his nephew's style of life and dress would become more and more apparent.

Published in February 1950, Lillian Ross's *New Yorker* profile of Hemingway at fifty captures much that begins to shift in his public presentation during the period, particularly with regard to dress. The article begins with his disingenuous statement to Ross that he doesn't want to have any publicity and that "not seeing news people is not a pose," even as he agrees to meet with her for the purpose of the profile (17). When she meets the Hemingways at the airport, he arrives carrying a beat-up briefcase, which

is covered with travel stickers, and accompanied by fourteen suit-
cases, half of which he has designed and which are embossed
with a *hierro* of his own design as well. The dilapidated state of
the briefcase signals Hemingway's disinterest in his appearance,
even as its stickers and the specially designed luggage proclaim
that he is a sophisticated, well-traveled man whose special needs
require special packaging. Ross reports that he is wearing "a red
plaid wool shirt, a figured wool necktie, a tan wool sweater-vest,
a brown tweed jacket tight across the back and with sleeves too
short for his arms, gray flannel slacks, Argyle socks, and loafers"
(17). While most of the items are continuant with his earlier style
as established in the 1930s, the combination of plaid shirt with
figured tie, of brown tweed with gray flannel, demonstrates a
further sartorial comment on his refusal to be bound by society's
rules. This unusual mix of clashing colors and patterns suggests
an even greater defiance against the post–World War II fashion of
the 1950s, with its emphasis on correctness, than his styles have
offered in the past.[9] In addition, too small clothing worn by an
adult is often interpreted as pointing out the differences between
the growing, maturing, and fully grown physique, displaying
power and control that simultaneously coincide with a sense of
defeat (Wright 54). Ross describes Hemingway's orange plaid
bathrobe as looking "too small for him" as well (27), suggesting a
rather disturbing pattern in his evolving self-presentation—one
that, for the first time, seems unintentionally ironic.

To add to the overall effect, Hemingway's hair is very long in
back, and he has a white mustache, a ragged white beard, and a
piece of paper pressed into service as a nose guard under the
nosepiece of his glasses. Perhaps Hemingway's longer hair and
luxuriant facial hair were his direct counter-response to Mary's
cropped blond hair and gray flannel slacks. The full description
of his appearance connotes a man who has stepped over the
bounds of sartorial comment and into a realm where he fails to
recognize his public subjectivity. He seems confused about the
connection between the way in which he represents himself
within that space and its effect upon his audience. Yet his repeated "How do you like it now, gentlemen?" also seems to indicate that he is painfully aware of his public as a contempo-

rary form of hovering furies whom he can no longer please or escape.

Ross's recount of helping Hemingway purchase a coat at Abercrombie and Fitch, the ultimate outdoorsman store, which Hemingway refers to as "this joint," takes up a considerable part of the article and is particularly mystifying. Hemingway seems to resist shopping for the item, even though he complains of the cold New York November weather, and he pronounces the first tan coat he selects to try as "hanging like a shroud" (31) before choosing a belted coat that he tests to be certain he can wear for hunting. The whole shopping incident indicates the casualness of Hemingway's approach to fashion, and yet the reader wonders why he invited Ross along for the excursion. After all, he knows that she is gathering information for her soon-to-be published profile. Hemingway's ambivalence about the importance of appropriate dress seems apparent as part of the underlying reason for, and tone of, the shopping excursion.

In this decade Hemingway often appears in a baseball cap with an unusually wide brim—even sporting one in the snow in Ketchum. If Hemingway isn't wearing a cap, he is often sporting hunting dress and gear, using a killed animal as a photographic accessory. When he was rescued from his safari plane crash in 1954, he carried two additional great-white-hunter props: a bunch of bananas and a bottle of gin. The combination of this image and Hemingway's published remarks inspired Ogden Nash to write a popular song that was recorded by Jose Ferrer and Rosemary Clooney (Raeburn 146). During this period Hemingway also accepted product endorsements when they fit the image he wanted to portray: he rejected ads for whiskey but pushed Ballantine Ale for those times "when you have worked a big marlin fast"; Barnum and Bailey Circus because the elephants don't "come crashing through the bush"; and the services of Pan American because it enhanced his globetrotter reputation (Raeburn 138). In each of these advertisements, Hemingway wears the appropriate masculine garb to confirm his status both as product endorser and as the, to borrow his term, "heavy-weight" writer.

Nowhere does Hemingway rely on the combination of hairstyles and clothing to help tell his story as in *The Garden of Eden,* which he was working on throughout the 1950s. When the novel opens, the young married couple are breakfasting in identical striped fishermen's shirts and shorts they have purchased from a marine supplies store. Other people did not wear such shirts, the narrator tells us, and Mrs. Bourne is the first girl whom he has ever seen wearing one. Avoiding the ostentatious of the new and gaining the relaxing comfort of the old, the girl has washed the shirts until they are soft and until their worn cloth displays her breasts. The novel devotes a good portion of its text to such descriptions of unisex clothing and to the cutting and dying of hair.[10]

As Anne Hollander points out, hair provokes stronger feeling than anything else in the history of clothing because it is always a part of both clothes and body representation and will "always do for any sort of rebellious expression; cutting it can be aggressive or denunciatory, and so can growing it . . . and the visual effects it creates may rely on immediate responses" (183). Hemingway uses the novel's heavy reliance on details of hairstyles as the essence of personal accessorizing to emphasize what is apparently one of the book's major themes: the dangers of transsexuality and the way in which it can destroy a man's Garden of Eden. Mark Spilka's chapter, "Papa's Barbershop Quintet," argues that the book allows Hemingway to admit how much he needs women through David's remarks, but in his epilogue Spilka avows that the novel can also be seen as "Hemingway's long adult quarrel with androgyny . . . and therefore as a revealing gloss on his own artistic struggles, his own self-definition as a writer with decidedly androgynous propensities" (335). The loud, public rejection of this androgyny is certainly reflected in the public dress Hemingway selected throughout his final decade.

In the twentieth century, military costume underwent many changes and is the "source for much of the male sexuality expressed in dress ever since" (Hollander 52). Hemingway's continued reliance on clothing that had military garb as its referent reflected his continued need to advertise his masculinity. Part of this reliance on minimalism of both language and dress, this attempt at a kind of masculine elegant simplicity, may also stem from Hemingway's indebtedness to French painting and taste.

His debt to Cézanne and the visual arts in general has been widely discussed, and he seems to have made similar connections between the aesthetics of clothing, identity formation, and literary technique.[11]

The links between the spare eloquence of Hemingway's prose and the understated fashions he donned and in which he dressed his more heroic fictional characters are both apparent and complicated—particularly as they are expressed in the androgynous fashions found in *The Garden of Eden*. Just as Hemingway's ostensible contempt for other writers and the fashionable world of New York masked his obsession for attention and praise from exactly those whom he criticized,[12] his need for public approval was so strong that he acknowledged it only by his repeated statements that it was unnecessary. Yet he instinctively adopted the public stance and attire guaranteed to attract and compel attention from the country he sought to represent as heavyweight writer. His professed distrust of the fashionable world and the world of fashion are key to his sex appeal both as writer and as man. Clothing and costume formed an integral part of Hemingway's doubt-free march to claim the literary reputation he felt he deserved.

If Robert Ruark's estimation of Hemingway's appeal is accurate, his writing and his public persona allowed vicarious adventures for men who had none because they lacked courage, or money, or both. Hemingway offered such Americans a code for manliness and proved them correct in their assumptions that "men aren't made at Yale or Harvard, but at the end of a .303, fly rod, or behind a dirty red cape" (quoted in Raeburn 169).

The clothing Hemingway promoted has become a public, visible sign of American, and perhaps international, masculinity. Its continued popularity seems proof that Americans still hold the intrinsic values it manifests. An advertisement on page sixty-seven of the Spring 1998 "Owner's Manual #60," published by J. Peterman, demonstrates the way the fashion of *machismo* remains with us—and its indebtedness to Hemingway.[13] Featuring a streamlined drawing of an item listed as "Hemingway's Cap," the ad tells us that Hemingway may have bought his at a gas station en route to Ketchum "next to the cash register, among the beef jerky wrapped in cellophane. Or maybe in a tackle shop." The writer uses Hemingwayesque prose and counts on the intended buyer's recognition of both the simulated writing style and the sacred Hemingway sites. Its appeal also rests on the sportsmanlike nature of the cap's original purchase.

Just in case the reader has missed the cap's intended masculine appeal, the writer proclaims that "the long bill, longer than I . . . ever saw before, makes sense." The combination of the exaggerated phallic symbol with the claim that such a symbol makes sense ties in with the pragmatic, masculine stance of *machismo*. The ad also insists that the cap will be unaffected by "repeated rain squalls," playing on both the phallic and sportsman images, before describing the cap's color as that of a "strong, scalding espresso, lemon-peel on the side, somewhere in the mountains of Italy." With the last phrase the ad connects the masculine sportsman and the cosmopolitan bon vivant who also appreciates the finer things in life; its ownership will allow a man to appear both masculine and urbane. This is not a cap for the man who wants to hunt with small-time, provincial types. He is a man of the world with a refined palate. The cap's "six brass grommets" remind the reader that such a man may also have seen military service at some point, or at least he can appear to be connected with the military through his choice of clothing. And the writer's final nod to Hemingway is the ad's insistence that the hat will not blow off "and into the trees."

This verbal tour de force, which requires something of an insider's knowledge of Hemingway, has been a successful selling device. The "Hemingway Cap" has been a featured item by the high-end, mail-order catalog company, which advertises in such publications as The *New Yorker*, for more than six years. It offers prospective owners a chance to "buy" some instant *machismo* and to feel slightly smug about their ability to recognize all the Hemingway allusions in the text. The cap, in fact, affords its owners a sense of being simultaneously a sportsman, a bon vivant, a cosmopolite, and an educated member of the literati—for a mere thirty-five dollars. As part of its stance of being honest and unpretentious, the ad's last remarks admit that Hemingway "probably got change from a five when he bought the original."

Peterman catalogs, the aisles of Banana Republic, middle-aged professors who sport curly white beards, or the physical appearance and dress of those attending Hemingway Society functions, whether consciously or unconsciously, offer a persuasive argument that his personal style remains viable. To dismiss either Hemingway or the fashion of *machismo* of which he continues to be the primary cultural representative is to dismiss the fullest portrayal in American literature of the complicated barriers American men feel obligated to present to the world. Like the men who so identify with him, Hemingway used ritual, codes, sport, symbols, and clothing as protective devices against the terror of loss he could not face directly. In so doing he seems to have tapped into the greatest male angst of the twentieth century: How can a man retain maleness when women insist on invading the world of the Papa at almost every social, economic, and artistic site?

Unlike many of his fans, Hemingway at least explored options before deciding, as he does in *The Garden of Eden*, that such women must be relegated to the world of the insane or designated as lesbian and, therefore, marginalized as "other." By interrogating the fashion of *machismo*, his final text moves to place him ideologically in the last half of the twentieth century where, as Marjorie Garber suggests, "the cultural fascination of crossdressing . . . is not always *consciously* [her italics] related to homosexuality, although homosexuality . . . might be viewed as the repressed that always returns" (5).

By the time Hemingway's final text appeared, however, the fashions of the 1980s proclaimed androgyny as an exciting option so that the fashion ideology of his final patriarchal garden seems hopelessly dated. Yet the *machismo* fashion he helped to establish remains—even though it is frequently adopted by women with little resulting stigma, marginalization, or madness. It still signals practicality, energy, physical fitness, and an "understated" nod toward desire—regardless of the sex or sexual orientation of its wearer. For the fashion of *machismo*, at least in the 1990s, has become a universal, signing sameness rather than a gender-specific difference.

NOTES

1. See John Raeburn for a thorough discussion of Hemingway's conscious role as "the architect of his public reputation" (7). While Raeburn does not discuss the role of clothing in this self-fashioning, he offers a convincing argument that Hemingway was fully cognizant that he was creating a public personality.

2. As Fred Davis points out, after World War I until the blue jeans movement of the 1960s when the political left and the bohemian culture coalesced in self representation, the prevailing "anti-bourgeois" style for American male leftists consisted of dark-hued, solid-color shirts worn tieless, unpressed corduroy or tweed jackets worn with corduroy, khaki, or tweed trousers, and a bare head or an occasional beret, often combined with hiking boots or workman's shoes. This description also seems apt as an overall assessment of Hemingway's dress once he marries Hadley and begins to choose his own clothing without the influence of his mother's more conservative guidance.

3. Calling Hemingway the Theodore Roosevelt of American literature, John Raeburn cites both men's reliance on famous nicknames as proof of the public's affection and their similar personal styles that combine the man of thought with the man of action. Both cultivated distinctive public personalities that readily attracted publicity, and both were especially appealing to their contemporaries precisely because they possessed such an unusual and volatile combination of qualities. Eventually both men were loved more for the legends they created about their lives than for their actual achievements (11).

4. This chronological description of Hemingway photographs is drawn primarily from Anthony Burgess's *Ernest Hemingway and His World* and Madelaine Hemingway Miller's *Ernie*.

5. According to Marjorie Garber, who cites the *New York Times* as her source, until World War I pink was thought to be a "stronger, more decided color" than blue and was, therefore, the accepted color for boys' attire (1). This historical use of color coding would seem to indicate that Grace was not trying to feminize her son to the extent argued by Kenneth Lynn.

6. I am indebted to Lieutenant Colonel David M. Owens and Lieutenant Colonel Michael Burke of the English department of the

U.S. Military Academy for pointing out details about Hemingway's attraction to military uniforms and their relation to his later style of dress and for their generous sharing of their knowledge about Hemingway's military friendships.

7. Mellow also reports that Hemingway was put off by Pound's bohemian dress, Ernest Walsh's raffish, romantic look, and F. Scott Fitzgerald's Brooks Brothers suits (289).

8. Both Mellow and Lynn cite Hemingway's repeated bragging about the number of men he had supposedly killed, further suggesting that he felt such killing a necessary credential for a man of his times. The period's cult of masculinity and fascination with the warrior role is also apparent, Douglas suggests, in women's postwar clothing styles. She points to such styles as "helmet or cloche hats" and loose-belted trench coats as adaptations of men's military garb; Greta Garbo's trench coat in *A Woman of Affairs* (1928), which became part of her signature style; and to the proliferation of women's sports clothing and suits (248).

9. In general the fashion of the 1950s expressed its dominant ideological values: gendered dress difference that upheld traditional femininity and domesticity (for an interesting look at the conflicting meaning represented by the New Look of the period along lines of class, see Partington).

10. Catherine Bourne's insistence on wearing pearls to sunbathe brings to mind those wonderful photographs of a similarly-attired Zelda Fitzgerald on the Riviera beaches and hints at Catherine's impending madness.

11. For discussions of the relationship between Hemingway's work and the visual arts, see Meyly Chin Hagemann, Kenneth G. Johnston, and Emily S. Watts.

12. See, for example, Hemingway's statement about his artistic aspirations and concerns in the preface to *Green Hills of Africa,* where he denounces the "writers in New York" as "angleworms in a bottle, trying to derive knowledge and nourishment from their own contact" and "afraid to be alone."

13. The scriptwriters of the popular television show *Seinfeld* created a character based on J. Peterman to serve as the character Elaine's eccentric boss. During the show's final two seasons, these two characters frequently employed Hemingwayesque dialogue and description to create part of the show's humor.

WORKS CITED

Barthes, Roland. *The Fashion System.* Trans. Matthew Ward and Richard Howard. Berkeley: University of California Press, 1983.

Burgess, Anthony. *Ernest Hemingway and His World.* New York: Scribner's, 1978.

Davis, Fred. *Fashion, Culture, and Identity.* Chicago: University of Chicago Press, 1992.

Douglas, Ann. *Terrible Honesty: Mongrel Manhattan in the 1920's.* New York: Farrar, 1995.

Garber, Marjorie. *Vested Interests: Cross Dressing and Cultural Anxiety.* New York: Harper, 1993.

Hagemann, Meyly Chin. "Hemingway's Secret: Visual to Verbal Art." *Journal of Modern Literature* 7 (1979): 87–112.

Hemingway, Ernest. *Dateline: Toronto—The Complete Toronto "Star" Dispatches, 1920–1924.* Ed. William White. New York: Scribner's, 1985.

———. *A Farewell to Arms.* New York: Scribner's, 1929.

———. *The Garden of Eden.* New York: Scribner's, 1986.

———. *Green Hills of Africa.* New York: Scribner's, 1963.

Hemingway photograph, *PM* 21 May 1944: 7.

Hollander, Anne. *Sex and Suits: The Evolution of Modern Dress.* New York: Knopf, 1994.

Johnston, Kenneth G. "Hemingway and Cézanne: Doing the Country." *American Literature* 56 (1984): 28–37.

Lynn, Kenneth S. *Hemingway.* New York: Simon and Schuster, 1987.

Mellow, James R. *Hemingway: A Life without Consequences.* Boston: Houghton Mifflin, 1992.

Miller, Madelaine Hemingway. *Ernie: Hemingway's Sister "Sunny" Remembers.* New York: Crown, 1975.

Partington, Angela. "Popular Fashion and Working Class Affluence." *Chic Thrills: A Fashion Reader.* Ed. Juliet Ash and Elizabeth Wilson. Berkeley: University of California Press, 1993. 145–161.

Raeburn, John. *Fame Became of Him: Hemingway as Public Writer.* Bloomington: Indiana University Press, 1984.

Ross, Lillian. "How Do You Like It Now, Gentlemen?" 1950. *Hemingway: A Collection of Critical Essays.* Ed. Robert P. Weeks. Englewood Cliffs, N.J.: Prentice, 1962. 17–39.

Rubinstein, Ruth P. *Dress Codes: Meanings and Messages in American Culture.* Boulder, Colo: Westview, 1995.

Sennett, Richard. *The Fall of Public Man.* New York: Knopf, 1974.

Simmel, Georg. "Fashion." *International Quarterly* 10 (1904): 294–95.

Spilka, Mark. *Hemingway's Quarrel with Androgyny.* Lincoln: University of Nebraska Press, 1990.

"*Vanity Fair's* Own Paper Dolls—No. 5." *Vanity Fair* Mar. 1934: 29.

Veblen, Thorstein. *The Theory of the Leisure Class.* New York: Mentor, 1953.

Watts, Emily S. *Ernest Hemingway and the Arts.* Urbana: University of Illinois Press, 1971.

Weeks, Robert P. "Introduction." *Hemingway: A Collection of Critical Essays.* Ed. Weeks. Englewood Cliffs, N.J.: Prentice, 1962. 1–16.

Wilson, Edmund. *The Shores of Light: A Chronicle of the Twenties and Thirties.* New York: Farrar, 1952.

Wilson, W., and the Editors of *Esquire. Man at His Best: "Esquire" Guide to Style.* Reading, Mass: Addison-Wesley, 1985.

Wright, Lee. "Outgrown Clothes for Grown-up People." *Chic Thrills: A Fashion Reader.* Ed. Juliet Ash and Elizabeth Wilson. Berkeley: University of California Press, 1993. 49–60.

Hemingway's Gender Training

Jamie Barlowe

Introduction

From 1899, the year that Ernest Miller Hemingway was born in
Oak Park, Illinois, until 1961, when he died by his own hand, public discussions of gender issues were as commonplace as they are
now in the last years of the twentieth century. Anachronistically,
many scholars and critics have read and interpreted the past as
without gender conflict, thus homogenizing, even silencing, the
contentious debates of the mid- to late nineteenth and early
twentieth centuries and replacing actual conditions with a nostalgic picture of the past. Other scholars have offered a portrait of
the past in which women did not assume the right to contest social norms, thus diminishing not only the nature and extent of
the public conflict, but also the history of all the women who,
like Hemingway's grandmother, mother, third wife, and two of
his mothers-in-law, were vocal and active. In such a sanitized
version of the past, then, particular individuals who challenged
or resisted the gendered social norms have been ignored, renamed as emasculators, or recategorized as exceptions to general
rules—and blamed—rather than seen as part of the complexly
structured social conditions. Not only did gender issues remain
publicly controversial and personally fraught for all of the years

of Hemingway's life, but they shaped his self-image, his goals and desires, his attitudes about men and women, and his fiction far more than has been demonstrated.[1] In this essay, I will attempt to reopen and explore the conflicted gendered cultural context that shaped Ernest Hemingway, as well as his parents, friends, and marriage partners; and then reread them in the light of this more complicated context.

Gendered History, Hemingway's Family and Childhood 1872–1917

Women's Suffrage

As early as 1872 Victoria Woodhull had run for president of the United States, and the arrest of fifteen women, "including Susan B. Anthony . . . in New York for trying to vote in [that] presidential election," was indeed newsworthy (Davidson and Wagner-Martin 954). As Anthony wrote in a letter to Elizabeth Cady Stanton on November 5, 1872: "Well, I have . . . gone and done it! positively voted . . . [I] registered on Friday, and fifteen other women followed suit in this ward, then in sundry other wards, some twenty or thirty women *tried to register,* but all save two were refused. . . . I hope morning telegrams will tell of many women all over the country trying to vote" (quoted in Frost and Cullen-DuPont 227–28). Not surprisingly, then, on November 16, 1872, the following notice appeared in the *New York Times:* "Warrants have been issued by United States Commissioner Sibris for the arrest of Susan B. Anthony and fourteen other females, who voted at the late election. The parties will probably be brought to court next week" (Frost and Cullen-DuPont 228). In court, however, Anthony was not allowed to testify in her own behalf, because as a woman the law prohibited her; thus, she was found guilty and fined $100.

A year later in a decision affecting Hemingway's home state of Illinois, the U.S. Supreme Court "upheld an Illinois state law which barred women from the practice of law in its state courts" (Frost and Cullen-DuPont 211). This decision was prompted by

Myra Bradwell's application for admission to the Illinois bar and followed up on an 1871 ruling of the Illinois Supreme Court that Alta Hulett be denied admission. The court's decision against Bradwell was "on the ground that as a married woman, she was not fully a free agent" (Wheeler 32).

Only nine years before Hemingway's birth, the National American Woman Suffrage Association (NAWSA) was formed— a merger of two earlier established suffrage groups, one led by Elizabeth Cady Stanton and Susan B. Anthony and one by Lucy Stone—its constitution stating that its "sole object is to secure for women citizens protection in their right to vote" (Frost and Cullen-DuPont 400). It would, however, be thirty years before the passage of the Nineteenth Amendment to the U.S. Constitution, which affirmed that the "right of citizens of the United States to vote shall not be denied or abridged by the United States or by any State on account of sex," although by that time "28 of the 48 states already had full or presidential suffrage for women" (McElroy 13). "Working through a network of state organizations between 1907 and 1916, NAWSA and its affiliates had helped secure suffrage" in eight states, including Illinois, and the Alaska territory (Frost and Cullen-DuPont 293), but in 1913 the governor of Illinois blocked a state referendum on full suffrage, allowing women in the state to vote only in presidential elections. In 1917, the year Hemingway was graduated from Oak Park High School, Illinois ratified suffrage, later granted nationally by the Nineteenth Amendment.

Along with many thousands of women in Illinois and across the country, Hemingway's mother, Grace Hall-Hemingway, and his grandmother, Adelaide Edmonds Hemingway, were engaged in this battle to win enfranchisement.[2] Suffragists participated in speeches, strikes, marches, meetings, and conventions, arguing their case and gaining support, as well as momentum. For example, in Oak Park, "400 women attended performances of 'How the Vote Was Won'" (Reynolds, *The Young Hemingway* 12–13). This play, which began as a pamphlet, was written by Cicely Hamilton and Christopher St. John and published in 1908 in England; it was first performed on April 13, 1909, at the Royalty Theatre London.[3]

The play opens with women everywhere going on strike and reporting to their nearest male relative to be supported. If men were going to argue that woman did not need the vote because they were "looked after" by men, then women should take men at their word and insist on being looked after. Confronted with a household of female relatives who have all given up their jobs and come to be supported, the anti-suffrage hero, Horace Cole . . . soon realises the error of his ways and rushes from the house to join the throngs of similarly converted men who are marching on Parliament to demand that the government gives votes to women—now! (Spender and Hayman 19)

Its longest run in the United States was "sixty-five straight nights" in Chautauqua, with Fola LaFollette's "barnstorming readings" (Auster 86). *How the Vote Was Won* and other suffragist dramas played a part in women gaining, first, political influence and, then, the vote.[4]

In addition to attending suffrage plays, women in Oak Park also "gave speeches, organized committees and rode in parade floats to rally support for suffrage at the local and state levels" (*Young Hemingway* 12–13). In 1910 the Women's Political Union held the first suffrage parade in New York City. A year later there was another one, with "3,000 marchers and perhaps 70,000 on-lookers" (Frost and Cullen-DuPont 289). That same year in Oak Park, women "won the vote on local issues. In a record turnout for the school board race, women out-voted men two to one, and local politics were never quite the same" (*Young Hemingway* 13). By 1912 there were 20,000 marchers and another 500,000 on-lookers for a parade in New York, and the 1913 suffrage parade "was even larger" (Frost and Cullen-DuPont 291). In 1913 Illinois became the "first state to get presidential suffrage by legislative enactment" (Wheeler 375). The popularity of the suffrage movement brought it more into the "mainstream" of American thought, making it "increasingly 'respectable' in its attitudes and goals" (McElroy 12). For some women activists this popularity compromised their more radical goals; for some it meant the possibility of achieving the right to vote: "By recognizing, emphasizing, and appealing to the differences that separated women, suffrage became the only common thread that tied together these diverse interests and goals" (Buechler 171).

Gender issues, then—as well as strong agreements and resistances—were part of the cultural air that Hemingway breathed. By the time he was a year old, the "majority of high school graduates were women," "'80 percent of the colleges, universities and professional schools in the nation admitted women,'" the birth rate had dropped to 3.56 per family, and there were five million working women in the United States, making up one-fifth of the American workforce (Davidson & Wagner-Martin 956; Rudnick 70–71).

Adelaide Edmonds Hemingway

The suffrage movement was "strongly influenced by the ideology of [white] middle-class women and social feminism. . . . Working women, Jewish women, and socialist women all found a home within the National Women's Trade Union League [1903–1947]. . . . The success of the NWTUL relied on the support that women from varied social, economic, and political backgrounds gave to each other" (Lewenson 37–39). Despite differences in assumptions and methods, both working- and middle-class women "believed that woman suffrage would assure them political, social, and economic equality. . . . Thus, for most women of the progressive reform era, regardless of their economic class, interest in obtaining suffrage rested in their desire to control their lives" (Lewenson 39).

For women like Hemingway's grandmother Adelaide—as religiously and economically conservative as she may have been—she had controlled her life enough to have "studied astronomy and botany at Wheaton College," to have been graduated, and to have been known as a "trained botanist" (Buske 214). Adelaide's six children, including her two daughters Nettie and Grace and son Clarence (Ernest Hemingway's father), were all graduates of Oberlin College, with its long history of civil rights advancements, from its founding in 1833 as America's first coeducational, multiracial institution (it began to admit women students in

1837), to the graduation of its first woman, Catherine E. Brewer, in 1840, to the first graduation in the nation of a black woman, Lucy Sessions, in 1850, to the graduation of seventeen women in 1855, and on into the twentieth century.[5] And although Wheaton College, Adelaide's alma mater, was a far more conservative institution, it boasted as its first president a well-known abolitionist and social reformer, Jonathan Blanchard. Adelaide's husband and Ernest's grandfather, Anson Hemingway, also was an agent for civil and social reform; he "receive[d] a commission in Natchez as a first lieutenant in the Seventieth U.S. Colored Infantry. When the war ended, he stayed in the South, serving as the acting Provost Marshal of the Freedman's Bureau in Natchez and primarily arranging contracts for freed slaves" (Nagel 9).

Feminism, Social Activism, and Reform

From the beginning of his life, then, civil rights and gender issues were in the air of Ernest Hemingway's home. His mother Grace not only earned enough money (perhaps as much as $1,000 a month) to help support the family by giving music lessons,[6] but she also was one of only twenty women in Oak Park who exercised her right to vote for university trustees in Illinois. She was a member of the Suburban Civics and Equal Suffrage Club as well, and grandmother Adelaide was the director of the club. "One of Ernest's early memories from a trip to Nantucket was going with Grace to a suffragist meeting" (*Young Hemingway* 106). Grace attended other feminist meetings on Nantucket when her family vacationed there (Spilka 22).

Early twentieth century feminism was based in social reform. Thus, the voting rights and higher education movements; the political movements that supported worker's compensation, higher wages, and legalization of trade unions and strikes; the "settlement house movement[;] the public health movement[;] and the modern nursing movement found women activists ready to improve the health and well-being of society. Women formed organizations to do some of the social housekeeping activities required of them to improve society" (Lewenson 266). Jane Addams of Hull-House, part of that group of women activists,

"played to a packed audience" when she spoke at the public library in Oak Park in 1907 (*Young Hemingway* 10)—the year that
the "proposal for municipal woman suffrage [in Chicago] lost by
only a single vote. . . . In the 1908 charter convention, suffrage
forces were led by Catharine McCulloch and Jane Addams with
the active support of nearly one hundred Chicago women's organizations" (Buechler 152).[7]

Another well-known Hull-House reformer, Florence Kelley,
became the "first factory inspector for the state of Illinois," and
later, Addams and Kelley "convinced President Taft to establish
the Children's Bureau" (Smith-Rosenberg 255). Chicagoans and
Oak Parkers also knew about the works and deeds of other
women reformers, such as Lillian Wald, Alice Hamilton, and
Grace and Edith Abbott. Social activism was also linked to paci-
fism, for example, in 1915. "Female pacifists, including Charlotte
Perkins Gilman and Jane Addams, founded the Women's Peace
Party. . . . Many black women's organizations, including the
NACW [National Association of Colored Women] and the National Federation of Afro-American Women, added strength and
mass to the suffrage cause" (Bredbenner 687–88). Grace Hemingway was interested as well in working against prejudice and discrimination, particularly that directed at Japanese Americans; she
also expressed interest, in a letter, in "Mary Bethune, the great
black educator who was the daughter of slaves" (Kert 79), and
Adelaide Hemingway "participated actively in the Women's Aid
Society" (Grimes 46).

However, at "the forefront of Oak Park reform stood Reverend William E. Barton, brother of Clara Barton, founder of
the Red Cross" (*Young Hemingway* 10), although, as Michael
Reynolds has documented, Barton's reform did not challenge the
social, economic, and racial privilege of his parishioners, except
at the level of moral responsibility and generosity, nor argue for
social equality. Barton's belief in democracy was profound; for
example, in an address he delivered on February 22, 1920, he said
that democracy "is more than a form of government: it is a philosophy of life" (1). Barton's influence on Oak Parkers and on the
Hemingways—and particularly on Ernest—has been traced by
various Hemingway scholars. For example, Larry Grimes de-

scribes Barton's theology as masculine and moral; Barton thought of it as "muscular"and connected to the democratic spirit; as he argued, "Nothing but human weakness (a failure of the will) can prevent the triumph of goodness in private lives or in the public domain" (quoted in Grimes 40). Rose Marie Burwell says that "after their marriage in 1896, Grace and Clarence had adopted a strenuous style of living that blended the spirit of muscular Christianity with that of the American frontier" (16).

Whether practiced by masculinists or feminists, the zeal for social reform and good works permeated life in Oak Park during Ernest Hemingway's childhood. Failure to participate yielded public scorn, and guilt was often the consequence for individuals like Hemingway who may have overtly rejected these ideals yet was shaped by them in ways he could never adequately suppress or repress. Even in high school Hemingway was rebelling against Oak Park's social and religious norms, as well as those he perceived as his family's. Oak Parkers were not all as conservative as Hemingway thought; in April 1917, for example, of the 7,586 men and women who turned out to vote, more than a third voted for a referendum on showing films on Sunday in the town's public theaters. However, almost three times more women than men voted against the issue (Goldstein 179–80).

Grace Hall-Hemingway

Hemingway viewed his mother's independence, activism, and successes as evidence of her desire to dominate and emasculate, and he spent a lifetime *not* working out the conflict between his intense desire for her approval and his often articulated hatred of her. For many men of the first two decades of the twentieth century, the social issues raised by women reformers and activists, and their insistence on the right to vote and function as citizens under the Constitution, were considered unfeminine. As Mark Spilka argues, "Grace brought a sense of personal and professional worth [to marriage and motherhood] which . . . critics have variously characterized as utter selfishness, a *grande-dame* manner, monstrous willfulness and self-delusion, frustrated careerism, and castrating Victorian momism" (25).

Grace Hemingway was not only an independent woman, singer, music teacher, and suffragist, but she was also a composer; some of her musical compositions were published by the Oliver Ditson Company in Chicago and Summy Company in New York (*Young Hemingway* 107). As Bernice Kert explains, even before Grace's marriage—but shortly after the death of her mother—she was determined to follow her career in music. The "renowned opera coach, Madame Louisa Cappianni . . . believed that Grace possessed a remarkable voice. She arranged an audition for her pupil with the authorities at the Metropolitan Opera and there was the possibility of a contract for Grace" (24–25). In order to pay for her lessons with Madame Cappianni, Grace used the proceeds from a concert she gave in Madison Square Garden in 1896 (which received good press notices), after which she accepted her father's invitation to go with him to Europe for the summer. By October of that year she had made a decision not to pursue a career in music but to marry Clarence Edmonds "Ed" Hemingway (Kert 25).

Pam Boker describes Grace as "an intensely ambitious woman who gave up her professional singing career to become a wife and mother" and argues further that "it is possible that Grace pushed her children to achieve the recognition that would make up for her own lost feeling of importance" (173). Rose Marie Burwell indicts Grace more severely, viewing her as "living her [own] mother's unfulfilled desire for a musical career" and as "far too self-involved to have provided the atmosphere in which [Ernest] could develop a self not contingent upon being the child she wanted him to be" and drawing attention to the fact that "Grace always identified herself as 'Grace Hall-Hemingway,' at a time when most married women dropped their maiden names" (25–26), although more than forty years earlier, in 1855, Lucy Stone had begun the practice of keeping her own name after she married. Reynolds relates that Grace was one of only three Oak Park women whose names appeared hyphenated in the newspaper; the other two were "Dr. Anna Blount, who led the suffragist movement in Oak Park and Illinois, and made contributions at the national level in the fight for the vote; and Belle Watson-Melville, a performer on the national Chautauqua circuit" (*Young Hemingway* 106–7).

Many Hemingway scholars and biographers simply blame Grace for most of Hemingway's problems, for his father's suicide, and even for Hemingway's eventual suicide, making it an easy leap from her independence to Ernest's unresolved issues. And, of course, Hemingway himself both blamed and hated his mother, refusing even to attend her funeral; as Burwell explains, quoting Hemingway: "true to his belief that his mother 'would be as dangerous dead as most women alive, I know I'd never go to her funeral without being afraid she was booby trapped.' Hemingway had remained in Cuba when Grace was buried near her Oak Park home" (129). Shortly before Grace died, on June 28, 1951, Ernest told Charles Scribner that "he would play the role of the devoted son if it pleased her. 'But I hate her guts . . . She forced my father to suicide. . . . I will not see her and she knows she can never come here'" (Kert 462). As Kert explains, for Ernest, "identifying with his father, bitterly critical of his mother, [Clarence's] suicide set off a continuing search for the villain. Eventually he cast Grace Hemingway in that role" (215).

However, complicating the simplistic self-serving blame of his mother on Hemingway's part (and continuing cycles of blame on the part of critics and scholars) is the larger historical and cultural context, which, from the perspective of the active women's movement at the time, would have celebrated and encouraged Grace's independence and interpreted her "self-involvement" as significant progress for women in a post-Victorian age. Social constructions of the female demanded that she have no interests or involvement outside the domestic sphere, but "typically, the New Woman was defined as having the attributes of independence, self-definition, physical adeptness, and mental acuity, qualities that allowed her to work, play, study, volunteer, and socialize with equal aplomb" (Rudnick 73). Further complicating these interpretations of progress, though, were the internal conflicts of the women—"Victorian conventions . . . were not easily let go of" (Rudnick 73)—as well as the fear-based perceptions of men that women would literally abandon their homes and children as they became more educated, independent, and involved outside their homes. For many, especially men in the early decades of the twentieth century, women were seen as incapable of being loving parents *and* having careers or outside interests, and this seems to be the interpretation that Ernest Hemingway adopted about his mother. He seemed, too, to have been terrified that his mother's independence of mind and purpose could undo his male self-construction.

Middle-class white men like Ernest were forced into male roles as often as girls and women were pressed into conformity to female social roles. In fact, men had far fewer challenges to the constructions of male identity than women did to female identity. The immensity and power of the women's movement offered corroboration that biology did not support the social codes and constructions of the female, and in some cases proved them lies. For example, the long held medical belief that women's wombs and brains were directly connected was being questioned; this medical commonplace viewed overstimulation of the brain (study, education, writing, participation in the world outside the domestic sphere) and overstimulation of the body (exercise) as inevitably resulting in the "woman's" disease of "hysteria," in inhibiting women's procreative capabilities, and, ultimately and literally, destroying the white race in America. The public conflicts and debates about the female gender in the United States at least provided some choices for women: they could choose to believe and conform unquestioningly or they could choose to question the validity of the claims that their social roles were inevitably tied to their biological development and to their "natures." Choosing the latter caused confusion, of course, at the personal, familial, and social levels, but at least it offered differing ways of self-identifying in light of the growing awareness that social codes, the construction of female identity, and female biology were not inevitably connected, any more than the biology and "natures" of Africans and African Americans had inevitably made them slaves, as slaveholders and supporters of slavery had argued for 400 years in the Americas. Also under contestation and debate were the continuously voiced arguments that the Christian God had foreordained people of color and women to be subservient, even to remain as property. Thus, the biological and theological claims that women's social and political status, as well as the status of race and class, were righteous, inevitable, and preordained were being exposed and separated. Disconnections of these long-held and deeply protected connections gave women, even before Hemingway's birth and certainly during his childhood (indeed, during his whole life), at least pause before they made their choices.

The social constructions of white, middle-class manhood, though, was not under much contestation or public debate, especially when a series of wars reinforced masculinized notions of duty, honor, and courage, and men like Teddy Roosevelt "taught a generation that life was strife" and that there was "nothing so low as the man 'who shirks his duty as a soldier'" (*Young Hemingway* 16). Even Grace Hemingway's notion of maleness was far less complex than that of femaleness, and some critics and biographers, particularly Spilka, claim that Grace gave an "edge" to "maleness," which was "not uncommon among turn-of-the-century women with advanced ideas" (47). Maleness, in fact, was constructed as the opposite of what was traditionally constructed as female; thus, to be a man was to be not-weak, not-passive, not-subservient, not-naturally-nurturing, not-forbearing, not-easily-overstimulated-and-nervous, not-intellectually-tied-to-biology, and so forth; hence, strong women were considered masculine.

In Hemingway's eyes, his father failed as often to live up to the social codes of white male identity as his mother failed to live up to the social codes designated as female. Interestingly, it was Clarence, not Grace, who was treated for the kind of nervous condition labeled hysteria in women and neurasthenia in men. As Reynolds says, "Dr. Hemingway's long and losing battle with his 'nervous condition,' as the children called it, began early, making him an increasingly moody and sometimes dark person, remote and demanding. By the time Ernest was twelve, the best days with his father were passed, leaving the son to wonder what had gone wrong and the father to wrestle with the demons of depression and paranoia" (*Hemingway: The American Homecoming* 146). Clarence even underwent the famous Dr. S. Weir Mitchell Rest Cure, usually reserved for women. In other words, as the argument went at the time in general, and as many Hemingway scholars have continued to argue specifically about the Hemingways: if

Grace had been a "better" mother/wife/woman, Clarence could have been a "better" father/husband/man. In this evaluation, "better" means strict adherence to social codes and constructions of gender. As Hemingway's character Robert Jordan says in *For Whom the Bell Tolls* about his parents, "He was just a coward and that was the worst luck any man could have. Because if he wasn't a coward he would have stood up to that woman and not let her bully him" (339).

Childhood to Manhood—1918–Marriage

By the time Ernest Hemingway first left home, at age eighteen in October 1917 to work for three months for the Kansas City *Star* newspaper, and then in early 1918, to go to Italy to drive Red Cross ambulances, his general and particularized notions of gender were both skewed and solidified. His general notions included his society's and community's ideas and conflicts about masculinity and femininity, maleness and femaleness, and socially constructed gender roles and codes. His more particularized perceptions were based in his parents' enactments and revisions of, as well as their resistances to, those constructed versions of men and women. All of the immense amount of thinking and rethinking Hemingway did for the rest of his life about these issues, both in his fiction and in his personal circumstances, was trapped in those early perceptions. He found many ways to rebel within the psychological constraints imposed by his unexamined perceptions, but he never found ways to resist them, even to revisit them as fear-based perceptions carried into manhood. Even his public and private rejections of gendered social codes and values ensnared him further, because of the guilt generated by his actions. His guilt can be interpreted as evidence that his rejections were merely superficial acts, unsupported by the kind of examination that would have freed him, socially and perhaps even psychologically. In fact, the very ideas that kept him trapped were the ones of which he could not let go, or even see, and the very ideas that he rejected were the ones that could have set him free.

In such psychologically and socially claustrophobic spaces, all of his decisions and actions further confirmed for him the power of those ideas, codes, and rules to which he had already assigned value and power. In other words, Hemingway moved forward from his childhood into manhood, hellbent upon proving to himself a set of ideas about gender that were not only skewed, but would lead to his self-destruction. Unable to allow himself to see how he could be wrong in his perceptions, he began his adult relationships with women, a series of alternating highs and lows, even disasters, which increased his guilt and painful, personal struggles. He also began to construct himself as a man, using as a mirror his skewed notions of masculinity, which he imposed not just on himself but on all men he ever met or knew, including the male characters in his narratives. Interestingly, though, his struggles in his writings with ideas of masculinity made his male characters far more compelling and complex than his female characters, who are either stereotyped versions of the absence of male traits or stereotyped versions of masculinized women. As "Nancy Walker states in 'Reformers and Young Maidens' . . . Hemingway's representations of the female define the limits of his ambiguous sense of masculinity" (Gilman 849). And, according to Denis Brian, "Readers got more myth than man, and that was what he wanted: he consciously created a larger-than-life hero behind which he hid . . . [he] strides through the pages of American literary history, a rugged, battered, and battering playboy. . . . The Hemingway hero was the face he wanted the world to see, the *man* he longed to be, and behind this mask of fiction he concealed himself" (4).

Hemingway, of course, did not consciously intend his own self-destruction, nor do we have much evidence that he was consciously aware of the consequences of his notions of gender, nor even, probably, consciously aware of the connections between his guilt-ridden bouts of depression and his refusal to reconsider his ideas about gender in twentieth century America. Leaving the country did not alleviate his worries and fears, nor mitigate his desires, as he may have hoped, any more than abandoning, rather than confronting, his problems with women did. Instead, after he abandoned each woman in his life, including his mother, he gave them money—although always creating situations that made it seem as though the women left him or forced him out of his home. "He never broke with a wife until her successor had committed herself to him and set in motion her arrangements for the life they would share" (Burwell 27). His financial responsibility—a component of his code of responsible masculinized behavior constructed, in part in opposition to his father's willingness to accept his wife's financial contributions and in part to his Americanized notions of paternal responsibility—I see as substituting for emotional responsibility, although I realize he probably would not have explained it in that way. As Comley and Scholes argue, Hemingway had a "powerful desire to pay his own way—or to convince himself and others that he had done so. . . . [G]iving [Hadley] the royalties of *The Sun Also Rises* [for example] . . . was a good and generous thing to do, but it was also a gesture interpretable in a code that makes emotional and economic things interchangeable" (27).

Agnes, Hadley, Pauline, Jane, Martha, Mary, and Adriana—1918–1961

When asked by Kurt Bernheim of *McCall's* in 1956 what he thought of as a "woman's role in a man's life," Hemingway said, "'A woman should be properly loved as one is able and according to her deserts. Men and women have their duties and pleasures and rewards, also the right to make mistakes if they are not intentional ones" (quoted in Bruccoli 107). Unable to convince himself that his mother deserved his love and with little experience with girlfriends, Hemingway met, first, Agnes von Kurowsky in Italy in 1918 and, then, in Chicago in 1920 Hadley Richardson. "The rejection of his own mother does not necessarily preclude a man's desire for certain qualities culturally defined as maternal. Agnes . . . the nurse in Milan whom Hemingway wanted to marry, was seven years his senior. He fell hard for her, but she jilted him. . . . Hemingway . . . married Hadley Richardson, who was eight years older than he" (Comley and Scholes 34).

Hadley was also a child of an ardently feminist and spiritualist mother; in fact, Florence Richardson was "one of St. Louis's leading suffragists—a plaque in her honor still stands in the city's Forest Park. She was one of the founders of the St. Louis Symphony and a popular lecturer on philosophy and social justice. A 1914 book, *Notable Women of St. Louis,* observed that she was "endowed with a fine, eager, receptive mind, and power in her hands has not been misplaced, for she has done much in advancing the cause of equality and education of women" (Diliberto 3).

Like Hemingway's mother, Florence Richardson was considered controlling and sexually repressed; thus, as with Grace, Florence's fierce independence and determination were renamed, putting a different spin on her purposes, intentions, and actions. Also like Grace, Florence Richardson has been blamed for her husband's problems—his weakness, alcoholism, insomnia, and eventual suicide—as well as for Hadley's breakdown and her sister Fonnie's "emotional problems" (Diliberto viii). Like Hemingway's father, James Richardson often maintained emotional distance from his family; also, like Clarence Hemingway—and later, Ernest—Richardson shot himself in the head.

Hadley's sister Fonnie was as staunchly feminist as her mother; in fact, it was at Fonnie's urging that Florence and Fonnie, along with Laura Gregg from the national headquarters of the Woman's Suffrage League in New York, formed the first St. Louis suffrage group. Hadley was not interested in her mother and sister's feminism, nor in her mother's spiritualism. Instead, she adapted herself to one of the primary social roles available to women: the invalid. "'Invalidism' was common in late nineteenth-century America—it was almost a career for some women. They were prone to headaches, fainting spells, and stomach ailments. Illness controlled their lives" (Diliberto 16). Hadley, then, was more of a "True Woman" than a "New Woman": the "True Woman was emotional, dependent, and gentle—a born follower" (Smith-Rosenberg 199).

Perhaps as a consequence of losing her father at age thirteen and, five years later, her sister Dorothea, who died of injuries received in a fire—and believing that her mother preferred and privileged her sister Fonnie and neglected her—as well as adopting invalidism, Hadley "dropped out of Bryn Mawr in 1912 after a nervous breakdown and lived at home in a state of emotional collapse, doing little except reading and playing the piano" (Diliberto vii). During 1919 and part of 1920 she nursed her mother until her death. In October 1920, on a trip to Chicago to visit her friend Kate Smith, Hadley met Ernest Hemingway. Less than a year later, on September 3, 1921, they were married and had a child, Jack, called "Bumby," on October 10, 1923. By 1926 Ernest had fallen in love with Pauline Pfeiffer, and by 1927 he and Hadley were divorced (April 14), and he had married Pauline (May 10). During their marriage, unlike her own mother and Ernest's, Hadley adapted herself completely to her husband's desires and needs. As Zelda Fitzgerald once remarked to Hadley, "'I notice in [your] family you do what Ernest wants.' Hadley told Zelda's biographer Nancy Milford, 'Ernest didn't like that much, but it was a perceptive remark'" (Diliberto 193). Pauline, too, at first was shocked by the way Hadley catered to Hemingway and the way Hemingway made her live. Eventually, though, Pauline convinced herself that Ernest was everything she had ever wanted and that she "would be better for him than Hadley" (Kert 170). Pauline accompanied the Hemingways to Shruns in the winter of 1925–1926, doing "everything to keep up the fiction that she was there to visit both Hemingways. . . . In spite of his later disclaimers, he was not the passive innocent, preyed upon by a scheming Pauline. He was sexually aroused by her and they were intellectually compatible. . . . Hadley was his good and devoted wife, but Pauline was the strange, wonderful new girl (as he later described her), and he did nothing to cool his infatuation" (Kert 172–73). Michael Reynolds describes the winter visit to Shruns as "papa and his harem, his ladies in waiting" (*Hemingway: The Paris Years* 342).

Like Ernest, Pauline was a product of the Midwest and, for a time, a practicing journalist and writer, and, like Hadley, grew up in St. Louis. Pauline attended the University of Missouri, majoring in journalism. Later, she lived with her wealthy family in Arkansas, after her father bought land there. Unlike Hadley and Ernest, Pauline was Catholic and had gone to a Catholic girls' school in St. Louis. Both women "had trust funds: Hadley's . . . provided about $2000 a year. Pauline's trust sent her $3600 a year, and her Uncle Gus was always providing windfalls. She was also quite capable of earning her own way in journalism" (*Paris Years* 317). Despite their shared hometown, Pauline and Hadley were not alike. Although they were friends for a time, Hadley became increasingly uncomfortable with Pauline's intrusion into their lives. Yet, she remained passive. "A more assertive woman would have sensed what was happening. . . . Hadley chose to ignore it. . . . She [later] told Alice Sokoloff, 'I *do* think I have a flaccid nature. I tend to give up before other people do'" (Diliberto 205). By the summer of 1926 Hadley was sure of the power of attraction between Ernest and Pauline.[8]

Neither Hadley nor Pauline seems to have benefited or learned much from the social and legal progress of women; during the years of Hadley's marriage to Ernest women's accomplishments were well known: for example, in the United States the first Ph.D.s were granted to African-American women (Georgianna R. Simpson, Sadie Tanner Mossell, and Eva Dykes); women's citizenship was no longer revoked for marriage to a foreigner; the first woman was appointed to the U.S. Senate (Rebecca Latimer Felton); the Equal Rights Amendment was first presented to Congress (by Alice Paul of the National Women's Party); the first female governor was elected (Ma Ferguson of Texas); the first case was argued before the U.S. Supreme Court by a black woman (Violette N. Anderson); the first woman swam the English Channel (Gertrude Ederle of New York); and the first black woman was appointed to serve in the U.S. legislature (Minnie Buckingham-Harper).

In France, where the Hemingways and Pauline Pfeiffer were primarily living during these years, one of the markers of a woman's independence was her short hair, which "symbolized a masculine character reflected in such 'virile' qualities as talent, logic, an ability to handle money, and fierce independence." This articulation of the "tomboy" or "bachelor girl," however, was controversial in both England and France; "Only revolutionary feminists, most notably schoolteachers affiliated with the CGTU, approved of the bachelor girl as an example of sexual equality" (Sohn 94). Although both Hadley and Pauline bobbed their hair, drank, and danced, they seem to have been driven by the kind of desire that eventually erased them as subjects, denying all agency, and leaving them primarily as subservient objects of Hemingway's whims and needs. Thus, Ernest was able to enact his earlier fantasy of the man made stronger by a weak, or at least fully submissive, woman. In so doing, he erased superficially the error he saw in his parents' marriage. In playing her role, Hadley, too, could rebel against everything her mother taught her.

Hadley also may have been influenced by the increased "social pressure for women to remain in the home" in France. In part in response to the sexual and personal liberation of women and in part in response to a declining birth rate in France, there was an urgency with regard to a mother's "duty to do whatever necessary to protect the 'race' and the nation" (Sohn 95). The pressure was particularly evident in France, because "many married women had careers. Any mother who did not wish to be branded 'an abomination of nature' was advised not to place her child in the hands of a paid wet nurse who might transmit a disease to the tender nursling. Breast-feeding meant that women had to stay home. Newspapers, novels, and politicians portrayed motherhood as the noblest of careers" (Sohn 96). Taking on the nobility of this notion of motherhood, as she had earlier taken on invalidism, may have also allowed Hadley the satisfaction of seeing her mother's rearing of her as neglectful and far less than noble. "The Ideal Mother . . . was expected to be strong, self-reliant, protective, an efficient caretaker in relation to children and home. She was to manage the family's day-to-day finances, prepare foods, make clothes, compound drugs, serve as family nurse" (Smith-Rosenberg 199).

It is clear that Hadley was concerned about nursing Bumby, especially during the ocean voyage from Canada back to France a month after his birth. As Hadley wrote Grace, "The least little fatigue or worry on my part so often pretty nearly ends the supply . . . and we feel that I *must* be able to nurse him on the ocean trip and until we can get a good formula for his milk in France where the milk is treated a little differently from here. I would prefer to keep him going all by myself until nine months are up anyway, but as I say, it is doubtful whether I shall be able to or not" (quoted in Diliberto 162). Hadley's earlier invalidism creeps into her newly constructed position as nursing mother, perhaps to give her justification if she failed. Ironically, though—given her refusal to adopt independence or self-determination—it was Ernest who quit his job as a journalist and Hadley's money that supported the family in France in the early years of Bumby's life.

By 1920, despite the propagandistic attempts to change them, women accounted for almost 40 percent of the workforce in France and were allowed to join labor unions without their husbands' consent. "Half of all French female workers were married in 1920, and the proportion had risen to 55 percent [by] 1936. . . . In France in the interwar period two-thirds of working women supported families. Outside the upper and upper-middle classes French women largely ignored the pro-family propaganda, then at its height, and pursued their own goals both in the home and in the workplace . . . only 10 percent—generally women with large families or working in unpleasant jobs—quit work permanently [when a child was born]" (Sohn 97–99, 114).

Despite Pauline Pfeiffer's upper-class status, education, and occupation as a journalist, she was, like Hadley, almost exclusively focused on Hemingway, not only as he transferred his affection to her from his wife, but during the whole fourteen years of their marriage. As Spilka explains: "Pauline is good-natured, as he is not; she calms him as he seethes, encourages him when he sags, prays for his success. . . . She serves him as Catherine Barkley serves Lieutenant Henry [in *A Farewell to Arms*]. She exhibits that 'desire to please' which Millicent Bell attributes solely to 'male fantasies of the ideal submissive partner'" (233). Reynolds supports this view of Pauline: "having made her husband her life's work, [she] tended him as carefully as her garden, writing the checks, arranging the house, managing the hired help, and raising their children" (*Hemingway: The 1930s* 260).

Thus, although at this time women's self-constructions could rely less on male fantasies and social codes unrelated to actual women's lives or psychologies, Hemingway's first two wives, as well as the women with whom he flirted and dallied (for example, Lady Duff Twysden and Jane Mason), functioned as though little or no progress had been made in the United States and as though in France the propaganda outweighed the reality of strong, self-supporting (and family-supporting) working women. "The typical woman of the interwar period was neither Ophelia nor the bachelor girl, neither a traditional housewife nor a blue-stocking; she had begun to throw off the yoke of nature and to claim her rights as a married woman even while [often] sacrific-ing herself, whether to motherhood or modernity" or to wife-hood (Sohn 119).

Not surprisingly, given Ernest's relationship with his mother and with at least two of his sisters, he worked hard to construct (or reconstruct) Hadley and Pauline in the image of *his* ideal of the sacrificing woman: as uncritical, inspirational, and sexual muses—in other words, in opposition to women of strength and indepen-dence, and certainly in opposition to his perception of his mother. So completely constructed by his ideals—and so completely im-mersed in the social and political propaganda in the United States and France—were these first two wives that while pursuing or with Hemingway they were mere extensions of his desire and his skewed notions of gender, mired in his fear-based perceptions of female strength, independence, integrity, and accomplishment.

Although at first so completely infatuated with Pauline's infat-uation with him that Hemingway betrayed Hadley for Pauline, he later blamed Pauline for his own desire and decisions, as he blamed his mother for his father's weaknesses, shortcomings, and illnesses. Ultimately, all women failed him and/or failed to live up to his notions of appropriate female behavior; it finally came down to "Hadley's deficiencies, Pauline's treachery, Agnes's betrayal, and his mother's tyranny" (Brenner 59).

When Hemingway and Pauline were married, they spent much of their time apart, and he continued his affairs, for exam-ple, with Jane Mason. Although he functioned with Jane in much the same way that he had with Pauline while married to Hadley, Pauline was not alarmed. Martha Gellhorn, however, presented a different story. "That Ernest was attracted to Martha from the moment he saw her was never in question. That Pauline was aware of his interest was equally obvious; she was accustomed to tolerating women . . . attracted to her husband" (*1930s* 257). In a bar named Sloppy Joe's in Key West, Florida, in December 1936, Hemingway and Gellhorn met. He knew of her work as a novelist and writer, particularly her recent collection, *The Trouble I've Seen*.

Amazingly, Gellhorn was also from St. Louis like Hadley and Pauline, was also a journalist and writer like Pauline, had a staunchly feminist suffragist mother and had attended Bryn Mawr like Hadley, although Martha left college for adventure and a career and Hadley left because she was ill. Martha's grandmother, Martha Ellis, became a teacher—"virtually an unheard-of act for a woman of her social prominence." Her family "was part of a nineteenth-century genteel society that [Martha Ellis] steadily and shrewdly undermined" (Rollyson 5). She also functioned as a self-styled social worker, since there were none in her time, and worked to change the curriculum in the St. Louis public schools to accommodate the poor as well as the privileged. She was part of the early suffrage movements, believing in "equal pay for equal work" (Rollyson 6). Gellhorn's mother, Edna, had been graduated from Bryn Mawr, was an ardent speaker and campaigner for suffrage and other causes, and, later, was one of the founders of the League of Women Voters. Unlike Hadley, Martha did not resent but reveled in her grandmother and mother's causes and work. Like Ernest's father, Clarence, but unlike Ernest or Hadley's father James Richardson, Gellhorn's father, George, was traditional in some ways, a physician (gynecologist and obstetrician) "proud and supportive of Edna's accomplishments."[9] George, though, "liked to accompany [Edna] to speaking engagements on behalf of women's suffrage. . . . He [also] gave a considerable amount of his time to establishing free prenatal clinics and other medical services for the poor" (Rollyson 7–8).

Unlike Hadley, Pauline, or even Agnes, Martha was younger than Hemingway. Also unlike Hadley or Pauline, "Martha was a professional, a dedicated writer" (*1930s* 257). By the time she met Hemingway she had worked for an advertising agency, the *New Republic*, the Albany *Times Union*, *Vogue*, *United Press*, and the St. Louis *Post-Dispatch;* she had also published articles in the *Spectator* and *La Lutte des jeunes* and had published a novel, *What Mad Pursuit* (1934), as well as a collection of stories, *The Trouble I've Seen* (1936). She had traveled extensively as a professional writer, including visits to Geneva "to see the League of Nations in session, [had] interviewed important women in League politics, and eventually worked up a series that was prominently featured" (Kert 286). She had lived and worked in the United States, France, Germany, Mexico, Italy, Spain, England, and Capri. In 1934 she was hired as a relief investigator for the Federal Emergency Relief Administration, and her first trip for FERA was to see the appalling conditions in a North Carolina textile town. She had also spent time with Franklin and Eleanor Roosevelt, in fact, living with them at the White House in 1935 while she worked on her first draft of *The Trouble I've Seen*. In 1936 she returned to Europe but came back to the States in November to spend Christmas with her mother—their first without her father, who had died in January. They decided to go to Key West with Martha's brother, Alfred, a medical student on vacation.

Also unlike Pauline, "whose sympathy for the working class was *noblesse oblige*, Martha was a born activist [with a] social conscience" (*1930s* 257). Gellhorn "came to Key West already interested in the Loyalist Spanish government and its fight against Franco's Nationalist rebels" (*1930s* 257). She was interested, too, in the fact that the "Spanish Republic came to stand in the forefront of the parliamentary democracies of Europe in granting women their rights. As early as 1931 Spanish women obtained the all-important right to vote." There were also changes in family law: "Within two years, the government had revamped Spanish law in the hope of changing the attitudes of the Spanish people" (Genevois 178, 180).

As war correspondents and filmmakers in Madrid during the fear and excitement of the leftist fight against Franco, Hemingway and Gellhorn lived in the Hotel Florida in the spring of 1937. As early as February 1936 General Franco "had proposed a seizure of power to the interim prime minister, and from then on, the plotting had continued without interruption. Despite the government's caution, rebellion broke out in July 1936" (Genevois 187).[10] In the midst of these civil war exigencies, as well as a result of their own needs and attractions, the relationship between Hemingway and Gellhorn, "tentatively begun, became a full-blown love affair" (*1930s* 263).[11]

Optimistic about his ability to maintain his marriage to

Pauline and continue his affair with Martha, Ernest was also optimistic about the defeat of Franco; as he said in May 1937, when
interviewed the day after his return, by the *New York Times:* "The
reason why Franco is out of luck . . . is that Madrid lies in this
big plateau, with all the defensive forces grouped together and
fighting from the inside. . . . The forces of the defenders of
Madrid increase their strength every week, and time is definitely
on their side. Franco has been hammering away at Madrid since
last November, and he lost his chance to take the city in that first
month'" (quoted in Bruccoli 8–9). On both counts—a continua-
tion of his marriage and a Loyalist victory—Hemingway was
wrong.

For the next year, Ernest withdrew from Pauline, his marriage, and his responsibility as a parent, although that responsibility he had always primarily given over to his wives. Critical of
his own father for the emotional distances he created between
himself and his children, Hemingway's distance from his own
children was both emotional and physical. In and out of Key
West, New York, Bimini, Spain, and France, he spent less time
with his family, increased his output of time and emotional energy on Martha Gellhorn, and became more focused on his various physical ailments.

In early 1938 he returned with Pauline to No Name Key,
"where he had been less than three weeks out of the previous
thirteen months." Ironically, at the same time, Martha Gellhorn
passed through Oak Park, "on a national speaking tour . . .
telling Hemingway's mother and other members of the Oak
Park's Nineteenth Century Club about the history of the Spanish
war" (*1930s* 282). Soon, both Hemingway and Gellhorn were back
in Spain, working again as war correspondents, from late March
until the end of May. During this time the rightist reform movement and the church attempted to reestablish authority, in part
by the founding of the Women's Falange, which "was intended
to return the women of the right to their subordinate place.
. . . Women . . . were being asked to submit once again to
the political and religious authorities." By the time Hemingway
and Gellhorn arrived in March, the government had "'liberated
the married woman from factories and work.' Along with this

'liberation' came maternity bonuses and a ban on women entering the professions. [Also in] 1938 the law on civil marriage was nullified, and the divorce law retroactively repealed. . . . The Church regained control of the schools. . . . When a Francoist victory became likely, the pro-Franco media began denouncing women of the left as 'viragos, sluts, monsters, and bloodsuckers' . . . they were responsible for the catastrophe . . . [they had] destroyed the Christian family and besmirched the chastity of the rest of Spanish women" (Genevois 189–91).[12]

Even early in the war, Hemingway viewed women's participation as problematic; he told a *Los Angeles Times* reporter in July 1937 that "women soldiers today are few. . . . In the early days of the [Spanish Civil] war, many women enlisted but proved a source of grave difficulty" (quoted in Bruccoli 11).

Although Hemingway, for one of the very few times in his life, was devoted to a political cause, Gellhorn's professional and personal relationship to the Spanish Civil War was far more complex and enduring. Hers was connected to her profound, lifelong commitment to worldwide struggles for women's and other human rights. She was already well known for her activism for women's rights all and for her stories based on "field interviews with destitute Americans gathered for the WPA [Works Progress Administration] that moved the President's wife, Eleanor Roosevelt, to do a public reading from the collection in New York and to recommend the book to readers of her newspaper column" (*1930s* 256–57).

For the rest of 1938 and most of 1939 Ernest and Pauline were more apart than together, and when together they argued incessantly. By May 1939 he was living in Cuba with Martha at the La Finca Vigía, because Martha erroneously believed his political and social commitments equaled hers. Hemingway was instead enamored of Gellhorn as his object of sexual desire and ready to move on to new woman/wife, although, as Reynolds claims, "Even if Martha Gellhorn had not appeared in his life, Ernest would have soon left Key West to its gaudy future, just as he always moved on . . . leaving behind the burden of the house and family, the intrusive friends whom he, of course, invited but complained about, and the burden of money" (*1930s* 303).

As Hemingway jettisoned each wife, he also jettisoned friends and places; "changing women mean[t] changing habits and habitats" (*1930s* 303). Yet his power and mastery as a writer did not suffer, nor did his professional reputation. The personal turmoil, incessant moving, and war experiences provided rich fodder for his fiction (*The Sun Also Rises, A Farewell to Arms, To Have and Have Not*, and numbers of short stories, including some of his best, "The Killers," "The Short Happy Life of Frances Macomber," and "The Snows of Kilimanjaro"), his autobiographical and experiential writings (*A Moveable Feast, Death in the Afternoon*, and *Green Hills of Africa*), his journalistic accounts, his speeches, and his play, *The Fifth Column*. By the time he moved in with Martha permanently, he had solid writerly credentials, was writing *For Whom the Bell Tolls*, and had sold the rights to *To Have and Have Not* to Hollywood.

On November 21, 1940, five days after they were married, a reporter for the Kansas City *Times* interviewed the newlyweds; Martha was preparing to go to New York in a few weeks to take a field assignment in Europe: "At any event," she said, "right now I'm the war correspondent in the family" (quoted in Bruccoli 24). Martha's work as a war correspondent placed her in a long line of distinguished women. For example, from 1847 to 1849, Margaret Fuller reported on the Italian revolutionary movement for the New York *Tribune*. "In the twentieth century, correspondents including Bessie Beatty . . . of the San Francisco *Bulletin*, Rheta Childe Dorr . . . of the New York *Mail* and Louise Bryant . . . of the Bell Syndicate, helped make American aware of the . . . revolutionary movement in Russia. . . . In the 1930s, Josephine Herbst . . . evoked vivid portraits of revolutionaries in Cuba, while Agnes Smedley . . . and Anna Louise Strong . . . wrote about revolutionaries in China" (Fishkin 758).

In other words, as Burwell notes, besides Ernest's mother, Gertrude Stein, and a very few other far less significant women in his life, only Martha Gellhorn was a "truly ambitious woman" (170). Burwell quotes Hemingway as saying: "[Martha] was the most ambitious girl I ever met. That doesn't mean much because I have not met many ambitious girls as they frighten me and I dislike them" (170). Gellhorn was also well known for her courage, a quality Hemingway deeply admired, although he would come to resent her fierce independence, ambition, and determination, qualities he associated with his mother. Burwell argues further that "Martha's absences for her work assignments with *Collier's* soon became the source of conflict [in their marriage]. Hemingway blamed his irascibility and inability to create on her not being at home" (27–28). Martha had qualms about marriage before she married Ernest, and after, she often felt confined by domesticity and Ernest's expectations, as well as "bored" and "ill-used" (Burwell 41).

As Stephen Cooper says, Martha "was eager to see and report on" World War II, but "Hemingway had no immediate desire to return to a warring Europe" (117). In fact, after she went back to Europe to report on the war, Ernest wrote that he refused to leave Cuba; she answered, "You have a life there because you have a useful work. It is what you believe in and feel right about doing. But I believe in what I am doing too and regret fiercely having missed seeing and understanding so much of it these years. I would give anything to be part of the invasion and see Paris right at the beginning and watch the peace. . . . I have to live my way as well as yours or there wouldn't be any me to love you with" (quoted in Kert 389). Ernest became increasingly resentful and drank heavily. After a tour at the Italian front and in North Africa—where she received numerous cables from Ernest that read "ARE YOU A WAR CORRESPONDENT OR WIFE IN MY BED"—Martha returned to the Finca (Kert 391). To punish her, Ernest decided to go to the war himself and "offered himself to *Collier's*, the magazine that had been hers since 1937. By the rules of the U.S. Press Corps in the European Theatre of Operations, a magazine was allowed only one front-line correspondent. 'Therefore,' said Martha, 'I was totally blocked . . . having taken *Collier's* he automatically destroyed my chance of covering the fighting war [in an official capacity]'" (Kert 392).[13]

Arriving in London before Martha—because he had taken the last seat on the plane, forcing her to come by ship—Ernest met Mary Welsh Monks, also a journalist, writing for *Time;* Mary was married to Noel Monks, a war correspondent in the South Pacific for the *Daily Mail,* but she was currently involved with Irwin

Shaw. By the time Martha's hazardous fog-bound, freezing voyage was over—in a ship loaded with explosives and no lifeboats—Hemingway was already dating Mary, and he had been in an auto accident that landed him in the hospital. Martha Gellhorn found him there, "holding court"; she was "tired and disgusted and coldly critical [and] stalked out of the room. . . . She told him . . . that she thought him contemptible and considered herself free and separate from him" (Kert 398, 410). Mary's later visit, then, provided him with a welcomed difference.

Although also born in 1908, like Gellhorn, and also a journalist, Mary's "origins were very different, not only from Marty's but from Hadley's and Pauline's as well" (Kert 398). Raised in a working-class family in Minnesota, Mary spent her summers living on a riverboat with her logger father. She attended Northwestern University, entirely supporting herself, and studied journalism. She quit college during a short (two-year) marriage and began working at a small magazine. In the early 1930s she worked for the *Chicago Daily News*, the managing editor of which was Paul Mowrer, Hadley Richardson Hemingway's second husband. By 1937 she was working for the *London Daily Express;* she married Noel Monks in 1938.

Ernest's affair with Mary, prior to his divorce from Martha, followed the same pattern as his earlier marriages/affairs/divorces. One difference was that Martha Gellhorn was happy they would be divorced; his affair with Mary signaled the coming breakup. Another difference was the way Ernest treated Mary; he was often angry and abusive. Unlike Martha, who refused any such treatment, and far more submissive than either Hadley or Pauline, Mary "found herself in the role of 'whipping boy' . . . react[ing] to his insults with a self-abasement that was puzzling" (Kert 408). After the war and after each divorced, Mary, whom he often referred to as "Small Friend," and Ernest went to Cuba. They were married March 14, 1946, after she agreed to "take over the management of the house, garden, food larder, and the accounts, and to type Ernest's manuscripts and take care of correspondence. All financial decisions would remain in his hands" (Kert 422).

Despite his self-serving arrangements and memory, his refusal to be accountable, his patronizing view of women (generally calling women "daughter"), his acts of revenge, his six-year obsession with Adriana Ivancich (a young woman, still a teenager, he met in Torcello, Italy), and his growing paranoia and depression, his marriage with Mary endured until his death in 1961. During those years, Ernest became increasingly exhibitionist, "sit[ting] around the pool or at meals and brag[ging] about his sexual conquests (real or imagined), and Mary, covering her embarrassment, would act as though she was proud of his manliness" (Kert 444). He also became increasingly abusive to Mary, even blaming her for an ectopic pregnancy. As their friend Bill Walton put it, "By refusing to march out when he was so abusive, [Mary] lost something upon which there can be no price — her self-respect" (Kert 455). Sometime after 1950, he remarked, referring to Mary as well as more generally, "I think most sterile women were clapped early and just didn't notice it. Most of them don't even know when they have the clap or the old rale and they give it to you with love and affection. They always have to be jealous of something and if you give them no cause for jealousy except your work they will be jealous of that" (quoted in Burwell 50). Ernest's physical illnesses and his delusions, depression, and paranoia mounted until 2 July, when he shot himself in the head.

Hemingway and Gender: Conclusion

Hemingway continued to hate his mother well past her death in 1951, despise Gertrude Stein and Zelda Fitzgerald, blame Pauline (who also died in 1951), and revile Martha. He blamed his often foul moods on the "'open wound' of loving women." As he wrote Buck Lanham, "What suckers we are for them. . . . As long as they have mens and womens, we will have plenty problems" (quoted in Kert 425). He wrote Maxwell Perkins that

> A man who suffers from women . . . has a more incurable disease than cancer. . . . A woman ruined Scott [Fitzgerald]. It wasn't just Scott ruining himself. But why couldn't he have

told her to go to hell? Because she was sick . . . and because they're sick you can't treat them as you should. The first great gift for a man is to be healthy and the second, maybe greater, is to fall [in] love with healthy women. You can always trade one healthy woman in on another. But start with a sick woman and see where you get. . . . If you leave a woman, though, you probably ought to shoot her. It would save enough trouble in the end even if they hanged you. (Baker 553–54)

Not surprisingly, then, as Burwell says, "writing was the only intimate human relationship Ernest Hemingway could sustain" (160). She and hundreds of scholars, critics, readers, filmmakers, and other aficionados of Hemingway have searched his life and his private and public/published and unpublished writings for clues about the nature and extent of his ideas about and experiments in gender, in intimate relationships, and in writing. Some of those interested in Ernest Hemingway have made forays into the larger gendered context: that set of social, legal, institutional, economic, and religious conditions that have insidiously and invidiously shaped and reshaped generations of girls and boys into women and men. However, most who have written about Hemingway have opted for a smaller, tighter focus on the family, the friends, the wives/lovers, and the man, often as though none was formed and informed, even controlled completely, by those larger, gendered conditions and forces, and as though gendered ideologies did/do not exist.

Yet, it seems clear that this complex, gendered set of conditions consciously and unconsciously motivated Ernest Hemingway, shaped his responses and attitudes, lay behind his fictionalized characters, inhabited and inhibited all his relationships, contributed to his immense guilt and to his various psychological strategies for avoiding guilt through blaming others, and finally made him so sad and lonely that he could not go on. Such insights complicate and broaden our understanding of Hemingway and ourselves as his readers, because they press us to recognize that individuals and families are shaped and controlled by social and historical forces that we may view as mere background to our lives. Instead, that background and what we have learned as foreground—some notion of conscious selves attempting to control our lives—cannot be separated into background and foreground. Nor can we de-link the conscious from the unconscious, the rational from the irrational, or ideology from the choices we make. All are complexly and inevitably intertwined. All exist on a continuum of shifting, multiple definitions, positions, beliefs, and ideas, which ideology endlessly reshapes as shared truths. In other words, Ernest Hemingway was the complex, male-gendered product not just of the generations of Halls and Hemingways, but also of endlessly interconnected social and historical gendered forces and conditions of which the Halls and Hemingways were also products.

Thus, as my essay urges, we have to examine the complex web of forces and conditions into which Ernest Hemingway was born and in which he existed. Understanding him, as he was socially constructed—and as he reconstructed himself as rebellious, self-made, and manly—then, requires us to begin to do such an examination. I have also been urging us to reconsider and reread the women in his life in light of these forces and conditions, and to ask why women were suffragists or activists or feminists—or not. It is far too simple to answer, as so many Americans and so many scholars have done, that they were bitches who hated men. It is not only embarrassingly simple, but also wrong to say that they caused men's breakdowns and problems. Thus, I have also urged us to reconsider the social and historical forces that rendered women as second-class citizens, at best, and to which so many women finally responded. In that space and light, then, we can also consider the consequences of such potentially radical social and legal changes for men who were accustomed to being in power. We can consider, too, the women—for example, those like Hadley, Pauline, and Mary—who were easily seduced back into ideological compliance with regard to a woman's "place" or who were never motivated to resist social codes and ideas about women at all.

In this essay, I have only briefly and sketchily probed the gendered social and historical forces and have only begun the work of reconsidering and rereading the writer and the man named Ernest Hemingway and those who peopled his life and writings.

As I and others have argued elsewhere, Hemingway offers us a valuable site for studying the contested, fraught, and interesting late nineteenth- and twentieth-century history of gender in the United States, as well as in the other countries where he lived, fought, reported, and wrote. That he offers this site of examination, even understanding, cannot be contested; that he *was* this site remains excitingly a source of debate.

NOTES

1. See Rose Marie Burwell, Gioia Diliberto, Bernice Kert, Michael Reynolds, Carl Rollyson, and Mark Spilka, for example, who find correspondences among Hemingway, his family, and the gendered social conditions and examine those conditions to some extent.

2. See Cooper, who downplays Grace's participation.

3. Hamilton had earlier published a bestselling book, *Marriage as a Trade*, and had written other plays, her first in 1890.

4. Early suffragist dramas were written by women involved in the British suffrage movement, but one of the most popular, *Votes for Women*, was written by "an American-born actress, Elizabeth Robins, who lived in England. . . . [It] was a compound of 'fallen women' melodrama and suffragist propaganda" (Auster 82). Hundreds of these plays were written, published, and produced in the United States, including ones by well-known writers such as Charlotte Perkins Gilman and by well-known female actors such as Mary Shaw.

5. On May 26, 1856, Susan Anthony "reported" to Elizabeth Cady Stanton that "she had been to dinner with Mrs. Finney, the wife of the president of Oberlin. After her husband denounced women's rights, 'Mrs Finney took me to another seat and with much earnestness inquired all about what we were doing and the growth of our movement. . . . Said she, you have the sympathy of a large proportion of the educated women with you. In my circle I hear the movement much talked of and earnest hopes for its spread expressed—but these women dare not speak out their sympathy'" (quoted in DuBois 50).

6. "Dr. Hemingway's income . . . between 1900 and 1920 grew from about $2000 a year to perhaps $5000 a year. If Grace Heming-

way had a large voice in the family's affairs, it was proportionate to her contribution" (*Young Hemingway* 106).

7. Jane Addams has been called one of the "two most widely known and respected American women in the 20th century," along with Eleanor Roosevelt (Rossi 599). Also in 1907 Addams published "Utilization of Women in City Government," considered both provocative and intelligent, but also controversial. In 1910 she published "Why Women Should Vote," in *Ladies' Home Journal*, as well as her book *Twenty Years at Hull-House*, which became a bestseller.

8. When Hadley broached the subject with Ernest, he "denied nothing, but . . . rebuked her sternly for bringing 'the thing' into the open. 'What he seemed to be saying to me,' recalled Hadley, 'was that it was my fault for forcing the issue. Now that I had broken the spell our love was no longer safe.' . . . She backed off immediately, hurt and confused, but determined to do what he asked, which was to go on as before" (Kert 178–79).

9. One of Edna's accomplishments was to found, along with a group of supporters and other parents, a progressive high school, named after the naturalist John Burroughs; it opened on October 2, 1923, "with ten teachers and seventy-five students. Martha Gellhorn was the first girl admitted. . . . Students who could not afford the tuition were provided with scholarships, and John Burroughs was regarded as setting a new standard for other schools, public and private, to follow (Rollyson 22–23).

10. Paradoxically, though, "the war furthered the cause of women. On the Republican side, there was a new urgency in proceeding with cultural and legislative changes. . . . Clearly, for many women, the civil war led to a profound change in outlook, as historical sociologists are now demonstrating with evidence formerly concealed by Franco's reconstruction of history (Genevois 188).

11. Despite Hemingway's patronizing of Gellhorn when she arrived in Spain—he said to her, with his hand on her head: "I knew you'd get here, daughter, because I fixed it so you could" (quoted in Rollyson 97)—and despite her being enraged in response, she fell in love with him. They continued to have bad moments, as, for example, when he locked her in her hotel room during a bombardment. "No one heard her banging and shouting until the shelling stopped. . . . Hemingway . . . confessed bashfully that he had locked her in 'so

that no man could bother her.' His 'possessiveness' annoyed her, but she also took pleasure in his sense of command" (Rollyson 98).

12. Although the "history of the repression of women under Franco [was] similar in most respects to that of men: exile, execution, prison, reeducation of their children, denunciation, professional blacklisting, and book burning were measures that affected all Republicans . . . women also endured rape, castor oil, shaved heads, and church prisons. Many paid with their lives. Exactly how many is unknown, but in Madrid in 1939 prisoners were being executed at the rate of 6,000 a month. . . . And of course women suffered for an offense that only they could commit, the crime of being the wife, widow, or mother of a 'vanquished' Republican" (Genevois 192).

13. Later, however, Gellhorn was able to find a way to get ashore during the D-Day invasion, and Hemingway was not, even though both were covering it, he on a landing craft and she on a hospital ship; she "managed to sneak ashore with the stretcher bearers to collect wounded men" (Elwood-Akers 70).

WORKS CITED

Auster, Albert. *Actresses and Suffragists: Women in the American Theatre, 1890–1920.* New York: Praeger, 1984.

Baker, Carlos, ed. *Ernest Hemingway: Selected Letters, 1917–1961.* New York: Scribner's, 1981.

Barton, William E. "George Washington: An Address." Oak Park, Ill.: Advance, 1920.

Boker, Pamela A. *The Grief Taboo in American Literature: Loss and Prolonged Adolescence in Twain, Melville, and Hemingway.* New York: New York University Press, 1996.

Bredbenner, Candice Lewis. "Political Organizations, 1900–1960." *The Oxford Companion to Women's Writing in the United States.* Ed. Cathy N. Davidson and Linda Wagner-Martin. New York: Oxford University Press, 1995.

Brenner, Gerry. *Concealments in Hemingway's Works.* Columbus: Ohio State University Press, 1983.

Brian, Denis. *The True Gen.* New York: Grove, 1988.

Bruccoli, Matthew, ed. *Conversations with Ernest Hemingway.* Jackson: University of Mississippi Press, 1986.

Buechler, Steven M. *The Transformation of the Woman Suffrage Movement: The Case of Illinois, 1850–1920*. New Brunswick, N.J.: Rutgers University Press, 1986.

Burwell, Rose Marie. *Hemingway: The Postwar Years and the Posthumous Novels*. Cambridge: Cambridge University Press, 1996.

Buske, Morris. "What If Ernest Had Been Born on the Other Side of the Street." *Ernest Hemingway: The Oak Park Legacy*. Ed. James Nagel. Tuscaloosa: University of Alabama Press, 1996.

Comley, Nancy R., and Robert Scholes. *Hemingway's Genders: Rereading the Hemingway Text*. New Haven, Conn.: Yale University Press, 1994.

Cooper, Stephen. *The Politics of Ernest Hemingway*. Ann Arbor, Mich.: UMI, 1987.

Davidson, Cathy N., and Linda Wagner-Martin, eds. *The Oxford Companion to Women's Writing in the United States*. New York: Oxford University Press, 1995.

Diliberto, Gioia. *Hadley*. New York: Ticknor, 1992.

DuBois, Ellen Carol. *Feminism and Suffrage: The Emergence of an Independent Women's Movement in America 1848–1869*. Ithaca, N.Y.: Cornell University Press, 1978.

Elwood-Akers, Virginia. *Women War Correspondents in the Vietnam War, 1961–1975*. Metchuen, N.J.: Scarecrow, 1988.

Fishkin, Shelley Fisher. "Reportage." *The Oxford Companion to Women's Writing in the United States*. Ed. Cathy N. Davidson and Linda Wagner-Martin. New York: Oxford University Press, 1995.

Friedl, Bettina, ed. *On to Victory: Propaganda Plays of the Woman Suffrage Movement*. Boston: Northeastern University Press, 1987.

Frost, Elizabeth, and Kathryn Cullen-DuPont. *Women's Suffrage in America: An Eyewitness History*. New York: Facts on File, 1992.

Genevois, Daniele Bussy. "The Women of Spain from the Republic to France." *A History of Women: Toward a Cultural Identity in the Twentieth Century*. Ed. Francoise Thebaud. Cambridge, Mass.: Harvard University Press, 1994.

Gilman, Sander. "Stereotypes." *The Oxford Companion to Women's Writing in the United States*. Ed. Cathy N. Davidson and Linda Wagner-Martin. New York: Oxford University Press, 1995.

Goldstein, Joel H. *The Effects of the Adoption of Woman Suffrage: Sex Differences in Voting Behavior—Illinois, 1914–21*. New York: Praeger, 1984.

Grimes, Larry E. "Hemingway's Religious Odyssey: The Oak Park Years." *Ernest Hemingway: The Oak Park Legacy.* Ed. James Nagel. Tuscaloosa: University of Alabama Press, 1996.

Kert, Bernice. *The Hemingway Women.* New York: Norton, 1983.

Lewenson, Sandra Beth. *Taking Charge: Nursing, Suffrage, and Feminism in America, 1873–1920.* New York: Garland, 1993.

McElroy, Wendy. "Introduction: The Roots of Individualist Feminism in Nineteenth-Century America." *Freedom, Feminism, and the State: An Overview of Individual Feminism.* Ed. Wendy McElroy. Washington, D.C.: Cato Institute, 1982.

Nagel, James. "The Hemingways and Oak Park, Illinois: Background and Legacy." *Ernest Hemingway: The Oak Park Legacy.* Ed. Nagel. Tuscaloosa: University of Alabama Press, 1996.

Reynolds, Michael. *Hemingway: The American Homecoming.* Oxford: Basil Blackwell, 1992.

———. *Hemingway: The 1930s.* New York: Norton, 1997.

———. *Hemingway: The Paris Years.* Oxford: Basil Blackwell, 1989.

———. "High Culture and Low: Oak Park before the Great War." *Ernest Hemingway: The Oak Park Legacy.* Ed. James Nagel. Tuscaloosa: University of Alabama Press, 1996.

———. *The Young Hemingway.* Oxford: Basil Blackwell, 1986.

Rollyson, Carl. *Nothing Ever Happens to the Brave: The Story of Martha Gellhorn.* New York: St. Martin's, 1990.

Rossi, Alice, ed. *The Feminist Papers: From Adams to deBeauvoir.* New York: Bantam, 1973.

Rudnick, Lois. "The New Woman." *1915, the Cultural Moment.* Ed. Adele Heller and Rudnick. New Brunswick, N.J.: Rutgers University Press, 1991.

Smith-Rosenberg, Carroll. *Disorderly Conduct: Visions of Gender in Victorian America.* New York: Knopf, 1985.

Sohn, Anne-Marie. "Between the Wars in France and England." *A History of Women: Toward a Cultural Identity in the Twentieth Century.* Ed. Francoise Thebaud. Cambridge, Mass.: Harvard University Press, 1994.

Spender, Dale, and Carole Hayman, eds. *How the Vote Was Won and Other Suffrage Plays.* London: Methuen, 1985.

Spilka, Mark. *Hemingway's Quarrel with Androgyny.* Lincoln: University of Nebraska Press, 1990.

Villard, Henry Serrano, and James Nagel. *Hemingway in Love and*

War: The Lost Diary of Agnes von Kurowsky, Her Letters & Correspondence of Ernest Hemingway. Boston: Northeastern University Press, 1989.

Wheeler, Marjorie Sprull. *One Woman, One Vote: Rediscovering the Woman Suffrage Movement.* Troutdale, Ore.: NewSage, 1995.

The Great Themes in Hemingway

Love, War, Wilderness, and Loss

Frederic J. Svoboda

The 1996 Richard Attenborough film *In Love and War* is only the most recent work of popular culture to remind us that Ernest Hemingway's appeal to the public far transcends his purely literary achievements. Hemingway has a place in American culture, even for many who have not read him. The Attenborough film was a workmanlike treatment of the young Hemingway's 1918 love affair with nurse Agnes von Kurowsky, the real-life prototype for Catherine Barkley in Hemingway's great novel of World War I, *A Farewell to Arms*. *In Love and War* had the singular misfortune to appear in the same season as Anthony Minghella's *The English Patient*, a far more effective treatment of similar themes. Even so, *In Love and War,* based on von Kurowsky's diaries of the time, still attracted considerable notice and prompted new attention to the facts—or stereotypes—of Hemingway's life and work. Why should such interest continue, more than thirty-five years after the author's suicide? Why should a respected director devote his time to such a production? Certainly a director of epics such as Attenborough is always in need of epic material, and the First World War and a love affair that may have propelled an author to world-class achievement might have seemed worthy of attention. Yet in this case, Attenborough did not produce an epic: *In Love and War* was no *Gandhi*. The film's battle scenes did not have epic sweep but were staged in near-dark, focusing on a single character's wounding. The love affair ended not with a crescendo of emotion, but with words spoken nearly too softly to be heard, as the lovers played by Chris O'-Donnell and Sandra Bullock parted at an Italian train station. The callow O'Donnell was no great lover, and several critics suggested that Attenborough would better have filmed *A Farewell to Arms* itself. Even so, the film did a decent business, and viewers paid attention. On the Internet Movie Data Base, a standard electronic resource, viewers polled it at 7.8 on a ten-point scale, only three-tenths less than *The English Patient*, with its nine Oscars.

It seems to me that the popularity of *In Love and War* can be explained by its thematic concerns, the same thematic concerns that have brought millions of ordinary readers to Hemingway's writing over the last seventy years. The makers of *In Love and War* got it half right in their title, for the great themes in Hemingway are: Love and War, Wilderness and Loss. All four themes show to one degree or another in the film, helping to assure its popularity.

I

Hemingway's position as a cultural icon seems a little puzzling when we consider that he began his literary career as an avant-garde writer, very nearly publishing his own writing in the early 1920s Paris of the Lost Generation. His only paying market was *der Querschnitt*, a German "little magazine" of new writing. Yet Hemingway also came to literature by way of journalism. Before going to war he had been a cub reporter on the Kansas City *Star*; after, a successful news correspondent covering Europe and the Balkans for the Toronto *Star* and Hearst's International News Service. So the mass market was not far from him. And, as Linda Wagner-Martin has pointed out, he was lucky to find his essential concerns rather early in life and even luckier that these concerns proved to be widely shared by the reading public.

Hemingway strove for a career as a man of letters. Among his writings are numerous short stories (considered by some to be his finest achievements), book-length satire, travel books, a somewhat esoteric study of bullfighting, and a Broadway play. But his publishers identified him early as a producer of epic novels and a popular personality. To a considerable extent he went along with their program, with still-visible results on public images of him. We see some of the crudest of these images near the end of *In Love and War*. In a meeting that never happened in real life, Bullock's Agnes comes to visit O'Donnell's Ernest after she has rejected him via a "Dear Ernest" letter and in turn has been rejected by the rich Italian suitor she had planned to marry. Agnes finds Ernest at home in a picturesque log cabin. The cabin is set beside a lake and surrounded by a wilderness of towering evergreens. Neither cabin nor setting bears much resemblance to "Windemere," the Hemingway family's prosaic frame cottage on northern Michigan's rather civilized Walloon Lake, in a region whose trees had been cut over in the late nineteenth century. O'Donnell plays all the Hemingway stereotypes: he is unshaven, drunk, and surly. When Agnes asks for forgiveness he throws her out in order to return to his bottle, his regret, and his budding career. The loss of Agnes explains it all, the film implies. Lose the girl, get drunk, and become a great writer. It's just that simple in the popular view of Ernest Hemingway, larger-than-life personality.

As it happens, Attenborough's film is just enough right to drive a Hemingway scholar to drink, himself, for certainly there were elements in Hemingway's life that did not measure up to the seriousness and balance of the author's best fiction. And there are definite patterns to Hemingway's work.

It turns out that Hemingway's protagonists tend to come paired with women, and in some of these pairings there may be links to the Hemingway/Agnes von Kurowsky romance. A partial listing would include the young Nick Adams and his almost fiancée Marjorie in "The End of Something" (1924), as well as Nick Adams and his Chippewa girlfriend Trudy Gilby in "Fathers and Sons" (1933). Both stories are set in the resort areas of northern Michigan. In the first the young Nick, Hemingway's closest fictional alter ego, rejects the rather conventional Marjorie and then unconvincingly pretends to himself that their relationship is not necessarily over as a result of his action, even though Marjorie has convincingly demonstrated her newfound independence as she pushes off and rows away, leaving Nick alone on the shore of Horton Bay. In the latter, a middle-aged Nick looks back from adulthood at his idyllic sexual initiation with Trudy. The latter story is suffused with nostalgia yet mostly redeemed from sentimentality by Nick's thoroughgoing realism about the comic inadequacies of his Victorian father's attempts at sex education. In both stories the destruction of Michigan's white pine wilderness parallels the interpersonal losses.

Then there is the war-wounded Jake Barnes, narrator and protagonist of *The Sun Also Rises* (1926), and his ever frustrated true love, Lady Brett Ashley. For a former aviator, in World War I parlance a "knight of the sky," Jake is notably non-heroic. He lives for small pleasures: eating and drinking, going to work, and taking a vacation. Of the world he expresses a prototypically existentialist concern: "All I wanted to know was how to live in it" (148). He intermittently appeals to and is rejected by Lady Brett, with whom he met and fell in love while he was a patient in a military hospital and she was a member of the British Voluntary Aid Detachment, a nurse's aide. At book's end, as Brett supposes that they might have had a wonderful relationship with each other had he not been rendered impotent by his wound, Jake answers, "Isn't it pretty to think so?" (247). Generations of critics have argued about whether that statement is intended to be read as harshly cynical and despairing or merely a realistic statement of the lovers' situation. Generations of readers have sympathized with the couple's plight.

Frederic Henry and Catherine Barkley in *A Farewell to Arms* (1929) of course are most directly related to Hemingway and Agnes. Death separates these two, as it does the piratical Harry Morgan and his wife in *To Have and Have Not* (1937), failing writer Harry Walden and his wife in "The Snows of Kilimanjaro" (1935), beautiful people on safari Francis and Margo Macomber in "The Short Happy Life of Francis Macomber" (1936), and guerrilla dynamiter Robert Jordan and his young lover Maria in Hemingway's novel of the Spanish Civil War, *For Whom the Bell Tolls* (1940). The middle-aged, dying Colonel Cantwell and his teenage Countess

Renata in *Across the River and Into the Trees* (*Across the River* [1950]) are similarly separated by Cantwell's fatal heart attack.

In posthumously published novels similar couples are painter Thomas Hudson and his actress ex-wife, separated first by divorce and then by death in *Islands in the Stream* (1970), as well as troubled newlyweds David and Catherine Bourne (and Marita, their shared lover and temptress) in *The Garden of Eden* (1986).

Ernest and his first wife Hadley in the posthumous memoir/novel of 1920s Paris, *A Moveable Feast* (1964), also find trouble in marriage and impending separation. The memoir's somewhat fictionalized young Ernest finds himself drawn simultaneously to Hadley and to the heiress who will become his second wife, Pauline Pfeiffer. The rapidly aging Ernest who writes the memoir idealizes Hadley and mourns the loss of her love—and of his youth and innocent poverty. Even *The Old Man and the Sea* (1952), very nearly a book without women, characterizes the old Cuban fisherman Santiago as a man who finds the death of his wife still so painful to contemplate that he keeps her photograph flat on a shelf under his folded spare shirt rather than in full view so that he will not be reminded of the loss of her.

In all of these works it is the loss of love, and often the memory of its loss, that is a core element in the appeal to a reader.

II

War often provides a parallel and resonance to these tales of the loss of love. Revolutions mark *In Our Time* (1925) and *To Have and Have Not*. The former is a collection of short stories arranged according to a chronology of twentieth-century history and unified by the recurrence of Hemingway's characteristic themes, as well as by the appearance of Nick Adams in many of the stories. In it we see upheaval in Greece and the generalized leftist striving toward revolution in Europe that followed the First World War. World War I also figures prominently in the collection (including a one-page fictionalization of the story of Ernest and Agnes entitled "A Very Short Story" and ending with the protagonist contracting gonorrhea in a Chicago taxicab), as does the Greco-

Turkish War of 1922. The fruits of love often become ominous in
In Our Time, with recurring images of women giving birth under
dangerous conditions—in a bunk in an isolated Michigan Indian
camp ("Indian Camp") or in the rain under blankets during a
military retreat ("On the Quai at Smyrna"). We also read of the
loss of autonomy that becomes the threatening concomitant of
romantic commitment, as in such stories as "Cat in the Rain"
(a view inside what is proving itself to be a decidedly ordinary
marriage from the woman's point of view) and "Cross-Country
Snow" (a view in contemplation of marriage from the point of
view of the would-be groom). In *To Have and Have Not* it is the
1933 revolution in Cuba against dictator Gerardo Machado, echoing 1930s leftism in the United States, that provides the background for Harry Morgan's amoral strivings. His double dealing
in the smuggling of booze and illegal immigrants between Cuba
and Key West leads to his fatal wounding and to his less than
completely revolutionary realization that "a man alone ain't
got no bloody fucking chance" (225). The true love offered by
Harry's wife, the rotund and sometimes bleached-blonde Marie,
is juxtaposed to the sterile relationships of the idle rich and members of the comfortable left wing. Marie offers Harry a relationship more authentic and more loving, but her love cannot save
Harry. She merely can mourn alone, feeling "empty like an
empty house" and unable even to bring herself to go to Harry's
funeral (257).

It is in *A Farewell to Arms* that the First World War is most directly treated, and the loss of love through Catherine Barkley's
death in childbirth is not merely paralleled by the war. In the novel
the many losses of the war become nearly equal in dramatic force
to the loss of love. (The failure of *In Love and War* to balance these
two great themes is at least in part a reason for the film's relative
failure as a work of art.) Attenborough's film focuses on Hemingway and Agnes, the lovers; Hemingway's novel comes more and
more to his fictionalized lovers as it progresses, but it convincingly
intertwines their fate with the war, beginning with early ominous
images of marching Italian infantrymen carrying pouches of am-
munition under their capes and so looking like women "six
months gone with child." Images of war, disease, and death are set

in counterpoint against the passing seasons in the mountain landscape of northern Italy in the novel's famous opening chapter. With winter comes the onset of cholera; the deadly aspects of World War I are suggested by the narrator's ironic comment that "only" 7,000 soldiers died of it (4).

The novel's narrator, Frederic Henry, is an American student of architecture in his twenties who has enlisted as a lieutenant in the Italian army's ambulance corps on a whim but who progressively finds himself involved in a very serious business indeed. He would like to make his war a matter of dispassionate whoring and drinking, and his first encounters with Catherine Barkley partake a good deal of what she calls "the nurse's-evening-off aspect of it" (26). Frederic conceptualizes their relationship as a game of bridge played with words rather than cards; he has no thought of loving her. He views his evenings with her merely as more pleasant alternatives to visits to the officers' bordello.

The lessons of unselfish love exemplified by a young Italian chaplain are easily overlooked by Frederic. "[The priest] has always known what I did not know and what, when I learned it, I was always able to forget" (14), Frederic writes in rueful hindsight. Frederic also tends to take for granted the comradeship of the enlisted men he commands, though he at least tries to be responsible for their well-being, even at some risk under enemy fire. Then, wounded and in a hospital bed, Frederic suddenly sees that he is in love with Catherine: he had not known it before, though Hemingway suggests that in the hospital comes not the moment of love, but the moment of the realization of a love that already exists, much against Frederic's conscious will. From this point the war begins to take on a new seriousness for Frederic and for the novel's readers. The stakes are raised by the lesson of Frederic Henry's own mortality, taught by an exploding trench mortar shell, by the lessons of love that he learns from Catherine's example, and by the ways in which the war works against his desire to return to her. In Book Three of the novel, Frederic returns to the front after a stay in the hospital where Catherine has cared for him. This stay threatened to become a romantic idyll—came close but ultimately did not do so, if only because of the opposition of the middle-aged nurse who serves as hospital administrator. His friction with this nurse over his drinking in the hospital results in the cancellation of Frederic's convalescent leave, and thus he reaches his unit one day before the Austrians and Germans launch the great Caporetto offensive of fall 1917 that will drive the Italian army back from the Alps almost to Venice.

During the retreat Frederic's identity as officer is stripped away as he successively discovers his failures: He is not needed as supervisor (the ambulance section runs quite well without him). He cannot protect his men: one dies in an ambush by panicked Italian troops, and Frederic shoots another, a straggler trying to go on alone when the ambulances become bogged in mud and must be abandoned. Frederic eventually is not even recognized as an officer: alone himself, separated from his men, he is waylaid by battle police and misidentified as a German spy because he speaks Italian with an accent. To escape summary execution he plunges into the flooded Tagliamento River and emerges on the other bank as a different Frederic, eventually fleeing the war with Catherine to neutral Switzerland. Reborn, he remains immature, indeed babyish. (His best friend, the Italian surgeon Rinaldi, is an early contrast to Frederic's ineffectuality. Though his good humor turns increasingly to despair at the losses of the war, Rinaldi continually improves his surgical skills and tellingly has nicknamed Frederic "baby.") Frederic escapes the war to a new idyll with Catherine in the Swiss mountains, and he does not often think of the war and comrades he has left behind. Only through Catherine's continuing example of unselfish love does he gradually grow toward maturity. Yet by novel's end this becomes a bitterly disappointed maturity indeed, as he walks in the spring rain away from the hospital where Catherine and his son have died in childbirth.

Chance has ruled Frederic's life—in his meeting with Catherine, in his wounding, in sending him back to the front at an inopportune moment, in the accident of obstetrics that hemorrhages away Catherine's life and chokes their son in her womb—and the war has conditioned all these chances. Losses build and interrelate; by the end of the novel Frederic's emotional reaction to loss would be nearly oppressive were he not protected by his affectless, dissociated state of mind. Only in retrospect, as he contemplates his losses, may Frederic be seen as approaching true maturity. (In this, he probably shows Hemingway's debt to Stephen Crane's similarly named Henry Fleming, protagonist of *The Red Badge of Courage* [1895], who only begins to come to maturity as he looks back to examine his actions in the American Civil War Battle of Chancellorsville.)

III

The Spanish Civil War of *For Whom the Bell Tolls* offers another tale of love and war, but the stakes of this war are different, and the lovers perhaps more positively viewed than those of *A Farewell to Arms*. The novel's protagonist, Robert Jordan, is a university instructor of Spanish from Montana who has come to fight for the Spanish Republic in the mountains north of Madrid. Of course, the Spanish Civil War often has since been characterized as representing democracy's last chance to oppose European fascism so as to avert World War II, so the stakes are very high, as Jordan recognizes. Yet the democracies sat out the war, leaving the fascist rebels (supported by Germany and Italy) and communist "republicans" (supported by the Soviet Union) to fight it out between themselves. This adds to Jordan's dilemma, for he understands at least a little of the war's tangled politics. He is much more a thinker than is Frederic Henry, and the novel's tone is far more introspective as a result. Also as a result, the meanings of the characters' actions are more easily accessible to readers. (*For Whom the Bell Tolls* was the first of Hemingway's novels to make the yearly top-ten bestseller list.)

Crossing behind enemy lines, Robert Jordan will have three days to prepare to blow a strategic bridge and so prevent fascist reinforcements from opposing a planned republican offensive. Apart from the questions of world politics that may hinge on the battle's result, the personal question Jordan faces—the question that Hemingway poses for him—is whether it is possible in three days for a person to live a life as full and meaningful as one might ordinarily live in the biblical threescore years and ten. And the posing of such a question makes the war accessible to readers in a way that political theorizing could not. It does turn out to be possible for Jordan to lead a meaningful life in these days, but only through the medium of Hemingway's prose, which continually points up the significance of Jordan's acts. The danger of Jordan's mission is always clear, as is his likely fate, and it is the members of a guerrilla band who will simultaneously represent the Spanish people for readers as well as become Jordan's family and help him toward a realization of his need for human connections. In *A Farewell to Arms* the soldiers who work under Frederic Henry's command become individuals, yet they are not at the center of the novel's concerns. In *For Whom the Bell Tolls*, where the novel's epigraph, taken from John Donne, proclaims "No man is an *Iland*, intire of it selfe," the individual members of the band become even more individualized and contribute more to Robert Jordan's fate. Most important of these is not Maria, the innocent young victim of fascist rape and the murder of her family. She will come to love Robert and to be loved by him in return. Rather, at the center of the novel's structure of meaning is Pilar, a middle-aged gypsy woman, ugly and intelligent, who reads Jordan's fate written on his face and in his palm. Pilar arranges Maria's first tryst with Jordan; it is her act of love and compassion for Maria and for Jordan, to both of whom Pilar is attracted despite the difference in their ages. It is also Pilar's attempt to remain connected to life and purpose at a time when her own lover, the band's drunken leader, Pablo, has nearly given up the battle against the fascists for a life of relative ease, drinking wine and cherishing the horses he has stolen from them.

The young lovers meet and come to know each other under the sometimes skeptical, sometimes envious eyes of the members of the guerrilla band, who by novel's end will seem to represent not just the Spanish people but humanity as a whole. In a famous scene in a mountain meadow under the Spanish sky, the earth moves for Robert and Maria in their lovemaking. They at least momentarily escape the limitations of their three-day affair. The earth moves because they are for a moment floating above it, outside the limitations of time and mortality, apart from the passage of time that is measured by the turning of the earth as well as apart from the other members of the guerrilla band. Then they come back to earth and soon are quizzed regarding their experience by the intrusive—yet guiding—Pilar. Ultimately it is the return to time and to connections to others that is more important than the two lovers' momentary escape.

Death separates the lovers at book's end as Robert, leg shattered in a fall from a horse, awaits with a Lewis machine gun the advance of fascist cavalry led by Lieutenant Paco Berrendo. Incapacitated from travel by his injury, Robert intends to buy time for the escape of the remaining members of the band, including Maria. In a characteristic Hemingway irony, Berrendo is the noblest of Robert Jordan's enemies and very nearly a Spanish analogue to him. It is clear that in the moment after the ending of the novel these two men who should have been brothers instead will kill and be killed by each other—a bitter loss of war, which Hemingway denounces irrespective of the right or wrong of political movements or causes. While the bridge has been blown, the battle will be lost, and the war lost as well, with implications obvious to Hemingway's readers at the time of the publication of the novel in 1940, the second year of World War II.

Yet something is saved here as well. While Frederic Henry is ambiguously reborn in his crossing of the Tagliamento but then loses all with the death of Catherine Barkley, Robert Jordan surely will be reborn through his love for Maria and through his act of responsibility for the members of the guerrilla band. "I go with thee," he says to Maria in their tortured parting moments. "As long as there is one of us there is both of us" (463). Following Jordan's wish, Pilar and Pablo take Maria away despite her desire to stay and to die with him. She and the band will escape to another mountain range, the Sierra de Gredos. Jordan will live in Maria's memory, in the memories of the members of the guerrilla band who have become like a family to him—and in the person of their yet to be born child, conceived in the sunlight of the mountain meadow. At the sunlit moment when the earth moved Maria saw nothing but light, while Robert Jordan saw the dark of the ground and his omened death. After the earth moves for them they return to the cycles of life, the same cycles that Hemingway highlighted in an epigraph to *The Sun Also Rises* that was drawn from the biblical book of Ecclesiastes: "One generation passeth away, and another generation cometh; but the earth abideth forever . . ." (Hemingway's ellipses). Jake Barnes, whatever his nobility and intelligence, has been rendered impotent. The immature Frederic Henry has lost a good deal of his identity and has seen death take his lover and child, but Robert Jordan finds himself and the meaning of his life in those natural cycles. And he achieves his immortality with Maria, as much immortality as anyone may hope for in the modern world as Hemingway portrays it.

IV

The Second World War also provided material for Hemingway, but less satisfyingly so. His *Across the River* proved a disappointment to most readers. Unlike *For Whom the Bell Tolls*, it was not set in the midst of war, but in the recollection of war by an embittered and aging American infantry colonel, veteran of the grinding Hurtgen Forest battles that Hemingway covered as war correspondent in 1944. Colonel Cantwell's hope for immortality involves the teenaged Rènata, whose name means "reborn" in Italian, but he seems to find only moments of immortality in his love for her, not something more involving for the reader. Tellingly, Cantwell is dying of heart disease; unfortunately, his lovemaking is described in terms of an infantry attack over difficult terrain. Also, his memories of battle tend toward the sorts of discussion of the corruption of higher levels of command that Hemingway dished out only sparingly—and after readers had come to identify with Robert and Maria—in *For Whom the Bell Tolls*. Of the texture of battle itself, there is little. Hemingway claimed to have gone beyond arithmetic to calculus in writing *Across the River*, but the tiny slices of perception that he offers in this novel are undercut by his unattractive protagonist and ultimately prove less convincing than the tiny "chapters" of *In Our Time*. The novel's best moments describe the natural world, Venice, and a nearly magical duck hunt.

The posthumously published *Islands in the Stream* moves from

the 1930s into World War II, but its explorations of Winslow
Homer–like painter Thomas Hudson are necessarily unfinished,
and the final (wartime) section of the novel, loosely based on
Hemingway's quixotic hunting of Nazi submarines in the waters
of the Gulf Stream off Cuba, seems to owe a little too much to
the traditions of Captain Marryat and similar Victorian spinners
of adventure yarns. The more impressive earlier sections deal
with the dilemmas of the creative artist, including a Hemingway-
like writer, a double to Hudson, and with the joys and burdens of
family love. They are at their best as they echo themes of *A Moveable Feast*, a more satisfying job of posthumous editing from
more nearly finished material.

The earth that abideth forever also lends resonance to tales of
love and war. It may be profaned or perverted, as by the cholera-
bringing rains of *A Farewell to Arms*. It may seem lost, as the cut-
over wilderness of Michigan seems to be lost irrevocably in the
stories of *In Our Time*. Yet without the weight of significance and
beauty that his readers discover in such natural worlds Hemingway would not be Hemingway, nor would his characters' stories
mean as much. Important locales to him are the north woods,
and all manner of mountains, and Africa, and the Gulf Stream
between Key West and Cuba. Even in urban moments that seem
far from nature, descriptions of fishermen on the Seine or of the
horse chestnuts outside a Paris café will remind his readers of the
importance of Hemingway's natural world.

At least part of this importance may derive from Hemingway's place in history, at a time when nature was being more and
more subordinated to the machine. That subordination certainly
did not begin in his time, but it was dramatized by the aftermath
of the cutting of the Michigan wilderness as well as by the First
World War, in which industrial processes tore the landscape and
overwhelmed old concepts of courage on the field of battle. In
1915 the teenaged Hemingway wrote a diary entry in which he
proposed becoming an explorer on one of earth's last frontiers,
but of course the great explorations were all finished by then.
Even so, in his life he revisited many of the frontiers of the nineteenth century, often recasting them in his fiction as if they still
really existed as frontiers. He had been born in the era of the

horse and buggy but grew up in the age of the automobile, and the tension between the two ages often is instructive. In "The End of Something" Nick and Marjorie lose their love while fishing near the site of a razed lumber mill; Marjorie spins fantasy visions of the mill as their castle, which Nick ignores in his discomfort at her show of sentiment. Horse-drawn cabriolets and modern automobile taxicabs coexist in Jake Barnes's 1920s Paris, and Jake's escape to an Edenic fishing trip in the mountains of northern Spain is made on a double-decker autobus that speeds him along a country road.

These contrasts between the older and newer worlds may seem prosaic, but other contrasts often become gripping in their intensity, and they increase our sympathy for Hemingway's characters. Remember, for example, Robert Jordan's injury at the ending of *For Whom the Bell Tolls,* when trying to escape a modern mechanized army on horseback, he and his mount are felled and his leg broken by the explosion of a tank's shell. In a fine moment in the posthumous *Islands in the Stream,* an idyll suddenly turns to nightmare. Thomas Hudson watches the fin of a hammerhead shark slice the ocean toward his swimming son and repeatedly fires a rifle at it—and repeatedly misses. The tension builds until just as suddenly an alcoholic friend rises to the occasion, killing the shark with an illegal tommy gun and saving the boy. The contrast between nature and the mechanical world takes a different direction in this last example, but is as clear.

Thus, another aspect of nature's importance may derive from the way in which the connection to nature also raises the stakes in Hemingway's writing. The ironies of nature are always there: the earth reliably turning, however else the lives of the characters of *The Sun Also Rises* may descend to chaos; the spring snow concealing Robert Jordan and Maria in their shared sleeping bag from a patroling fascist cavalryman in *For Whom the Bell Tolls* but also dooming members of another republican guerrilla band when it reveals the tracks of their horses in the snow to the fascist patrol.

The stakes particularly are raised when nature is a real or imagined wilderness, with all that depiction of wilderness implies of innocence and of the loss of innocence. This is true of the depictions of Michigan's lost woodlands in *In Our Time,* where little Nickie Adams grows to young manhood, continually surrendering his innocent illusions only to find that other illusions remain to be lost in their turn, yet where Nick as a young man finds a refuge from war and responsibility in a fishing trip to a burned-over wilderness in the last story of *In Our Time:* "Big Two-Hearted River." It is true of the depictions of the Spanish countryside in *The Sun Also Rises* and *For Whom the Bell Tolls,* where the beauty of the landscape is often in contrast with the ignorance or savagery of mankind. It is true of the American West, from which Hemingway drew elements of *For Whom the Bell Tolls* as well as such stories as "Wine of Wyoming" and "The Gambler, the Nun and the Radio," a relatively early attempt to deal with the social issues of the 1930s. It is true of an Africa of hyenas, lions, water buffalo, and elephants in such works as "The Snows of Kilimanjaro," "The Short Happy Life of Francis Macomber," and the elephant story that David Bourne is writing within *The Garden of Eden.* It is true of the Gulf Stream we read of in *To Have and Have Not* and *The Old Man and the Sea* and the letters Hemingway wrote for *Esquire* magazine in the 1930s and in *Islands in the Stream.*

Indeed, the Hemingway protagonist often seems to exist like Hemingway in a moment after: after the nineteenth century, after wilderness, after innocence, after loss. In *The Garden of Eden,* another posthumous novel, an Edenic honeymoon is corrupted by modern ambiguities of sexual roles and by the jealousy of a young wife for the creativity of her writer husband, a creativity that shuts her out. Here Hemingway builds upon material that might have belonged in or followed *A Moveable Feast,* including his perceptions of his and of Scott and Zelda Fitzgerald's doomed relationships. As with a good deal of his later, mostly unfinished work, *The Garden of Eden* was much edited in the process of preparation for publication. Its consideration of sexuality and of gender roles comes through clearly, and it reaches a positive ending, one probably not inherent in its drafts. The novel's consideration of the dilemmas of the creative artist is perhaps more muted, though still present. *The Garden of Eden* has achieved considerable popular attention because it seems to hint at a Hemingway persona less assured and macho than the one constructed during the writer's life, though little in it really surprises readers of Hemingway's earlier novels. But even in its published state, the achievements of David Bourne, its protagonist, come at a very great cost to himself and to those he loves.

Eventually, whether we think of love or of war or of wilderness as we read the great themes in Hemingway, it probably is loss that produces the final effect upon the reader. There is no question that Hemingway as writer is a realist in subject matter as well as a modernist in form. A World War II veteran, part of the second generation to read Hemingway, once remarked to me that even before that war Hemingway was teaching members of the veteran's generation how to bear the burdens that they expected to have to bear. The veteran doubted whether Hemingway would continue to mean as much to baby boomers and generation Xers. Yet Vietnam War veterans have suggested to me that the experience of reading Hemingway's stories is like being dropped behind enemy lines, with everything to be figured out in an instant. These veterans have found the disillusioned World War I veteran Krebs of "Soldier's Home" reflecting accurately their experiences of ambiguous and unsatisfying homecoming. And lest we mistake Hemingway as a writer only for and about men, younger women have valued Catherine Barkley's courage in *A Farewell to Arms* as well as the struggles of Catherine and David Bourne and Marita to solve the riddles of gender in *The Garden of Eden*. In Hemingway's modern world much is open to question, and we still live in a recognizably similar world.

It may be a mistake to read too much Hemingway at one time, simply because the patterns of the author's reiterated concerns—love, war, wilderness, and loss—perhaps become too clear and seem too neat taken one after another. What is a fairly consistent though developing world view may come to seem pat. Perhaps the stereotypes of Hemingway that so mar *In Love and War* (and that seem to circulate in the culture, making "Hemingway" a term of opprobrium to some) derive from such reading as much as from the press agent's view of Hemingway that circulated during his lifetime. A pattern so clear is more easily felt and appreciated one book or story at a time.

A part of the difficulty of *In Love and War* certainly derives from the casting of Chris O'Donnell as the young Hemingway. O'Donnell might be credible in his role as Robin, the Boy Wonder, in the most recent of the Batman movie series. O'Donnell manages petulance well, but in Hemingway's stories it is not any sort of emotionalism that carries the reader's interest. Rather it is the sense that, whatever the position in which his characters may find themselves, living their lives with authenticity in a world that makes such lives nearly impossible is what is most important. Hemingway's protagonists may sometimes begin as immature or adolescent, as is the case with Nick Adams and Frederic Henry, or even with Francis Macomber, the rich boy-man on safari of "The Short Happy Life of Francis Macomber." They do not stay that way. Their losses do not come cheaply, no more than their victories, and their victories are often far more partial than readers might hope for. But generally there are victories, even if victories so high priced as Frederic Henry's maturity or Robert Jordan's immortality as I have defined them above. That essential sense of the seriousness of life—and sometimes of its joy—is underscored by its occurring against a backdrop of love and war, certainly two of the world's most serious undertakings. And the losses of love and war, and the loss of the beauty of wilderness, all underscore the value of Hemingway. If sometimes the man was less than his characters, we probably can forgive him, for which of us lives in a world as finely shaped as a work of art? In any case, Hemingway early found an audience among ordinary people who appreciated the seriousness of his concerns, and he has kept it. If even a great director such as Richard Attenborough did not quite achieve the seriousness and appeal of the best of Hemingway when he directed *In Love and War,* at least Attenborough recognized that seriousness and appeal, as do all Hemingway's serious readers.

WORKS CITED

Hemingway, Ernest. *Across the River and into the Trees.* New York: Scribner's, 1950.

———. *A Farewell to Arms.* New York: Scribner's, 1929.

———. *For Whom the Bell Tolls.* New York: Scribner's, 1940.

———. *The Garden of Eden.* New York: Scribner's, 1986.

———. *Islands in the Stream.* New York: Scribner's, 1970.

———. *A Moveable Feast.* New York: Scribner's, 1964.

———. *The Old Man and the Sea.* New York: Scribner's, 1953.

———. *The Sun Also Rises.* New York: Scribner's, 1926.

———. *To Have and Have Not.* New York: Scribner's, 1937.

In Love and War. Dir. Richard Attenborough. Dmitri Villard Productions/New Line Cinema, 1996.

"In Love and War." *Internet Movie Database.* Online. Internet. Available: http://us.imdb.com/Title?In+Love+and+War+(1996).

von Kurowsky, Agnes. *Hemingway in Love and War: The Lost Diary of Agnes von Kurowsky, Her Letters, and Correspondence of Ernest Hemingway.* Ed. Henry Serrano Villard and James Nagel. Boston: Northeastern University Press, 1989.

The Intertextual Hemingway

Linda Wagner-Martin

M uch of Hemingway's writing gives the reader such a feeling of personal authenticity that it has often been considered autobiographical. All the more surprising, then, is the actual aesthetic situation: that at least some parts of his fiction are drawn from other literature—that during the 1920s and the 1930s particularly, Ernest Hemingway was pioneering in what has today become known as "intertextuality."[1] Tracing an author's borrowings—whether thematic correspondences, stylistic effects, parodies, or parallel characters or scenes—has today become a kind of critical method. Scholars acknowledge that such echoes, such borrowings, do not breech ethical norms. Indeed, using materials that could be found in writing by established authors may be a highly complimentary practice; for American modernist writers like Hemingway, such borrowing might also be ironic.

Considering a Hemingway novel from the perspective of an earlier, similar fiction allows the critic to assess the author's difference from the model. Hemingway's choices help the reader establish his own definition of what good fiction is supposed to be. Much of what made Ernest Hemingway so intrinsically "modern" was his deep and rich background in the established literature of the nineteenth century. By knowing what had been written, he could see ways to reinscribe those themes and subjects in order, in a sense, to remodel them for his twentieth-century readers, or the readers he hoped to attract. One of Hemingway's great gifts as a writer was that he had an accurate notion of what readers contemporary with him wanted to read.

Hemingway and Henry James

For example, at the turn of the century, one of the most popular literary forms for elite readers in both the United States and England was the expatriate novel of manners. Henry James was the author most responsible for, in effect, creating this category. One of his earliest novels, *The American,* set a successful U.S. businessman (named *Christopher*—with echoes of Columbus—*Newman,* a pointed underscoring of the promise of American democracy) adrift within a severely classed French society he had no way to understand. Similarly, in *The Portrait of a Lady,* the American woman Isabel Archer, despite her intelligence and her fortune—or, perhaps, because of them—is bested by an expatriate American man who uses European conventions to conquer her spirit. In one of James's last great novels, *The Ambassadors,* he again moved American characters into European circles where their politeness, coupled with their own sometimes foolish self-confidence, kept them from asking the right questions, from getting the information that would have, perhaps, kept them from becoming victims. Europe as predator, even when populated chiefly by other Americans, became one central trope of the expatriate novel.

Between 1907 and 1910 the New York edition of James's novels was published and many readers bought the volumes by subscription. Living in Paris, Gertrude Stein and Alice B. Toklas purchased a set of the white-covered books. James was one of the authors both Stein and her brother Leo, whom Hemingway knew separately from Gertrude through the Paris café scene, praised consistently (Jane Austen was another); and in 1917 another of Hemingway's mentors, Ezra Pound, had edited a special issue of the *Little Review* that was devoted exclusively to essays written in praise of James. There was little question about

James's standing within the postwar culture of expatriates from the United States.

Having established himself as a writer of short stories, poems, and poetic vignettes, Hemingway in the mid-1920s was clearly looking for something on which to base a novel. The intertextual method shows how plausible it is that Hemingway used James's *The Ambassadors* as he shaped *The Sun Also Rises*, which Hemingway had begun as a travel diary of his and Hadley's first and second Pamplona visits. While there are a number of clear similarities, Hemingway's recalcitrance to accept James's characterizations of Americans as naive colored his approach; with the confidence of an American in his mid-twenties, able to not only belong to the elite expatriate Paris culture but to captivate it, Hemingway drew for his novel U.S. characters who were too smart to become the victims of Europeans.

No reader would ever pity Jake Barnes, even if he could not normally consummate his love. True to the narrative expectations of romance, at the end of *The Sun Also Rises* Jake almost succumbed to Brett's need; but his cryptic withdrawal, his laconic "Isn't it pretty to think so?"[2] marked his refusal to become the romantic object. For what Hemingway most disliked about Henry James's Lambert Strether, the central "ambassador" of the impressionistic and self-conscious observation of Europe's tangled webs of friendships, adulteries, and same-sex liaisons, was his passivity. Not only was the aging and stiflingly polite Strether financially dependent on his backer/lover in the States, Mrs. Newsome, but he was emotionally enchained not so much by his love for her but by his omnipresent sense of propriety. Clouded by the admittedly provincial attitudes of Woollett, Massachusetts, Strether yet was man enough to see the values of—to admire what was "wonderful" about—Paris, the French, and Europeans in general. Caught in his obligations to Mrs. Newsome—to visit Paris and spy on her son Chad and then report back to her—Strether could still understand "freedom" (*The Ambassadors* 215).

Strether's own narrative, however, is so hedged with personal moral convictions, or what he describes as moral convictions, that he himself can never act. His conversations with Little Bilham and the perceptive and loving Maria Gostrey show that he is a man of understanding, understanding even for the most grotesque of James's American figures, Waymarsh (who, despite his own lack of sensitivity, *does* manage to act). Yet the tragedy of Strether's journey as an ambassador from Massachusetts to France is that he returns from it, marked forever by his knowledge and therefore unable to accept the role he had begun that odyssey convinced he wanted—to become Mrs. Newsome's consort, a kind of subordinate Mr. Newsome-Strether.

Determined to be seen as "modern," Hemingway stripped his Strether—Jake Barnes—of his gentility right off the bat by using the short, rough form of that character's given name, Jacob. He then stripped him of the most apparent of his sexual qualifiers, his penis, with a kind of ironic commentary on the use normally-equipped male characters might not have made of their God-given rights as men. (The fact that *The Sun Also Rises* contains a dialogue devoted to Jake's impotence juxtaposed with comments about what a good writer Henry James is, despite his apparent emasculation, lends a writerly subtext to this discussion; perhaps more important is that the dialogue occurs between Jake and Bill Gorton, the two closest male friends in Hemingway's work.) Hemingway then wrote an entire novel around what might be seen as a deftly embroidered casting and recasting of Lambert Strether's admonition to Little Bilham:

> . . . don't forget that you're young—blessedly young; be glad of it on the contrary and live up to it. Live all you can; it's a mistake not to. It doesn't so much matter what you do in particular, so long as you have had your life. If you haven't had that what *have* you had? (*The Ambassadors* 215)

Taking his cue from one of James's best-known passages, then, in *The Sun Also Rises*, Hemingway attempts to force a festival of experience—bullfighting, traveling, fishing, bicycle racing, eating, drinking, church going, dancing, loving, fighting, drinking, eating, and, that most American of themes, searching for (and perhaps finding) the self—into one short novel. And rather than create a mellowed-by-experience observer like James's Lambert

Strether, Hemingway gives us the brash (but still writerly, still sensitive) journalist, Jake Barnes. Impatient with Robert Cohn's literary romanticism—that he find a better country, find a better woman, write a better book—Jake demands that people find their pleasures where they are, realize what is "wonderful" about their current lives, and stop the endless café talk about what might be possible. As Jake answers Cohn, even to the point of having to fight with him, so *The Sun Also Rises* answers *The Ambassadors*.

The most important difference, of course, is that Jake has not been *sent* to Europe by anyone. Even though Hemingway was at that time living off his first wife Hadley's inheritance, he could believe that he was independent because he was convinced that he would eventually earn his way by writing. *The Sun Also Rises* makes clear that there are no puppet strings attached to Jake Barnes, just as Hemingway's first novel attempts to cut whatever strings of influence the young writer might have felt were being attached to him. It is no accident that his parodic novel *The Torrents of Spring* appeared just before this one, for in his ill-conceived take-off on both Sherwood Anderson and Gertrude Stein, Hemingway reminded the literary world that he was an original, that he did not like his work being coupled with that of either Stein or Anderson. *The Sun Also Rises* was his gesture of farewell to both of those writers, as well as to the meditative American novel, the interminable dialogic text that pondered, pondered, pondered. Anderson's *Poor White* as well as Stein's *The Making of Americans*, which Hemingway had typed some parts of in order to publish it in *transatlantic review*, were both in the Jamesian mode.

But even as he tried to leave the stylistic and narrative model of the long novel of manners, Hemingway found much about the form useful. He too, like James, wanted to vaunt his intimate knowledge of France (and Spain), knowledge philosophical and religious as well as anthropologic and geographic. He also wanted to champion the innocence of Americans who were less cynical and jaded than their European counterparts. And he especially wanted to impress his readers with the assurance of his own, Jake Barnes's own, sophistication. While the avuncular

James radiated his cosmopolitanism, the handsome, intentionally rugged, young American writer searched for ways to exude that same quality.

More directly, from James's *The Ambassadors* Hemingway took the sexuality and centrality of Madame de Vionnet; at thirty-eight, she is the seductively beautiful prototype of the *femme du monde*, the civilizing woman. Unfortunately, in James's novel, she is a woman who loved unwisely. While Brett Ashley transmuted the gentility of de Vionnet into a sexual energy that James left to the reader's imagination, a more recognizable Hemingway *femme du monde* character appeared later as Catherine Barkley in his *A Farewell to Arms*. But there were uses to be made of de Vionnet in Brett as well, and what moved James's figure into the "modern" in Hemingway's first novel was Brett's utter lack of hypocrisy. Although she slept with many men, she did not care who knew it. She thought sexual experience with her might be "good" for them, and until she fell in love with the very young Pedro Romero (which makes her a closer parallel with Madame de Vionnet), she was usually unharmed by her liaisons.

What was perhaps most "modern" about Brett Ashley was her androgynous character. Like Jake, she ate well, drank a lot, enjoyed the bullfights, wanted to be at the center of the vigor of life. In contrast to the veiled and mysterious sexuality of Madame de Vionnet, Brett's female being came closer to the male in its aggression, its lack of subtlety, and its visible appetites (see Barlowe, Elkins [both in this volume]). Or perhaps, if the reader follows the lead of Mark Spilka in his important book, the issues of femaleness and maleness were also blurred enough for Hemingway that he was borrowing more from the character of Strether—especially Strether in his relation to Little Bilham—than *The Sun Also Rises* made clear. The mirror scene, in which Jake acknowledges and mourns his neutering, becomes central in the reader's determining what role Jake is really to play in Hemingway's tapestry.

In point of structure, *The Sun Also Rises* is *The Ambassadors* writ modern. A group of men come together in Europe, their lives defined to a great extent by their friendships. Their action consists largely of determining what their role is in relation to the female energy of the culture—whether that energy be provided by Madame de Vionnet or Brett Ashley or Paris itself. And there are complicating negative sources of female energy—Frances, Mrs. Newsome, Sarah Pocock (to some extent), Woollett; the presence of these entities makes the positive sources stand out brilliantly. In *The Sun Also Rises*, typical of the commonness of the male center, Jake, male friendships sort themselves out through battle, in a bloodshed that would be unseemly in James's text (especially in Gloriani's garden). In *The Ambassadors*, the violence remains hidden under the facade of socially acceptable behavior, but its damage is done nonetheless. That the old sculptor, Gloriani, shares his wisdom and his own sexual energy during his "queer old" garden party, his welcoming face offering the bemused Strether an "open letter in a foreign tongue"[3] (197, 99), gives depth to Hemingway's characterization of the Spanish mentor, Montoya, whose knowledge of the mysterious Spanish culture with its rites and rituals similarly attracts Jake. By the 1940s Hemingway would return to the idea of glorious gardens and same-sex friendships and pursue issues of sexuality and moral loyalties more fully.

It might also be said, coming to the end of both *The Sun Also Rises* and *The Ambassadors*, that Lambert Strether was not the only male protagonist who relinquished what he could have loved so that he could return, in a sense, to his natively moral beginnings.

Some Possible Sources of Hemingway's
Spanish Imaginary

Because France and Italy had long been a part of the American literary scene, as had Germany, Hemingway in his search for the new—the truly exotic, at least for U.S. readers—moved to a practically undiscovered country. Spain provided not only the bullfight as a focus of highly ritualized action, complete with its roots in religious rite, which was increasingly important to Hemingway, but the novelty of a culture that was considered "primitive." Not only the Catholicism, but the bacchanalian emphasis on drink, dance, fiesta, sex (evident in the existence of numerous children in every family), and the obvious otherness of the language and the skin color made the Spanish more similar to the black American culture, at least as Hemingway understood it, than to a white. By choosing Spain as setting, Hemingway could mark out new territory, even as he benefited from the current aesthetic interest in African and African-American (Harlem inspired) art, customs, dance, and behavior. Aware that his knowledge of blacks was limited, he also knew better than to trade on the information that Gertrude Stein, Carl Van Vechten, Jean Toomer, Nella Larsen, and many others possessed; Spain provided him a means not of competing with them but of drawing on the partly psychological, partly emotional interests in what were considered more primitive cultures. After all, *The Torrents of Spring* was a parody of Sherwood Anderson's 1925 novel, *Dark Laughter,* a book in which Anderson focused on the American black culture's amusement at the machinations of the supposedly superior whites' sexual behaviors.

There was also Rene Maran's Prix Goncourt–winning novel, *Batouala,* one of the few books that Hemingway ever reviewed. Published in 1921 in an edition of only 1,050 copies, the book—then titled *Batouala: A Negro Novel from the French of Rene Maran*—was reissued in 1922 by Jonathan Cape in London. Maran had spent six years in the French Congo; this book was, according to his preface, "a witness," an "entirely objective" account of what he had observed (12). Rife with bloody ceremonies (circumcision, murders), the novel included a long festival scene—marked by feasting, sex, and ritualized dancing—that might well have been the model for the raiu raiu scene in *The Sun Also Rises*. Maran's novel also includes a section in which an enemy is planning Batouala's death ("hunting accidents! They are frequent enough for people to give them a little thought from time to time! // What! You aim at an animal, and you kill a man! It is not granted to everyone to be skilful! The best shot can miss his target" [135]—or hers, as Hemingway's later story "The Short Happy Life of Francis Macomber" showed).

It helped a great deal too that the Hemingways were among the earliest Americans to visit the Pamplona festival; drawing on information they garnered from Stein and Toklas, who may have been the first Americans to see the festival there, they found those July weeks both sensual and forbidding. Spain, then, with its sonorous customs and language, seemed to be a country crying out for delineation.

And there was the body of fiction that already existed about the bullfight and the people of Spain. I have written elsewhere, as has Susan Beegel, about Hemingway's evident knowledge of—and admiration for—the writing of Spanish-Argentinian novelist Blasco Ibañez. Few non-Western authors were so popular among American readers, and even as the literati (John Dos Passos among them) scoffed at his bestsellers such as *The Naked Maja* (1906), *Blood and Sand* (1922), and *The Four Horsemen of the Apocalypse,* the last became the 1921 film of the same name, selling to Hollywood for $200,000 and making Rudolph Valentino a star. Valentino also made the 1922 film from Ibañez's bullfighting novel, *Blood and Sand.* Ibañez's own stardom consisted of a triumphal tour through the United States in 1919–1920, during which he received medals and honorary degrees.

Typical of one pattern of Hemingway's borrowings here is the fact that he joined Dos Passos in the critical denigration of Ibañez, whose work surely provided a number of characters (among them, the androgynous, tough woman of *The Enemies of Women,* a novel that went through twenty-one printings during two months in 1920) and themes for Hemingway's own work. As I have suggested elsewhere, not only the title of Hemingway's bullfighting novel but many of its scenes, details about costume, behaviors, and cultural importance could have come directly from Ibañez's work. So too could much of the intermixed love and war narrative that was the brilliance of *A Farewell to Arms* have come from Ibañez's antiwar novel, *Four Horsemen of the Apocalypse,* in which the nurse Marguerite and Julio Desnoyers meet in the Garden of the Chapelle Expaitoire. When Marguerite renounces her love for Desnoyers in order to care for her blind husband, a casualty of the brutal war, the foreign-born Desnoyers throws himself passionately into battle. Nothing but his death will erase the loss of his beloved.

There may have been several other sources as well for information about bullfights, Spanish culture, and non-Western women. One of the raconteurs Hemingway admired on the

Parisian café scene was Frank Harris, a legend past his own time—an Oscar Wilde biographer, novelist, and short story writer who in 1900 published *Montes the Matador and Other Stories*. Written ten years earlier, the collection uses the device of Montes telling bullfighting stories on his deathbed; "the deed talks—louder than any words," so the collection profiles a number of matadors, brave and cowardly, as well as a number of bulls (6). Montes is expert at judging bulls, an essential ingredient for a long-lived matador. One of Harris's stories reads like Hemingway's "The Undefeated"; another suggests "The Killers." The book also defines terms, a tactic Hemingway would adopt for his own manual of bullfighting, *Death in the Afternoon*; and it deals with themes of honor, friendship, betrayal, and how a man meets death. Several of the shorter tales are subtitled "A Mere Episode"; that these tend to be the most somber stories calls attention to Harris's ability to use structure ironically. In "The Interpreter" a man's suicide is treated as if it were worth only a paragraph of newsprint, despite the fact that Harris writes graphically of "his brains scattered on the pillow and the wall" (164).

As *For Whom the Bell Tolls* would prove, the attraction of the Spanish world was permanent in Hemingway's life. When he felt his aesthetic drive failing, he returned to what remained one of his constant fascinations. Personified this time in the women of the novel, both Pilar and Maria, the spirit of the sensual Spanish stoicism flowered to give him what was perhaps his best-realized book. Quibbling about Maria's Spanish nickname aside, the pines that mark the landscape, the intricate details of village life, and the almost nihilistic severity of the moral tenor of the novel make it Hemingway's last masterpiece.

The Integrity of War: Facing Death Another Way

Few works, regardless of author, tap into the mainstream of reader interest as well as Hemingway's second important novel, *A Farewell to Arms*. The 1920s were filled with literary treatments of World War I, although many of those treatments were not written by Americans. While Hemingway's friend John Dos Passos had published two war novels, *One Man's Initiation* and *Three Soldiers,* and e.e. cummings had had success with his memoir of imprisonment in France, *The Enormous Room,* most of the significant treatments of the European war were written in other languages and therefore had to be translated. Through Frank Harris if not on his own, Hemingway would have found perhaps the most moving book about the war, Henri Barbusse's *Le Feu* (Harris devotes a chapter to Barbusse and his book in his *Latest Contemporary Portraits*). Again, whenever Hemingway commented on war novels, his approbation of Stephen Crane's *The Red Badge of Courage*—a narrative of a remote conflict, written by a man who had never seen war—might well have been intentionally misleading.

Part of the appeal of Barbusse's novel was its authenticity. Translated and subtitled as *Under Fire: The Story of a Squad,* the book was dedicated to "the memory of the comrades who fell by my side at Crouy and on Hill 119, January, May and September 1915." Reliving his own experiences under fire, Hemingway recognized the bloodshed as Barbusse described it—one of the reasons readers objected to the book—but considering his antiwar stance, Barbusse's bleak and sometimes unbearable details add to the novel's sense of authenticity:

And little Godefroy—did you know him?—middle of his body blown away. He was emptied of blood on the spot in an instant, like a bucket kicked over. Little as he was, it was remarkable how much blood he had, it made a stream at least 50 meters long. Gougnard got his legs cut up by one explosion. They picked him up not quite dead. That was at the listening post. I was there on duty with them. But when that shell fell I had gone into the trench to ask the time. I found my rifle, that I'd left in my place, bent double, as if some one had folded it in his hands, the barrel like a corkscrew, and half of the stock in sawdust. The smell of fresh blood was enough to bring your heart up. (49)

Jammed into a single paragraph (which included two other deaths as well), these fearsome details attempt to remain objective. The horrible similes are undercut by the short terse sentences. In this kind of description, as well as in Barbusse's reliance on physical descriptions of the less dramatic lives of the soldiers, the inherent drama of the scene is tonally calmed. For instance, Barbusse's focus on clothing:

> The uniforms of these survivors are all earth-yellowed alike, so that they appear to be clad in khaki. The cloth is still with the ochreous mud that has dried underneath. The skirts of their greatcoats are like lumps of wood, jumping about on the yellow crust that reaches to their knees. Their faces are drawn and blackened; dust and dirt have wrinkled them anew; their eyes are big and fevered. (48)

While *Le Feu* claims to be objective, it also reflects the author's sentiments about the waste of war; there are disquisitions about "fair" and "unfair" ways to kill and about the use—or the lack thereof—of innumerable men's deaths. There are comments about the falsity of the soldiers as they return home, reduced to "false swearing" as they tell about the war, hoping to find some modicum of understanding in the civilians that remained there (308). Some of the descriptions hardest to read are Barbusse's accounts of what death in the trenches is like, whether men are drowned in trenches turned to lakes or trapped in them, run through from behind, nailed to planks by bayonets, or literally fragmented by explosions. And there is this account of a man's mind/consciousness being blown through the air by such an explosive force:

> Suddenly a fearful explosion falls on us. I tremble to my skull; a metallic reverberation fills my head; a scorching and suffocating smell of sulphur pierces my nostrils. The earth has opened in front of me. I feel myself lifted and hurled aside— doubled up, choked, and half blinded by this lightning and thunder. But still my recollection is clear; and in that moment when I looked wildly and desperately for my comrade-in-arms, I saw his body go up, erect and black, both his arms outstretched to their limit, and a flame in place of his head! (173)

Although Hemingway's *A Farewell to Arms* never tries to narrate the European war, it is punctuated with brutal scenes of evacuation, execution, and Frederic Henry's own wounding—all of which have some relationship to the effective writing of Henri Barbusse.

But the themes of Hemingway's 1929 novel make the reader consider the book as less a war novel than a meditation on the existence of war, perhaps on the way men's philosophies of life lead them to either brutality or beyond. In fact, the book might almost be categorized as a romance rather than a war novel, so dominant is the story of the love between the traumatized Catherine and the young convalescent ambulance driver. In this mixture, Hemingway had the models of Ibañez's *The Four Horsemen of the Apocalypse,* as well as one of the great romantic British novels of the 1920s, Hugh Walpole's *The Young Enchanted,* which was subtitled *A Romantic Story.* While we know that Gertrude Stein borrowed the 1921 novel from Sylvia Beach's library and that she and Hemingway discussed it, we know only that Hemingway owned other of Walpole's books. What is most relevant about this novel is that Walpole has named his hero Henry, and in Part IV of the novel, "Knight Errant," a section in which the brave "warriors" that fighting men must be are rewarded with the hands of their princesses, Walpole announces,

> I have called this a Romantic Story because it is so largely Henry's Story and Henry was a romantic Young Man. He felt that it was his solemn duty to be modern, cynical and realistic but his romantic spirit was so strong, so courageous, so scornful of the cynical parts of him that it has dominated and directed him to this very day (283).

In line with Mark Spilka's tracing of the Victorian fiction that Hemingway had devoured and loved during his boyhood, Walpole's sentimental book—like his aside to the reader here— might not have been objectionable to Hemingway. (Stein, too, seemed capable of "liking" a quantity of popular work, from Gene Stratton Porter's *A Girl of the Limberlost* to mystery novels.) And perhaps the transfer of "Henry" from the given name of

Walpole's character to the family name of Hemingway's is an indication that *A Farewell to Arms* does extend the "family" of the romance novel, tongue-in-cheek if not in earnest.

There are other novels of the 1920s that Hemingway would have known. Solita Solano, a key member of the American expatriate community through her love affair with *New Yorker* correspondent Janet Flanner ("Genet"), saw E. P. Dutton publish her *The Uncertain Feast* in 1924. Aside from the echoingly similar title of Hemingway's posthumously published memoir, *A Moveable Feast*, Solano's novel also tells a romantic story—this one marked by betrayal, miscegenation, and the death of the estranged couple's child. After their child dies, however, Dan Fiske ends his liaison with his secretary, Miss Elliot, and returns to his wife, Amy.

The "war" novels of Willa Cather and Virginia Woolf—*One of Ours* and both *Jacob's Room* and the Septimus Smith story in *Mrs. Dalloway*—thread through the texture of *The Sun Also Rises*, which is often read as a postwar narrative, and *A Farewell to Arms*. The connection with Woolf (who had reviewed him unfavorably) is particularly obvious in his first novel, when Hemingway gives the reader the ironically peripheral information that "Jacob" is a Flemish name, surely a play on Jacob Flanders, the hero of Woolf's *Jacob's Room*, a character given to the very kind of introspection to which Jake finally succumbs before his bedroom mirror.

Adding to that mix is D. H. Lawrence's *Sons and Lovers* (1922), less for its influence on the themes of war than for its notion of the tragically crippling powers of love. In some ways, Hemingway too continuously saw himself as that deprived and embittered son, working hard to be loved by other suitable women to make up for his relationship with Grace Hall-Hemingway. And while the struggle such a mother-son entanglement created was less obvious in *The Sun Also Rises*, it may have influenced the depiction of Frederic Henry as a student of Catherine's wisdom in the later novel.

Hemingway and Ford Madox Ford

The most likely urtext for Hemingway's *A Farewell to Arms*, however, remains Ford Madox Ford's *The Good Soldier.* While Hemingway's dislike of Ford is obvious in both his 1926 novel and in his personal comments, it also is clear that he was not above borrowing from Ford. Ford's 1923 *Women and Men*, a treatise on what he called the "new gospel" of Otto Weininger and the privileging of sex in that author's *Sex and Character*, appeared from Three Mountains Press books, as did Hemingway's *in our time*. In 1927, changing the arrangement of words for ironic and perhaps disingenuous effect, Hemingway titled his second story collection *Men without Women*.

In Ford's World War I novel, *The Good Soldier*, the themes of love and war are carefully, if ironically, intertwined. One cannot exist without the other; yet the ostensible tone and texture of the work belie its subtitle, *A Tale of Passion*. It was Hemingway's comment on Ford's use of the word "passion" that was lost when he followed Fitzgerald's advice and cut the opening sections of *The Sun Also Rises*. As Frederic Svoboda quotes the unpublished section, Ford—named "Braddocks" in the Hemingway novel—continues to irritate the Jake Barnes character:

> In Braddocks's novels there was always a great deal of passion but it took sometimes two and three volumes for anyone to sleep with anyone else. In actual life it seemed there was a great deal of sleeping about among good people [,] much more sleeping about than passion. . . . Who knew anything about anybody? You didn't know a woman because you slept with her any more than you knew a horse because you'd ridden him once. . . . Besides you learned a lot about a woman by not sleeping with her. (Svoboda 85)

Especially for a novel written during the war (Ford began the novel in 1913, deciding to prove on his fortieth birthday what kind of a writer he truly was), well before the decade of the world's great sexual revolution in the 1920s, Ford's representation of passion stands as accurate. But by the time Hemingway is viewing the sexual arrangements of postwar Paris, particularly from his chosen perspective—of belittling whatever Ford Madox Ford had done, including his conception of the *transatlantic review*—his targeting the word *passion* is not only logical but likely.

Given Hemingway's inherent competitiveness with all men, Ford's heavy body and what appeared to the conventional young American as his unusual romantic success with women had to become objects of ridicule. For Ford to be the authority on sexuality also amused Hemingway. Rather than point to Ford's presentation of war and postwar conflict in his own borrowings from *The Good Soldier*, then, Hemingway chose to focus on the relentless romance plot. It was this plot that had led Ford to title an early version of the novel "The Saddest Story."

While Charles L. Ross makes a good case for Hemingway's having been influenced by Ford's *The Good Soldier* during his writing of *The Sun Also Rises*, in retrospect it becomes clear that the real reworking of Ford's masterpiece comes in both Hemingway's *A Farewell to Arms* and in his posthumously published *The Garden of Eden*. By 1929, when *A Farewell to Arms* is published, Hemingway is out of favor with his Paris friends—partly because of his own meanness and partly because of his leaving Hadley and their child for Pauline Pfeiffer. Hemingway did not care who recognized the heavy borrowings, the ironic twisting of Ford's very moral narrative into a much less ironic, and in some ways much less modern, tale.

That Hemingway became famous on the back of one of his borrowed and rewritten passages from *The Good Soldier* is itself ironic. In Ford's novel, the narrator Dowell comments about the seductive power of patriotism, saying that "all good soldiers are sentimentalists" and that eventually their speech is filled with "the big words—'courage,' 'loyalty,' 'honor,' 'constancy'" (26–27); in Hemingway's *A Farewell to Arms*, Frederic Henry stands apart from those good and patriotic soldiers in order to reflect cynically, "I was always embarrassed by the words sacred, glorious, and sacrifice, and the expression in vain. . . . Abstract words such as glory, honour, courage, or hallow were obscene beside the concrete names of villages, the numbers of roads, the names of rivers, the numbers of regiments and the dates" (184–85). It is as if Hemingway is juxtaposing Dowell's comment (which does not, after all, reflect that character's views) with the dedication of the Barbusse novel, in which the place names of battles and the dates are given. The implication is that *Le Feu* was a real war novel; *The Good Soldier,* only a pastische of the same.

Hemingway would also use Dowell's word "sentimentalists" against Ford and his work; in fact, there is probably a version somewhere in which Hemingway titled *A Farewell to Arms* "The Bad Soldier." Who, in military terms, could be a worse soldier than a deserting one—and one deserting less from revulsion at the morally unprincipled mandates that soldiers must kill than from a need for sheer creature comforts (being able to eat, drink, be clean, sleep at night, and live with one's beloved)? What is there, finally, about Frederic Henry's decision to desert that is admirable? The quixotic behavior of the Italians on the bridge is no direct cause: in war, one side destroys the other, that is the way the game is played. What impetus leads to Frederic's decision— except his need to have his lover and his child safe in some location with him? Somewhere in Hemingway's consciousness is Teddy Roosevelt's censure, that the lowest man is he who "shirks his duty as a soldier" (*The Young Hemingway* 16). To write a novel about a deserter was surely a modernist tour de force.

Neither is there any hint that Frederic Henry wants to protect Catherine in the later stages of her pregnancy: where would she be better cared for than in her own hospital? Why must she attempt with him to row across a lake, where their boat might capsize, they be taken prisoner, or they be arrested for desertion? Their escape to some other country—a fallacy from the start— has certainly not been undertaken with Catherine in mind.

There is no defense either in the argument that Catherine had already lost a lover to the war and that Henry's escaping the threat to his own life was necessary to her sanity. Calm and serene, Catherine seems able to withstand worry over the whereabouts of the father of her child; even the solicitous Fergie does not use that argument with Henry. What she argues is that he needs to marry Catherine, so that she is not subjected to the treatment society will mete out if he is killed before they marry and she is left with a bastard child. The only scene in which Catherine dislikes herself or feels any guilt is that in the whorish hotel room, where the social disapprobation of her behavior is imaged clearly. If a belief in love makes one sentimental, then both Catherine and Henry are guilty.

But Frederic Henry may be guilty of much more than sentiment, and his cowardice might well be the overriding consideration for the romantic flight into a separate country, in search of that separate peace that has been haunting Hemingway since the vignettes of his *In Our Time*. The irony, then, of a comparison between Ford's *The Good Soldier* and Hemingway's protagonist in *A Farewell to Arms* is deep. Tragically unhappy at the loss of his beloved, whether that loss be in person or in love, as Nancy's telegram suggests, Ford's character Edward Ashburnham stoically kills himself with the penknife, "quite a small penknife," not in a field of battle but in his own stable yard (256). And even as Dowell calls his friend a sentimentalist—he does, after all, believe in enduring love, and that his own human happiness depends on that love, which he has relinquished—Dowell also puts himself into that category.

In contrast, Hemingway creates a novel in which the great lovers of the Western world—Catherine and Frederic Henry— are somehow caught by fate, or fated to be caught, and it is Catherine's death in childbirth that gives *A Farewell to Arms* its resonance. It is the comparatively simple Catherine, guilty herself in believing in the romantic myth, who pays the price. While Henry might be morose, and might walk alone in the rain, he lives to find another love and, perhaps more important, to tell another story.

Hemingway's other story, published long after his death, is the unexpectedly sexual *The Garden of Eden*. In this work, the true complications of Ford's *Good Soldier*'s many liaisons come home to roost—and the number, and variety, of those liaisons when compared with what are usually heterosexual, monogamous situations in Hemingway's fictions seem bewildering. But if the younger writer were once again borrowing from the convoluted narrative of Ford Madox Ford's *The Good Soldier*, it is clear that Hemingway's *Garden* is, if anything, somewhat less complex.

Ford's novel uses Edward Ashburnham and his several affairs as its center. Married to Leonora, Edward has carried on liaisons with other women throughout their marriage, including his affair with Dowell's wife, Florence. She commits suicide, so Dowell himself is free to fall in love again. Unfortunately, both Dowell and Edward are passionately in love with Leonora's young niece, Nancy. There are suggestions in *The Good Soldier* that Leonora's relationship with Nancy may be sexual; at any rate, there is such an emotional bond between aunt and niece that Leonora is able to poison Nancy against the love of her husband (and Nancy's erstwhile uncle), Edward. It is this triangle (discounting the presence of Dowell, easily cut away from the liaison because of his lack of sexual prowess) that Hemingway replicates in *The Garden of Eden.*

In *The Garden of Eden,* David and Catherine honeymoon in almost complete isolation—until the beautiful and supposedly lesbian Marita becomes their companion. Attracted initially by Catherine, Marita eventually succumbs to David's charm, and the novel ends with Marita and David becoming a passionate, heterosexual couple. By this time, Catherine has gone mad. The extra couple—Barbara and Nick—that appeared in the full version of the novel were cut by the work's editor; so Hemingway's sexual text seems comparatively straightfoward. In effect, Marita's dangerous lesbian or bisexual tendency is changed through her love for the typically masculine David. She is a satisfied good lover of the heterosexual variety.

In Ford's *The Good Soldier,* it is after Leonora has plotted to remove Nancy from their lives, sending her to Ceylon to visit her father, that Edward kills himself. Upon hearing of his suicide, Nancy goes mad. Leonora marries someone else and bears a child. Dowell, then, is left to care for the insane, catatonic Nancy as though she were his betrothed—without any response, satisfaction, or even acknowledgment from her. If Hemingway were incensed that Ford's narrator, Dowell, was such a passive and effete character, his drawing his David as a virile, commonsense writer/artist figure would have been the kind of rebuttal he had chosen to use before.

It was important to Ernest Hemingway that any reader see that his men were cut from a different pattern than those of either Henry James or Ford Madox Ford. After all, it is Hemingway at about this time (1949) who writes to his publisher and friend,

Charlie Scribner, that he "started out trying to beat dead writers that I knew how good they were" (*Letters* 673). After successfully taking on Turgenev, Maupassant, Henry James, and Cervantes, Hemingway is thinking next of Tolstoy, Melville, Dostoevsky— if he lives to be sixty. As he closes his mocking but perhaps not parodic letter, "Know this sounds like bragging but Jeezoo Chrise you have to have confidence to be a champion and that is the only thing I ever wished to be (*Letters* 673)." Or, as Michael Reynolds writes in this volume, "All his writing life, [Hemingway] insisted that his best writing was what he made up, but readers refused to believe it." As this essay has tried to suggest, to "what he made up" one might legitimately add the phrase "or borrowed."

NOTES

1. The best example of a critic's finding reasonable—even striking—corespondences between Hemingway's work and that of earlier novelists is Myler Wilkinson's *Hemingway and Turgenev: The Nature of Literary Influence.* Wilkinson makes an impressive case for Isaac Babel as well as Chekhov, Dostoevsky, and Tolstoy.

While the central thrust of Mark Spilka's 1990 book *Hemingway's Quarrel with Androgyny* is not delineation of intertextuality, his early chapters describe relationships between Hemingway's works and those of nineteenth-century British writers: Dinah Mulock Craik (*John Halifax, Gentleman*), Frances Hodgson Burnett (*Little Lord Fauntleroy*), Rudyard Kipling, John Masefield, and Captain Frederick Marryat—as well as Mark Twain's *Huck Finn* and Emily Brontë's *Wuthering Heights.*

2. *The Sun Also Rises,* 247. Earlier manuscript versions of this line include "Isn't it nice to think so?" and "It's nice as hell to think so" (Hemingway Collection, John F. Kennedy Library, Boston).

3. Donald Pizer also privileges Gloriani, seeing the character as "a resplendent mix of freedom and energy . . . explicitly in tune with the new 'geography' of Paris" (5).

WORKS CITED

Barbusse, Henri. (*Under Fire: The Story of a Squad*). Trans. Fitzwater Wray. New York: Dutton, 1917. Trans. of *Le Feu.* 1917.

Beegel, Susan. "'The Undefeated' and Sangre Y Arena: Hemingway's Mano a Mano with Blasco Ibañez." *Hemingway Repossessed*. Ed. Kenneth Rosen. Westport, Conn.: Praeger, 1994. 71–85.

Blasco Ibañez, Vicente. *Blood and Sand*. New York: Grosset & Dunlap, 1922.

———. *The Enemies of Women*. Trans. Irving Brown. New York: Dutton, 1920.

———. *The Four Horsemen of the Apocalypse*. Trans. Charlotte Brewster Jordan. New York: Dutton, 1919.

Ford, Ford Madox. *The Good Soldier*. Introduction by Ford. New York: Random, 1951.

Harris, Frank. *Latest Contemporary Portraits*. New York: Macaulay, 1927.

———. *Montes the Matador and Other Stories*. London: Grant Richards, 1900.

Hemingway, Ernest. *Ernest Hemingway: Selected Letters, 1917–1961*. Ed. Carlos Baker. New York: Scribner's, 1981.

———. *A Farewell to Arms*. New York: Scribner's, 1929.

———. *For Whom the Bell Tolls*. New York: Scribner's, 1940.

———. *The Garden of Eden*. New York: Scribner's, 1986.

———. *The Sun Also Rises*. New York: Scribner's, 1926.

James, Henry. *The Ambassadors*. New York: Penguin, 1986.

Maran, Rene. *Batouala: A Negro Novel from the French of Rene Maran*. London: Donathan Cape, 1922.

Pizer, Donald. *American Expatriate Writing and the Paris Moment*. Baton Rouge: Louisiana State University Press, 1996.

Ross, Charles L. "*The Good Soldier* and *The Sun Also Rises*." *Hemingway Review* 12 (Fall 1992): 26–34.

Solano, Solita. *The Uncertain Feast*. New York: Dutton, 1924.

Spilka, Mark. *Hemingway's Quarrel with Androgyny*. Lincoln: University of Nebraska Press, 1990.

Svoboda, Frederic Joseph. *Hemingway & "The Sun Also Rises": The Crafting of a Style*. Lawrence: University Press of Kansas, 1983.

Tyler, Lisa."Passion and Grief in *A Farewell to Arms*: Ernest Hemingway's Retelling of *Wuthering Heights*." *Ernest Hemingway: Seven Decades of Criticism*. Ed. Linda Wagner-Martin. East Lansing: Michigan State University Press, 1998.

Wagner-Martin, Linda. "*Favored Strangers*": Gertrude Stein and Her

Family. New Brunswick, New Jersey: Rutgers University Press, 1995.

———. "Kiki of Montparnasse and Hemingway's *A Moveable Feast.*" *Hemingway Review* 9 (Spring 1990): 176–77.

———. "'The Secrecies of the Public Hemingway." *Hemingway: Up in Michigan Perspectives.* Ed. Frederic J. Svoboda and Joseph J. Waldmeir. East Lansing: Michigan State University Press, 1995. 149–156.

Walpole, Hugh. *The Young Enchanted.* New York: Doran, 1921.

Wilkinson, Myler. *Hemingway and Turgenev: The Nature of Literary Influence.* Ann Arbor, Mich.: UMI, 1986.

ILLUSTRATED
CHRONOLOGY

Hemingway's Life

July 21, 1899: Ernest Miller Hemingway born, and—during the fall—is taken to Windemere Cottage on Walloon Lake in mid-Michigan, where he will spend summers for the next eighteen years.

1905: Hemingway begins first grade in Oak Park, Illinois, public schools.

1906: Grace Hall-Hemingway uses inheritance from her father to build the family a new home at 600 N. Kenilworth Avenue in Oak Park.

Ernest and Marcelline with their parents, Grace Hall-Hemingway and Clarence. Hemingway's relationship with his strong, feminist mother has been the topic of much discussion. Here, before the other four children were born, the Hemingways present an idyllic picture of health and stability. Photo used courtesy of the Hemingway Collection, John F. Kennedy Library.

Historical Events

1899: Hemingway is born into an imperialist nation; the Spanish-American War (Feb.–Aug. 1898) brought the United States Puerto Rico and the Philippines.

1899: Kate Chopin (1851–1904), *The Awakening;* Thorstein Veblen (1857–1929), *The Theory of the Leisure Class.*

1900: An average of 3.56 children are born to each U.S. woman; Theodore Dreiser (1871–1945), *Sister Carrie.*

1901: Booker T. Washington (1856–1915), *Up from Slavery.*

1902: Henry James (1843–1916), *The Wings of the Dove.*

1903: W. E. B. Du Bois (1868–1963), *The Souls of Black Folk.*

1905: Edith Wharton (1862–1937), *The House of Mirth.*

1906: Upton Sinclair (1878–1968), *The Jungle,* instrumental in passage of the Pure Food and Drug Act.

1909: Sigmund Freud's first lectures in the United States; National Association for the Advancement of Colored People founded; Gertrude Stein (1874–1946), *Three Lives.*

The Oak Park Agassiz Club. Under the leadership of his father, Dr. Clarence Hemingway, Oak Park boys could participate in one of the many Agassiz clubs. Named for the pioneering naturalist Louis Agassiz, the clubs introduced young boys to the scientific study of the natural world. The young Ernest is second from the left. Photo used courtesy of the Hemingway Collection, John F. Kennedy Library.

1913: Hemingway and his older sister Marcelline begin high school in Oak Park. He will write for the newspaper, *The Trapeze,* and the literary magazine, *Tabula.*

1917: After graduation from Oak Park High School, Hemingway takes a job as a cub reporter on the Kansas City *Star* (Kansas City, Missouri).

1918: Hemingway enlists in the American Red Cross as an ambulance driver; arrives in Italy on June 4 and volunteers to staff the Piave River front canteen. Wounded by a trench mortar shell on July 8, he is hospitalized for five months in Milan and falls in love with a nurse, Agnes von Kurowsky.

"Babes in the Wood" advertisement. As is evident in this commercial ad for the Woods automobile, the concept that children need fresh air and outside exercise was being inscribed in the turn-of-the-century culture. Reproduced and used by permission of the Hemingway Collection, John F. Kennedy Library.

Some of the shrapnel pieces that were removed from Hemingway's legs. Fashioned into a ring, the heavy metal fragment—like the other fragments that are arranged here—shows clearly how damaging the wounds from more than 220 such pieces could be to the young ambulance driver. Reproduced and used by permission of the Hemingway Collection, John F. Kennedy Library

Hemingway's Italian medal. Awarded after World War I had ended and at the close of his convalescence in Italian hospitals, the medal was one of Hemingway's prized possessions. Reproduced and used by permission of the Hemingway Collection, John F. Kennedy Library.

1910: An estimated 8 million immigrants arrive in the United States; Hamlin Garland (1860–1940), *Other Main Travelled Roads.*

1911: Triangle Shirtwaist Company fire, with loss of 146 lives.

1912: British oceanliner *Titanic* sinks on its maiden voyage; in Chicago, Harriet Monroe founded *Poetry: A Magazine of Verse.* First electric washing machine introduced.

Teddy Roosevelt. America's "roughrider" president (for two terms, from 1901 to 1909) was an icon of masculinity for much of the early twentieth century. His fighting in the Spanish Civil War, his big-game hunting and his general "outdoorsy" manner were much publicized. Even as a young child, Hemingway was encouraged to be a sportsman and a soldier.

Buy Liberty Bonds. *A typically alluring World War I poster suggests the hard-sell campaign that created the atmosphere of unquestioning patriotism against which Hemingway rebelled in his 1929 novel,* A Farewell to Arms.

1913: The Armory Show.

1914: Archduke Ferdinand of Austria assassinated in Sarajevo and World War I begins; Margaret Anderson founds *The Little Review.*

1915: Nevada's easy divorce law enacted; Provincetown Players formed.

1916: Ring Lardner (1885–1933), *You Know Me, Al;* Carl Sandburg (1878–1967), *Chicago Poems.*

1917: United States enters World War I on the side of the Allies; T. S. Eliot, *Prufrock and Other Poems;* Joyce's *Ulysses* appears in *Little Review.*

Early Twentieth-century Feminists. *While women's rights movements garnered much public support in both the United States and England, they were also the topic of harsh criticism and crude humor. Cartoon used courtesy of* Life *magazine.*

1919: January 4, Hemingway is discharged from Red Cross and arrives in New York January 21; in March Agnes breaks off their engagement. He convalesces in Petosky, Michigan, trying to write seriously.

1920: From January to May, Hemingway works in Toronto, Ontario, and freelances for the Toronto *Star.* On his July birthday, Grace asks him to leave Windemere; Hemingway moves to Chicago and works for *Cooperative Commonwealth.* There he meets writers as well as Hadley Richardson of St. Louis.

Ernest and Hadley at their September 3, 1921, wedding at Horton Bay, Michigan. Wearing his fashionable white flannels, Hemingway planned and implemented his wedding to Hadley Richardson of St. Louis as if to answer his mother's earlier complaints that he was immature. Photo used courtesy of the Hemingway Collection, John F. Kennedy Library.

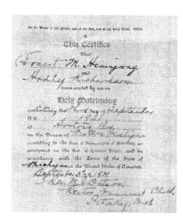

(Above) Ernest and Hadley's Marriage License. Reproduced and used by permission of the Hemingway Collection, John F. Kennedy Library.

(At right) Heningway and Hadley, 1922. After some early years of writing in Chicago and Michigan, Hemingway began his career in fact with his move to Paris in late 1921. He is shown here with his first wife, Hadley Richardson. Photo used courtesy of the Hemingway Collection, John F. Kennedy Library, Boston.

Gertrude Stein and Alice B. Toklas, Bumby's godmothers. Hemingway's relationship with Stein extended to involving her, with her companion Alice Toklas, in his most intimate family life; Stein was also the godmother of Pablo Picasso's son. Photo used courtesy of the Hemingway Collection, John F. Kennedy Library.

1921: September 3, Hadley and Hemingway are married at Horton Bay, Michigan; in December they sail for Paris, with introductory letters from Sherwood Anderson.

1922: The Hemingways rent 79 rue Cardinal Lemoine on the Left Bank. Writing for the *Star,* he covers Genoa Economic Conference in Italy, the Greco-Turkish War from Constantinople, and the Lausanne peace conference. Writing seriously, he develops friendships with Ezra Pound, Gertrude Stein, and other Paris notables. He and Hadley travel to Switzerland, Austria, Italy, the Black Forest, and Chamby, skiing and bobsledding. Hadley carries his manuscripts to Switzerland, and they are stolen en route.

1918: "Fourteen Points" Armistice signed; Willa Cather (1873–1947), *My Antonia.*

1919: President Wilson supports League of Nations; ratification of the Eighteen Amendment (the Volsted Act) begins Prohibition; Sherwood Anderson (1876–1941), *Winesburg, Ohio.*

1920: Ratification of the Nineteenth Amendment enacts women's suffrage; Sinclair Lewis (1885–1951), *Main Street;* F. Scott Fitzgerald (1896–1940), *This Side of Paradise.*

1921: The first Miss America Pageant is held in Atlantic City.

1923: Travels continue, including Madrid, where they see bullfights. Robert McAlmon publishes *Three Stories & Ten Poems* (some of which have appeared in *Poetry*). Hadley and he return to Toronto, where Hemingway works for the *Star* and is therefore in the States at the time of the birth of their child (John Nicanor "Bumby") in October.

Bullfighting Programs and Newspapers. Hemingway's extensive collection of bullfight memorabilia [here, these items dating from 1923 (top right), 1924 (above right), and 1926 (above left)] contributed to both his 1926 novel, The Sun Also Rises, *and his treatise on the bullfight.* Death in the Afternoon. *Reproduced and used by permission of the Hemingway Collection, John F. Kennedy Library.*

(Left) The Hemingways–Hadley, Ernest, and Bumby. As Barlowe's essay makes clear, Hadley Richardson came from a long line of independent women. Photo used courtesy of the Hemingway Collection, John F. Kennedy Library. (Right) Ernest Hemingway's passport photo. As Hemingway's photo suggests, his identity when he and Hadley first arrived in Europe, soon after their 1921 wedding, was as an American journalist. Passport reproduced and used with the permission of the Hemingway Collection, John F. Kennedy Library.

The 1925 Expatriate Group in Pamplona, Spain. Ernest is second from right, sitting between his wife Hadley and Pauline Pfeiffer, who would eventually become the second Mrs. Hemingway. Gerald and Sarah Murphy are seated to the left. Photo used courtesy of the Hemingway Collection, John F. Kennedy Library.

1924: The family returns to Paris in January and rents 113 rue Notre-Dame-des-Champs. Hemingway works as associate editor on Ford Madox Ford's little magazine, *transatlantic review,* and publishes fiction. *in our time* is published in the spring. He and Hadley visit the San Fermin festival in Pamplona, Spain; the magazine fails; they travel to Schruns, Austria, for skiing.

1925: Liveright accepts the expanded *In Our Time* for U.S. publication. Meeting the Fitzgeralds and the Murphys, the Hemingways are a part of the Paris young literary set; they go back to Pamplona in the summer. Hemingway is writing *The Sun Also Rises,* as well as *The Torrents of Spring,* which he uses in the fall to break his Liveright contract and go to Scribner's.

1926: Pauline Pfeiffer joins the Hemingways for winter skiing at Schruns; Scribner's publishes *Torrents of Spring* after Hadley and Hemingway spend a summer at the Murphy's and in Pamplona and decide to separate so that, after 100 days, Pauline and Hemingway can be together. *The Sun Also Rises* is published in the autumn.

1927: The Hemingways divorce and, in May, Pauline and Ernest are married in a Catholic church in Paris. They summer in Spain, and *Men without Women* appears in October.

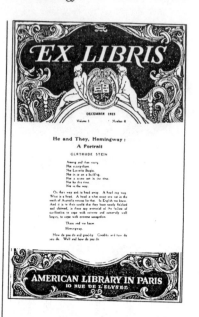

Gertrude Stein's "He and They, Hemingway." At the height of Hemingway's welcome to the Parisian expatriate colony, Gertrude Stein published her word "portrait" of him in the international little magazine Ex Libris, late 1923. Like Ezra Pound, Stein became an influential mentor for the young American—at least for a few years.

1922: James Joyce's *Ulysses;* T. S. Eliot's *The Waste Land;* Benito Mussolini comes to power in Italy.

1923: Margaret Mead (1901–1978), *Coming of Age in Samoa;* Wallace Stevens (1879–1955), *Harmonium;* Jean Toomer (1894–1967), *Cane.*

1924: Congress acts to give Native Americans citizenship; Eugene O'Neill (1888–1953), *Desire under the Elms.*

1928: After beginning *A Farewell to Arms*, Hemingway injures his eye and has the skylight accident with resultant head injuries. He and Pauline leave France for Key West and Piggott, Arkansas; Patrick is born there June 28. In December, Clarence Hemingway commits suicide and Hemingway returns to Chicago for his funeral.

1929: *A Farewell to Arms* appears after being serialized in *Scribner's Magazine* (the magazine is banned in Boston); the Hemingways are back in Madrid and Paris.

1930: *The Sun Also Rises* is republished; the Hemingways live in Key West and visit both Arkansas and Cooke City, Montana. Film sale for *A Farewell to Arms* (after a stage adaptation). Hemingway injures his right arm in an accident near Billings, Montana, and is hospitalized for a month.

1931: With Pauline's uncle (Gus Pfeiffer) funding the purchase, the Hemingways buy the house at 907 Whitehead in Key West; they return to Spain during the summer so that *Death in the Afternoon* can be finished. Gregory is born in November in Kansas City.

1932: *Death* published to mixed reviews; Hemingway writes short stories (many of which will appear in *Winner Take Nothing*) and refuses to attend the world premier (in Piggott) of the Gary Cooper and Helen Hayes version of *A Farewell to Arms*.

1925: The Scopes Monkey Trial pits evolution against creationism; F. Scott Fitzgerald, *The Great Gatsby;* John Dos Passos (1896–1970), *Manhattan Transfer;* Theodore Dreiser, *An American Tragedy;* William Carlos Williams (1883–1963), *In the American Grain;* Alain Locke, ed., *The New Negro: An Interpretation.*

1926: The Book-of-the-Month Club organized, has 40,000 subscribers to begin; Langston Hughes (1902–1967), *The Weary Blues;* William Faulkner (1897–1962), *Soldiers' Pay.*

1927: Nicola Sacco and Bartolomeo Vanzetti, anarchists, executed for an alleged murder.

1928: D. H. Lawrence, *Lady Chatterley;* Nella Larsen (1893–1964), *Quicksand;* Robert Frost (1874–1963), *West-Running Brook*

1929: U.S. stock market crashes, initiating the Great Depression.

1930: Sinclair Lewis is first American to win the Nobel Prize in Literature; William Faulkner, *As I Lay Dying;* Hart Crane (1899–1932), *The Bridge.*

1932: The Lindbergh baby kidnapping case (child is found dead after ransom paid).

1933: Hemingway writes for *Esquire*, becomes friends with its publisher, Arnold Gingrich. After fishing in Cuban waters and spending the summer in Spain and Paris, Pauline and Hemingway sail for Nairobi for a two-month safari.

1934: Hemingway buys the *Pilar* and brings it to Key West but lives mostly in Cuba as he writes *Green Hills of Africa.*

1935: *Scribner's* serializes *Green Hills of Africa* before it is published in October, again to mixed reviews. Hemingway's time is spent working on *To Have and Have Not*, fishing, and bear hunting. In December he meets Martha Gellhorn.

1936: Writing for North American Newspaper Alliance, Hemingway works to cover the Spanish Civil War, spending two months in Madrid, living at the Hotel Florida with Martha and other Americans. *The Spanish Earth* is shown in New York and the Roosevelt White House in July; he returns to Madrid in autumn. *To Have and Have Not* appears, again to mixed reviews.

1937–1938: Hemingway spends the years in Spain, or writing about Spain, or with either Martha or Pauline. *The Fifth Column and the First Forty-Nine Stories* appears in October 1938.

1933: Prohibition is repealed; Gertrude Stein, *The Autobiography of Alice B. Toklas.*

1934: Adolf Hitler combines presidency and chancellorship of Germany.

1935: Pearl Buck (1892–1973) is first U.S. woman to win the Nobel Prize in Literature; John Steinbeck (1902–1968), *Tortilla Flat;* Federal Writers' Project, till 1939.

1936: William Faulkner, *Absalom, Absalom!;* Margaret Mitchell (1900–1949), *Gone with the Wind;* James M. Cain (1892–1977), *The Postman Always Rings Twice;* Federal Theatre Project begun.

1937: Zora Neale Hurston (1901–1960), *Their Eyes Were Watching God;* John Steinbeck, *Of Mice and Men.*

1938: John Dos Passos, *U.S.A.;* Richard Wright (1908–1960), *Uncle Tom's Children.*

1939: Start of World War II; John Steinbeck, *The Grapes of Wrath.*

1940: 52 percent of U.S. households have mechanical refrigerators and/ or washing machines; Thomas Wolfe (1900–1938), *You Can't Go Home Again;* Richard Wright, *Native Son.*

Hemingway and His Three Children-and All Those Fish. Much of the writer's interaction with his sons—Jack ("Bumby"), Patrick, and Gregory—centered around fishing and hunting. Photo used courtesy of the Hemingway Collection, John F. Kennedy Library.

1939: As Hemingway writes *For Whom the Bell Tolls*, Martha rents La Finca Vigía outside of Havana. Martha goes to Finland as *Collier's* correspondent; Pauline leaves Key West with the children.

1940: *For Whom the Bell Tolls* is published in October to good reviews; it is a Book-of-the-Month Club Selection and receives a $100,000 film bid. Pauline's divorce from Ernest is final in November, and Hemingway and Martha are married November 21 in Cheyenne, Wyoming. They buy the Cuban house, La Finca Vigía, in late December.

1942: Under President F. D. Roosevelt's executive order, more than 110,000 Japanese Americans are placed in internment camps; William Faulkner, *Go Down, Moses*.

1943: T. S. Eliot, *Four Quartets*.

1945: World War II ends after the U.S. atomic bombing of Hiroshima and Nagasaki; Gertrude Stein, *Wars I Have Seen;* Eudora Welty (1909–), *Delta Wedding;* Gwendolyn Brooks (1917–), *A Street in Bronzeville;* Tennessee Williams (1911–1983), *The Glass Menagerie*

1941: Martha and Hemingway travel in China (he is writing for *PM* on conditions there) and then spend the autumn in the Sun Valley Lodge. They return to Cuba for Christmas.

1942: Hemingway is patroling Cuban waters in the *Pilar;* Martha travels for *Collier's* and lives and writes in Cuba.

1943: Hemingway remains in Cuba all year; Martha goes to Europe in the autumn for *Collier's* and urges Ernest to come as a war correspondent also.

1944: He finally takes the *Collier's* correspondent job in March, which leaves Martha without a way to get back to the European front. He goes to London, meets Mary Welch, and is convalescing from a concussion (another auto accident) with friends when Martha arrives. Their marriage ends, and Hemingway begins liaison with Mary. Jeep accident in August re-injures his head, which bothers him for the following year.

1945: Hemingway sues Martha for desertion in divorce proceedings. Mary's divorce is also in process.

1946: In March, Hemingway marries Mary; in August she nearly dies of a burst fallopian tube. They try living in Ketchum, Idaho.

1946: Ann Petry (1908–1997), *The Street;* Elizabeth Bishop (1911–1979), *North and South;* Robert Penn Warren (1905–1989), *All the King's Men.*

1948: Norman Mailer (1923–), *The Naked and the Dead;* Truman Capote (1924–1984), *Other Voices, Other Rooms;* Ezra Pound (1885–1972), *The Pisan Cantos;* T. S. Eliot is awarded the Nobel Prize in Literature.

1949: The first bikini bathing suit makes its appearance; Nelson Algren (1909–1981), *The Man with the Golden Arm.*

1950: William Faulkner is awarded the Nobel Prize in Literature; U.S. troops invade North Korea; McCarthy investigations begin.

1951: J. D. Salinger (1919–), *The Catcher in the Rye;* Rachel Carson (1904–1964), *The Sea around Us.*

1952: Ralph Ellison (1914–1994), *Invisible Man;* Flannery O'Connor (1925–1964), *Wise Blood.*

1953: Ethel and Julius Rosenberg are executed for allegedly passing U.S. secrets to Russia; James Baldwin (1924–1987), *Go Tell It on the Mountain;* Arthur Miller (1915–), *The Crucible.* The Korean War armistice is signed.

(Left) *Martha Gellhorn and Hemingway visiting China in 1941. The third Mrs. Hemingway was already a well-known journalist before she married Ernest, and the pressures of two vital careers soon led to their separation. Photo used courtesy of the Hemingway Collection, John F. Kennedy Library.* (Right) *Hemingway during World War II. Hemingway's fascination with the military was more than romantic, and during 1944–1945 he served in the European sector as a reporter for Collier's magazine. As he had during World War I, when he drove ambulances for the Italian services, he wore what he thought was appropriate military clothing. Photo used courtesy of the Hemingway Collection, John F. Kennedy Library.*

Hemingway's World War II Overseas Visa and Officers' Club Card. Being accepted by other military men was crucial to Hemingway, particularly as he aged. Reproduced and used by permission of the Hemingway Collection, John F. Kennedy Library.

1947–1949: Hemingway is writing on a "long" novel, living between Cuba and Idaho. He and Mary travel through Italy, where he meets Adriana Ivancich (the model for Renata in *Across the River and Into the Trees*). More travel in France and Italy.

1950: Returning to Cuba, Hemingway finishes *Across the River,* which appears in September to negative reviews. Adriana and her mother come for a visit; Mary thinks of divorce.

1951–1952: Grace Hall-Hemingway dies in July; Pauline dies October 1; Charles Scribner, in February 1952. In September, *Life* magazine publishes *The Old Man and the Sea,* for which they paid $40,000, to rave reviews.

1954: *Brown v. Board of Education of Topeka* finds racial discrimination in schools unconstitutional; Hemingway is awarded the Nobel Prize in Literature.

1955: Rosa Parks is arrested after failing to give up her bus seat in Montgomery, Alabama; three out of five households have television sets; Vladimir Nabokov's *Lolita*.

1956: John Barth (1930–), *The Floating Opera;* Allen Ginsberg (1926–1997), *Howl and Other Poems*.

1957: Jack Kerouac (1922–1969), *On the Road;* Ann Bannon (unknown), *Odd Girl Out*.

Hemingway with his fourth wife, Mary, both in hunting gear. Part of the attraction of the American West is the informality of its appropriate attire. Photo used courtesy of the Hemingway Collection, John F. Kennedy Library.

1953: The novella wins the Pulitzer Prize; Spencer Tracy is filming it in Cuba. Mary and Hemingway travel to Spain, France, and Africa.

1954: Plane crashes on safari. Hemingway receives the Nobel Prize for Literature, and his photo is the cover of *Time* magazine.

1955–1956: Despite much illness, Hemingway finishes the African book. With Mary, he travels to Spain and France.

1957–1958: Traveling in France and living in Cuba, Hemingway alternates between working on his memoirs *(A Moveable Feast)* and *The Garden of Eden*. The Hemingways move to Ketchum.

1959: Castro takes over Cuba. Hemingway buys the Ketchum house but goes to Spain for the summer, writing *The Dangerous Summer*.

1960: Much of this year Hemingway fights serious depression; in December, under an assumed name, he enters the Mayo Clinic and receives electroconvulsive shock treatment, through January.

1961: After two suicide attempts in April, Hemingway is readmitted to Mayo Clinic. In June he is released and taken by car to Ketchum. July 2, he commits suicide there.

Hemingway wearing the long-billed cap (still available from menswear catalogs). As Ernest aged and was bothered increasingly by physical illness, being able to set styles that were comfortable was itself a comfort. Photo used courtesy of the Hemingway Collection, John F. Kennedy Library.

1959: Lorraine Hansberry (1930–1965), *A Raisin in the Sun*, Broadway play; Grace Paley (1922–), *The Little Disturbances of Man;* Saul Bellow (1915–), *Henderson the Rain King.*

1960: John Updike (1932–), *Rabbit, Run;* Sylvia Plath (1932–1963), *The Colossus and Other Poems;* Anne Sexton (1928–1974), *To Bedlam and Part Way Back;* Charles Olson (1910–1970), *The Maximus Poems.*

1961: Joseph Heller (1923–), *Catch-22;* Walker Percy (1916–1990), *The Moviegoer;* Kurt Vonnegut, Jr., (1922–), *Mother Night.*

Bibliographical Essay

Lies, Damned Lies, and Hemingway Criticism

Kelli A. Larson

The best authors convince their audience that the hard work of creating flawless prose comes naturally. Yet, as any struggling writer can attest, the easiest writing to read is often the most difficult to produce. Hemingway proved no exception. Though he remains a powerful presence in American literature today and is perhaps one of the few American modernists whose name is known throughout the world, Hemingway wrestled mightily with his writing, carefully crafting both his subject matter and style. His perseverance and willingness to take risks taught him how to write "naturally." And his readers are the beneficiaries of his literary legacy, as we settle back in our comfortable armchairs ready to enjoy another adventure with one of his timeless heroes, those characters imbued with Hemingway's own indomitable passion for life.

For critics and scholars, Hemingway's legacy presents more than a good "read," however. Papa's distinctive and indelible mark on American literature has provided seemingly endless opportunities for critical exploration, investigation, and evisceration. Literally thousands of studies written in numerous languages have appeared over the past eighty years, on both the man and his work. Hemingway was wary of and distrusted critics, often feeling violated or misunderstood by them. One need examine only briefly his relationships with critics such as A. E. Hotchner, Charles Fenton, or Philip Young for a more complete understanding of the author's reservations regarding those who have made Hemingway their "business."[1] Yet, ironically, those same critics, often English teachers, have helped to keep Hemingway alive both in and out of the classroom. By teaching his texts, they continuously introduce new generations of potential teachers, scholars, and aficionados to the mastery of Hemingway's art. Yet the simple act of including Hemingway on reading lists holds even greater ramifications for the field of Hemingway studies as a whole. Many critics agree, for example, that *The Sun Also Rises* is Hemingway's most written about novel not only because it is arguably his best, but also because it is his most popular classroom novel, included on more high school and college syllabi than any other of his works. Since scholars write about what they know well, such familiarity with *The Sun Also Rises* quite naturally leads to increased critical attention as scholars share their ideas with others via publication. Thus the cycle of critical debate begins anew with the opening of each semester and attests most clearly to Hemingway's "re-readability" down through the years.

The recent burgeoning of the field in the past few decades can be directly linked to the foundation of the Hemingway Society in 1980, coinciding with the establishment of the Hemingway Collection at the John F. Kennedy Library in Boston that same year. Smaller collections of the author's correspondence and manuscripts are held at various universities across the country, including the University of Delaware; Princeton, Stanford, and Indiana Universities; and the Harry Ranson Humanities Research Center (Austin, Tex.). However, the principal collection of materials, including drafts, typescripts, letters, and pictures, is housed at the John F. Kennedy Library. Interested researchers can easily access the extensive collection through Jo August's compilation of a two-volume *Catalog of the Ernest Hemingway Collection at the John F. Kennedy Library.*[2] Library staff are particularly pleased with the increasing number of high school and college students who make use of the collection for class projects, proving that the field of Hemingway studies has reached beyond the traditional academic researcher (Desnoyers 108).

The biannual publication of the *Hemingway Review,* a journal devoted solely to the study of the author, concretely reflects the growing interest in Papa and his work. Founded in 1979 under the title *Hemingway Notes,* the journal began with just thirty original subscribers. Currently, the *Hemingway Review* enjoys a circulation of well over 1,000 in twenty-eight nations. In addition to publishing articles devoted to all aspects of the man and his work, the *Review* regularly includes book reviews, current bibliographical checklists, and updates on the collection at the Kennedy Library. The computer literate can also keep in touch with the latest in the field by visiting sites devoted to the author on the Internet and World Wide Web. Surely Hemingway, adventurer and world traveler, would have reveled in his entry into cyberspace.

With the deluge of books and essays appearing on Hemingway, bibliographies and checklists have necessarily entered the fray, recording for present scholars all of the past research and, thus by omission, directing the course of future study. Audre Hanneman's *Ernest Hemingway: A Comprehensive Bibliography* (1967) and her *Supplement* (1975) list primary and secondary materials through 1973. Linda W. Wagner's *Ernest Hemingway: A Reference Guide* (1977) is an annotated bibliography with summary annotations of critical studies through the mid-1970s. Beginning where Wagner leaves off, Kelli A. Larson's annotated bibliography, *Ernest Hemingway: A Reference Guide* (1990), includes materials as recent as 1989. And as previously noted, each issue of the *Hemingway Review* carries a current bibliographical article containing one of the most up-to-date checklists of criticism available. The *Modern Language Association International Bibliography,* available both in print and on CD-ROM, lists annually the most recent primary and secondary materials. For those seeking an overview of the scholarship, *American Literary Scholarship: An Annual* devotes a chapter to Fitzgerald and Hemingway each year, reviewing notable trends in the criticism as well as identifying important individual studies that might otherwise have been buried beneath the sheer volume of criticism. In a field that has evolved into nothing short of an industry, the guidance offered by such surveys of the literature proves invaluable in circumnavigating the maze of critical mass production.

In reviewing the author's fluctuating reputation with critics and scholars over the years, two contributors should not be overlooked. Their pervasive influence permanently changed the nature and direction of Hemingway studies—which until their appearance had been largely dominated by the personal and informal. In 1952 the publication of Philip Young's *Ernest Hemingway* and Carlos Baker's *Hemingway: The Writer as Artist* raised the level of critical discourse from the casual to the academic. Their thoroughly researched and carefully reasoned analyses heralded a new era of serious Hemingway scholarship. Young's early psychoanalytical approach to Hemingway's fiction has earned him the distinction of being one of the most often cited scholars in the field. Interestingly, Young's wound theory—that Hemingway's fiction represents the author's lifelong struggle to psychically purge himself of the wound he received while in Italy during World War I—is nearly as widely known as the fiction itself. Ironically, Young's highly influential wound and "code-hero" theories have made *him* the subject of critical analysis, beyond the conventional book review.[3] No doubt Hemingway would have delighted in the skewering of his most famous critic: "Hoist with his own petard!"

Though numerous studies devoted to Hemingway's stylistic development and artistic aesthetic have appeared since Baker's "classic" volume, his will be remembered as the first major Hemingway book. Baker's close reading of the author's novels and short fiction reveals Hemingway's careful craftsmanship and attention to detail. However, I would be remiss if I failed to mention Baker's other invaluable contribution to the field of Hemingway studies, his editing of *Ernest Hemingway: Selected Letters, 1917–1961*. Despite criticism by some for going against the author's expressed wish that none of his correspondence be published, Baker's judicious selection and editing of 600 letters from the estimated 6,000 to 7,000 that Hemingway wrote during his lifetime have provided scholars and the general reading public with a solid understanding of the man and his art, revealing the real Hemingway beneath the legendary mask. As reviewers have pointed out, these letters serve as Hemingway's posthumous autobiography. And who better to compile such a volume than

Hemingway's authorized biographer, Carlos Baker, whose 1969 *Ernest Hemingway: A Life Story* remains a standard in the field, though dated. Still, with numerous newly "discovered" letters coming to light each year, researchers continue to hope for the eventual publication of a comprehensive collection of all of Hemingway's correspondence, including the thousands of letters not included in Baker's edition.

Also compiled posthumously are selections of Hemingway's journalistic writings, entitled *By-Line: Ernest Hemingway* and *Dateline: Toronto*, both edited by William White. *By-Line* includes less than one-third of all of Hemingway's identified newspaper and magazine articles, spanning the author's lifetime. *Dateline* concentrates on Hemingway's apprentice years while writing for the Toronto *Star*, prior to achieving legendary status. Both provide excellent fodder for the critical mill, exhibiting Hemingway's developing technique and distinctive style. Despite the author's claim that his journalism was separate from his creative efforts, White's collections confirm that a portion of these pieces do indeed prefigure later works such as *In Our Time* and *The Sun Also Rises*. In a related matter, the *Hemingway Review* has published thirty dispatches the author wrote for the North American Newspaper Alliance (NANA) while in Spain covering the Spanish Civil War. This special issue [7.2 (Spring 1988)] includes an introduction to NANA and to the dispatches, as well as maps and photographs.

Sadly, Hemingway's literary reputation has declined with the posthumous publication of his other works, perhaps unjustly so. In their efforts to bring the author's final books (*A Moveable Feast, Islands in the Stream, African Journal, The Dangerous Summer,* and *The Garden of Eden*) to the reading public, editors have altered, deleted, added, and rearranged substantial amounts of material from Hemingway's often unformed and unfinished writings. Though scholars are grateful for these additions to the Hemingway canon, they also recognize the problematic nature of their appearance. No one will ever know, for example, how and to what extent the author himself would have changed and revised his own manuscripts had he been allowed the opportunity.

Despite Mary Hemingway's contention that her husband completed *A Moveable Feast* in 1960 in Cuba, drafts show that, prior to its publication in 1964, she herself changed, deleted, and reconfigured significant portions of Hemingway's memoir of his early Paris years. We know, for example, that she "created" a "Preface" for the book, rearranged the sequence of chapters, reinserted passages that the author had explicitly deleted, and cut others (Brenner). Equally disturbing are the "cuts" and alterations Hemingway's widow, Charles Scribner, Jr., and Carlos Baker made to the manuscripts to form *Islands in the Stream*, Hemingway's sea novel. As with *A Moveable Feast*, the lack of clearly expressed editorial criteria and notes makes it difficult to know just how much was left out or changed. We do know that salient issues regarding the narrative perspective of the novel had been left unresolved at Hemingway's death, thus requiring the editors to weld the three sections comprising the novel into a coherent structure. Such editorial intervention certainly calls into question the legitimacy of Mary Hemingway's claim in her opening "Note" to the novel that "The book is all Ernest's." Still, Gerry Brenner's acknowledgment of Mary's editorial efforts in his careful examination of the *Feast* manuscripts might equally apply to *Islands:* "Many scholars and students will frown at her failure to abide by her duty as executor—to publish only her husband's 'completed' work—or at least to be loyal to her own second 'principle of procedure.' But she chose the more difficult and questionable task of salvaging some excellent writing that might otherwise have ended up as miscellany, were it ever to see print at all (543)."

The two remaining novels brought forth in the mid-1980s may present the thorniest textual challenges for readers and scholars. Not until a handful of years after publication was it even widely known that A. E. Hotchner had edited Hemingway's bullfighting novel, *The Dangerous Summer*, cutting close to half of the original 120,000-word manuscript. Ironically, Hotchner's "condensed" version was itself cut in half by editors for later publication in *Life*, proving once again that what "goes around, comes around." And *The Garden of Eden*, the most recent addition to the Hemingway bookshelf, has also garnered its fair share of criticism and controversy. Tom Jenks edited Hemingway's 1,500-page manuscript of androgyny, sexuality, and love down to just 247 pages, claiming that "everything in here is his [Hemingway's]. I cut and rearranged, but I added nothing, rewrote nothing" (quoted in Pooley 50). However, scholars poring over Hemingway's original manuscript lament Jenks's extensive cutting of important scenes and subplots that tie the narrative together. As Michael Reynolds sums up, the novel "bears so little resemblance to the book Hemingway wrote that scholars can speak only to the manuscript versions" (4).

Only *African Journal*, based on the author's 1953–1954 safari, is well documented and footnoted. The editor, Ray Cave, provides an accurate account of the cutting and rearranging that resulted in the publication of only one-fourth of Hemingway's original 850-page manuscript. With the remaining posthumous texts, we must depend on scholars working with the collections at the Kennedy Library and elsewhere to unearth what the author had produced and perhaps intended. Ironically, it will be those very scholars and critics whom the author distrusted who will ultimately take on the responsibility of recovering and preserving the authentic Hemingway from the editorial distortions of these posthumous publications.

Distortions, misrepresentations, and errors in Hemingway texts do not fall under the sole purview of the posthumous works, however. After all, the publishing process necessitates that even Hemingway had to work with editors. Clearly, the author himself was concerned with accuracy in his published texts, remarking in the *New York Times Book Review*, "After I have written a book I only wish to see it published exactly as I wrote it and have as many people read it as possible" (58). Using the manuscripts available at the Kennedy Library, several important studies have shown the overwhelming need for definitive, or at the very least revised and corrected, editions of Hemingway's texts. For example, Jim Hinkle's exhaustive comparison study of Hemingway's finished typescript of *The Sun Also Rises* with Scribner's published edition reveals more than 4,000 differences, including substantial deletions and sentence and word changes. Scott Donaldson finds in his manuscript examinations that some of the more puzzling textual problems in *A Farewell to Arms* and the short fiction, such as disappearing characters and contradictions, can be directly attributed to the editor's blue pencil. Such revelations do not always come easy to critics who have occasionally constructed elaborate interpretations upon errata, but most agree that the need for clarity and accuracy in the Hemingway canon is long overdue.

On a final note, since we are examining erroneous suppositions, the latest edition of Hemingway's short fiction, *The Complete Short Stories of Ernest Hemingway: The Finca Vigía Edition,* is neither complete nor limited to short stories. Oddly, it fails to include five easily accessible stories published in Peter Griffin's 1985 biography while it does include three previously unpublished excerpts from novels. No doubt old magazines and other periodicals, as well as manuscript collections, will continue to yield "finds" for years to come, thus making the compilation of a comprehensive anthology a difficult and arduous task. However, though welcomed for its convenience, this edition is not the most up-to-date volume for which scholars have longed.

To assist those who wish to explore further Hemingway's life and work, an extended bibliographical checklist completes this essay. To give as full and comprehensive a picture of the research and scholarship as possible, all important published book-length contributions, including significant synthetic studies reflecting the author's literary, social, political, or cultural environment, have been included. A simple alphabetical organization by author's last name has been adopted for ease in locating specific works.

NOTES

1. See, e.g., Philip Young. "Hemingway and Me: A Rather Long Story," *Kenyon Review* 28 (January 1966): 15–37; Philip Young, "On Disremembering Hemingway," *Atlantic Monthly* 218 (August 1966): 45–9; A. E. Hotchner, "Postscript" to *Papa Hemingway: The Ecstasy and Sorrow* (New York: Quill, 1983).

2. It is hoped that a revised and updated edition of August's *Catalog* will be completed by the time this study goes to print. Scholars can access the collection's online catalog through the John F. Kennedy Library's web site.

3. See, e.g., Charles Stetler and Gerald Locklin, "De-coding the Hero in Hemingway's Fiction," *Hemingway Notes* 5.1 (Fall 1979): 2–10.

WORKS CITED

August, Jo, comp. *Catalog of the Ernest Hemingway Collection at the John F. Kennedy Library.* 2 vols. Boston: G. K. Hall, 1982.

Baker, Carlos. *Ernest Hemingway: A Life Story.* New York: Scribner's, 1969.

———. *Hemingway: The Writer as Artist.* Princeton, N.J.: Princeton University Press, 1952.

Beegel, Susan F. "From the Editor." *Hemingway Review* 15.2 (Spring 1996): 137–39.

Brenner, Gerry. "Are We Going to Hemingway's Feast?" *American Literature* 54.4 (Dec. 1982): 528–44.

Desnoyers, Megan Floyd, Lisa Middents, and Stephen Plotkin. "News from the Hemingway Collection." *Hemingway Review* 12.1 (Fall 1992): 106–8.

Donaldson, Scott. "The Case of the Vanishing American and Other Puzzlements in Hemingway's Fiction." *Hemingway Notes* 6.2 (Spring 1981): 16–19.

Griffin, Peter. *Along with Youth: Hemingway, the Early Years.* New York: Oxford University Press, 1985.

Hanneman, Audre. *Ernest Hemingway: A Comprehensive Bibliography.* Princeton, N.J.: Princeton University Press, 1967.

———. *Supplement to Ernest Hemingway, A Comprehensive Bibliography.* Princeton, N.J.: Princeton University Press, 1975.

Hemingway, Ernest. *By-Line: Ernest Hemingway, Selected Articles and Dispatches of Four Decades.* Edited by William White. New York: Scribner's, 1967.

———. *The Complete Short Stories of Ernest Hemingway: The Finca Vigía Edition.* New York: Scribner's, 1987

———. *Dateline: Toronto—The Complete Toronto "Star" Dispatches, 1920–1924.* Ed. by William White. New York: Scribner's, 1985.

———. *Ernest Hemingway: Selected Letters, 1917–1961.* Ed. by Carlos Baker. New York: Scribner's, 1981.

———. "Success, It's Wonderful." Ed. by Harvey Breit. *New York Times Book Review* 3 Dec. 1950: 4, 58.

Hinkle, James. "'Dear Mr. Scribner'—About the Published Text of *The Sun Also Rises.*" *The Hemingway Review* 6.1 (Fall 1986): 43–64.

Larson, Kelli A. *Ernest Hemingway: A Reference Guide, 1974–1989.* Boston: Hall, 1990.

Pooley, Eric. "Papa's New Baby: How Scribner's Crafted a Hemingway Novel." *New York* 28 April. 1986: 50–60.

Reynolds, Michael. "Prospects for the Study of Ernest Hemingway." *Resources for American Literary Study* 21.1 (1995): 1–15.

Wagner, Linda W. *Ernest Hemingway: A Reference Guide.* Boston: Hall, 1977.

Young, Philip. *Ernest Hemingway.* New York: Rinehart, 1952.

BIBLIOGRAPHY

Aldridge, John W. *After the Lost Generation: A Critical Study of the Writers of Two Wars.* New York: McGraw, 1951.

Arnold, Lloyd R. *High on the Wild with Hemingway.* Caldwell, Idaho: Caxton, Ltd., 1968. Rev. ed. New York: Grossett, 1977.

Aronowitz, Alfred G., and Peter Hamill. *Ernest Hemingway: The Life and Death of a Man.* New York: Lancer, 1961.

Asselineau, Roger, ed. *The Literary Reputation of Hemingway in Europe.* Lettres Modernes, no. 5. Paris: Minard, 1965.

Atkins, John. *The Art of Ernest Hemingway: His Work and Personality.* London: Peter Nevill, 1952.

August, Jo, comp. *Catalog of the Ernest Hemingway Collection at the John F. Kennedy Library.* 2 vols. Boston: Hall, 1982.

Baker, Carlos. *Ernest Hemingway: A Life Story.* New York: Scribner's, 1969.

———. *Hemingway: The Writer as Artist.* Princeton: Princeton University Press, 1952. Rev. ed. 1956. Rev. 3rd ed. 1963. Rev. 4th ed. 1972.

———, ed. *Ernest Hemingway: Critiques of Four Major Novels.* New York: Scribner's, 1962.

———, ed. *Hemingway and His Critics: An International Anthology.* New York: Hill & Wang, 1961.

Baker, Sheridan. *Ernest Hemingway: An Introduction and Interpretation.* New York: Holt, 1967.

Bakker, J. *Ernest Hemingway in Holland, 1925–1981: A Comparative Analysis of the Contemporary Dutch and American Critical Reception of His Work.* Amsterdam: Rodopi, 1986.

———. *Ernest Hemingway: The Artist as Man of Action.* Assen, Neth.: Van Gorcum, 1972.

———. *Fiction as Survival Strategy: A Comparative Study of the Major Works of Ernest Hemingway and Saul Bellow.* Amsterdam: Costerus, 1983.

Baldwin, Marc D. *Reading "The Sun Also Rises:" Hemingway's Political Unconscious.* New York: Lang, 1997.

Beach, Joseph Warren. *American Fiction: 1920–1940.* New York: Macmillan, 1941.

Beegel, Susan F. *Hemingway's Craft of Omission: Four Manuscript Examples.* Ann Arbor, Mich.: UMI, 1988.

———, ed. *Hemingway's Neglected Short Fiction: New Perspectives.* Ann Arbor, Mich.: UMI, 1989.

Benson, Jackson J. *Hemingway: The Writer's Art of Self Defense.* Minneapolis: University of Minnesota Press, 1969.

———, ed. *New Critical Approaches to the Short Stories of Ernest Hemingway.* Durham: Duke University Press, 1990.

———, ed. *The Short Stories of Ernest Hemingway: Critical Essays.* Durham: Duke University Press, 1975.

Benson, Jackson J., and Richard Astro, eds. *Hemingway in Our Time.* Cornvallis: Oregon State University Press, 1974.

Benstock, Shari. *Women of the Left Bank: Paris, 1900–1940.* Austin: University of Texas Press, 1986.

Bloom, Harold, ed. *Brett Ashley.* New York: Chelsea, 1991.

———, ed. *Ernest Hemingway.* New York: Chelsea, 1985.

———, ed. *Ernest Hemingway's "A Farewell to Arms."* New York: Chelsea, 1987.

———, ed. *Ernest Hemingway's "A Farewell to Arms."* Broomall: Chelsea, 1996.

———, ed. *Ernest Hemingway's "The Old Man and the Sea."* Broomall: Chelsea, 1996.

———, ed. *Ernest Hemingway's "The Sun Also Rises."* New York: Chelsea, 1987.

———, ed. *Ernest Hemingway's "The Sun Also Rises."* Broomall: Chelsea, 1996.

Boker, Pamela A. *The Grief Taboo in American Literature: Loss and Prolonged Adolescence in Twain, Melville, and Hemingway.* New York: New York University Press, 1996.

Bradbury, Malcolm, and David Palmer, eds. *The American Novel and the Nineteen Twenties*. Stratford-Upon-Avon Studies, no. 19. London: Edward Arnold, 1971.

Brasch, James Daniel, and Joseph Sigman. *Hemingway's Library: A Composite Record*. New York: Garland, 1981.

Bredahl, A. Carl, Jr., and Susan Lynn Drake. *Hemingway's "Green Hills of Africa" as Evolutionary Narrative: Helix and Scimitar*. Lewiston, N.Y.: Edwin Mellen, 1990.

Brenner, Gerry. *Concealments in Hemingway's Works*. Columbus: Ohio State University Press, 1983.

————. *"The Old Man and the Sea:" Story of a Common Man*. Twayne's Masterworks Studies, no. 80. Boston: Twayne, 1991.

Brian, Denis. *The True Gen*. New York: Grove, 1988.

Bridgman, Richard. *The Colloquial Style in America*. New York: Oxford University Press, 1966.

Broer, Lawrence R. *Hemingway's Spanish Tragedy*. Tuscaloosa: University of Alabama Press, 1973.

Bruccoli, Matthew J. *Fitzgerald and Hemingway: A Dangerous Friendship*. New York: Carroll & Graf, 1994.

————. *Scott and Ernest: The Authority of Failure and the Authority of Success*. New York: Random, 1978.

————, ed. *Conversations with Ernest Hemingway*. Jackson: University Press of Mississippi, 1986.

Bruccoli, Matthew J., ed., with the assistance of Robert W. Trogdon. *The Only Thing That Counts: The Ernest Hemingway/Maxwell Perkins Correspondence, 1925–1947*. New York: Scribner's, 1996.

Bruccoli, Matthew J., and C. E. Frazer Clark, Jr., comps. *Hemingway at Auction, 1930–1973*. Detroit: Gale Research, 1973.

Buckley, Peter. *Ernest*. New York: Dial, 1978.

Burgess, Anthony. *Ernest Hemingway and His World*. New York: Scribner's, 1978.

Burrill, William. *Hemingway: The Toronto Years*. Toronto: Doubleday, 1994.

Burwell, Rose Marie. *Hemingway: The Postwar Years and the Posthumous Novels*. Cambridge: Cambridge University Press, 1996.

Capellán, Angel. *Hemingway and the Hispanic World*. Ann Arbor, Mich.: UMI, 1985.

Castillo-Puche, José Luis. *Hemingway in Spain*. Trans. Helen R. Lane. Garden City, N.Y.: Doubleday, 1974.

Civello, Paul. *American Literary Naturalism and Its Twentieth-Century*

Transformations: Frank Norris, Ernest Hemingway, and Don DeLillo.
Athens: University of Georgia Press, 1994.

Comley, Nancy R., and Robert Scholes. *Hemingway's Genders: Rereading the Hemingway Text.* New Haven: Yale University Press, 1994.

Conrad, Barnaby. *Hemingway's Spain.* San Francisco: Chronicle, 1989.

Cooper, Stephen. *The Politics of Ernest Hemingway.* Ann Arbor, Mich.: UMI, 1987.

Corkin, Stanley. *Realism and the Birth of the Modern United States: Cinema, Literature, and Culture.* Athens: University of Georgia Press, 1996.

Cowley, Malcolm. *A Second Flowering, Words and Days of the Lost Generation.* New York: Viking, 1973.

De Falco, Joseph. *The Hero in Hemingway's Short Stories.* Pittsburgh: University of Pittsburgh Press, 1963.

De Koster, Katie, ed. *Readings on Ernest Hemingway.* San Diego: Greenhaven, 1996.

Diliberto, Gioia. *Hadley.* New York: Ticknor, 1992.

Dolan, Marc. *Modern Lives: A Cultural Re-reading of "The Lost Generation."* West Lafayette: Purdue University Press, 1996.

Donaldson, Scott. *By Force of Will: The Life and Art of Ernest Hemingway.* New York: Viking, 1977.

———, ed. *The Cambridge Companion to Hemingway.* Cambridge: Cambridge University Press, 1996.

———, ed. *New Essays on "A Farewell to Arms."* New York: Cambridge University Press, 1990.

Donnell, David. *Hemingway in Toronto: A Post-Modern Tribute.* Windsor, Ont.: Black Moss, 1982.

Eisinger, Chester E. *Fiction of the Forties.* Chicago: University of Chicago Press, 1963.

Farrington, S. Kip, Jr. *Fishing with Hemingway and Glassel.* New York: McKay, 1971.

Fellner, Harriet. *Hemingway as Playwright: The Fifth Column.* Ann Arbor, Mich.: UMI, 1986.

Fenton, Charles A. *The Apprenticeship of Ernest Hemingway: The Early Years.* New York: Farrar, 1954.

Ferrell, Keith. *Ernest Hemingway: The Search for Courage.* New York: Evans, 1984.

Fiedler, Leslie. *Love and Death in the American Novel.* New York: Stein and Day, 1959.

Fitch, Noel Riley. *Walks in Hemingway's Paris: A Guide to Paris for the Literary Traveler.* Boston: St. Martin's, 1990.

Fleming, Robert E. *The Face in the Mirror: Hemingway's Writers.* Tuscaloosa: University of Alabama Press, 1994.

Flora, Joseph M. *Ernest Hemingway: A Study of the Short Fiction.* Boston: Twayne, 1989.

———. *Hemingway's Nick Adams.* Baton Rouge: Louisiana State University Press, 1982.

Fuentes, Norberto. *Hemingway in Cuba.* Trans. Consuelo E. Corwin. Secaucus, N.J.: Lyle Stuart, 1984.

Gaggin, John. *Hemingway and Nineteenth Century Aestheticism.* Ann Arbor, Mich.: UMI, 1988.

Gajdusek, Robert E. *Hemingway and Joyce: A Study in Debt and Repayment.* Corte Madera, Calif.: Square Circle, 1984.

———. *Hemingway's Paris.* New York: Scribner's, 1978. Rev. ed. 1986.

Garcia, Wilma. *Mothers and Others: Myths of the Female in the Works of Melville, Twain, and Hemingway.* New York: Lang, 1984.

Gellens, Jay, ed. *Twentieth Century Interpretations of "A Farewell to Arms": A Collection of Critical Essays.* Englewood Cliffs, N.J.: Prentice, 1970.

Giger, Romeo. *The Creative Void: Hemingway's Iceberg Theory.* Bern, Switz.: Francke, 1977.

Graham, John, ed. *Merrill Studies in "A Farewell to Arms."* Columbus, Ohio: Merrill, 1971.

Grebstein, Sheldon Norman. *Hemingway's Craft.* Carbondale: Southern Illinois University Press, 1973.

———, ed. *Merrill Studies in "For Whom the Bell Tolls."* Columbus, Ohio: Merrill, 1971.

Griffin, Peter. *Along with Youth: Hemingway, the Early Years.* New York: Oxford University Press, 1985.

———. *Less Than a Treason: Hemingway in Paris.* New York: Oxford University Press, 1990.

Grimes, Larry E. *The Religious Design of Hemingway's Early Fiction.* Ann Arbor, Mich.: UMI, 1985.

Gurko, Leo. *Ernest Hemingway and the Pursuit of Heroism.* New York: Crowell, 1968.

Hanneman, Audre. *Ernest Hemingway: A Comprehensive Bibliography.* Princeton, N.J.: Princeton University Press, 1967.

———. *Supplement to Ernest Hemingway, A Comprehensive Bibliography.* Princeton, N.J.: Princeton University Press, 1975.

Hardy, Richard E., and John G. Cull. *Hemingway: A Psychological Portrait*. Sherman Oaks, Calif.: Banner, 1977. Rev. ed. New York: Irvington, 1988.

Harmon, Robert. *Understanding Ernest Hemingway: A Study and Research Guide*. Metuchen, N.J.: Scarecrow, 1977.

Hayashi, Tetsumaro. *Steinbeck and Hemingway: Dissertation Abstracts and Research Opportunities*. Metuchen, N.J.: Scarecrow, 1980.

Hays, Peter L. *A Concordance of Hemingway's "In Our Time."* Boston: Hall, 1990.

———. *Ernest Hemingway*. New York: Continuum, 1990.

Hemingway, Gregory H. *Papa: A Personal Memoir*. Boston: Houghton, 1976.

Hemingway, Jack. *Misadventures of a Fly Fisherman: My Life with and without Papa*. New York: McGraw, 1986.

Hemingway, Leicester. *My Brother, Ernest Hemingway*. Cleveland: World, 1962. 3rd ed. Sarasota, Fla.: Pineapple, 1996.

Hemingway, Mary Welsh. *How It Was*. New York: Knopf, 1976.

Hemingway, Patricia Shedd. *The Hemingways: Past and Present and Allied Families*. Baltimore: Gateway, 1988.

Hily-Mane, Geneviève. *Ernest Hemingway in France: 1926–1994; A Comprehensive Bibliography*. Reims, France: CIRLEP, 1995.

Hotchner, A. E. *Hemingway and His World*. New York: Vendome, 1989.

———. *Papa Hemingway: A Personal Memoir*. New York: Random, 1966. Rev. ed.

———. *Papa Hemingway: The Ecstasy and Sorrow*. New York: Quill, 1983.

Hovey, Richard B. *Hemingway: The Inward Terrain*. Seattle: University of Washington Press, 1968.

Howell, John M., ed. *Hemingway's African Stories: The Stories, Their Sources, Their Critics*. New York: Scribner's, 1969.

Hurley, C. Harold. *Hemingway's Debt to Baseball in "The Old Man and the Sea:" A Collection of Critical Readings*. Lewiston, N.Y.: Edwin Mellen, 1992.

Idema, Henry III. *Freud, Religion & the Roaring Twenties: A Psychoanalytic Theory of Secularization in the Novels of Anderson, Fitzgerald & Hemingway*. Lanham, Md: Rowman & Littlefield, 1990.

Isabelle, Julanne. *Hemingway's Religious Experience*. New York: Vantage, 1964.

Jobes, Katharine T., ed. *Twentieth Century Interpretations of "The Old Man and the Sea:" A Collection of Critical Essays.* Englewood Cliffs, N.J.: Prentice, 1968.

Johnston, Kenneth G. *The Tip of the Iceberg: Hemingway and the Short Story.* Greenwood, Fla.: Penkevill, 1987.

Joost, Nicholas. *Ernest Hemingway and the Little Magazines: The Paris Years.* Barre, Mass.: Barre, 1968.

Josephs, Allen. *"For Whom the Bell Tolls:" Ernest Hemingway's Undiscovered Country.* New York: Twayne, 1994.

Kazin, Alfred. *On Native Grounds: An Interpretation of Modern American Prose Literature.* New York: Harcourt, 1942.

Kennedy, Gerald J. *Imagining Paris: Exile, Writing, and American Identity.* New Haven: Yale University Press, 1993.

Kenner, Hugh. *A Homemade World: The American Modernist Writers.* New York: Knopf, 1975.

———. *The Pound Era.* Berkeley: University of California Press, 1971.

Kert, Bernice. *The Hemingway Women.* New York: Norton, 1983.

Kiley, Jed. *Hemingway: An Old Friend Remembers.* New York: Hawthorne, 1965.

Killinger, John. *Hemingway and the Dead Gods: A Study in Existentialism.* Lexington: University of Kentucky Press, 1960.

Klimo, Vernon (Jake), and Will Oursler. *Hemingway and Jake: An Extraordinary Friendship.* Garden City, N.Y.: Doubleday, 1972.

Kobler, J. F. *Ernest Hemingway: Journalist and Artist.* Studies in Modern Literature, no. 44. Ann Arbor, Mich.: UMI, 1984.

Kvam, Wayne E. *Hemingway in Germany: The Fiction, the Legend, and the Critics.* Athens: Ohio University Press, 1973.

Kyle, Frank. *Hemingway and the Post-Narrative Condition: An Unauthorized Commentary of "The Sun Also Rises."* Huntington, W.Va.: University Editions, 1995.

Larson, Kelli A. *Ernest Hemingway: A Reference Guide, 1974–1989.* Boston: Hall, 1990.

Laurence, Frank M. *Hemingway and the Movies.* Jackson: University Press of Mississippi, 1981.

Lee, A. Robert, ed. *Ernest Hemingway: New Critical Essays.* Totowa, N.J.: Barnes & Noble, 1983.

Leff, Leonard J. *Hemingway and His Conspirators: Hollywood, Scribners, and the Making of American Celebrity Culture.* Lanham, Md.: Rowman & Littlefield, 1997.

Leland, John. *A Guide to Hemingway's Paris.* Chapel Hill, N.C.: Algonquin, 1989.

Lewis, Robert W. *"A Farewell to Arms:" War of the Words.* Twayne's Masterwork Studies, no. 84. Boston: Twayne, 1991.

———. *Hemingway on Love.* Austin: University of Texas Press, 1965.

———, ed. *Hemingway in Italy and Other Essays.* New York: Praeger, 1990.

Limon, John. *Writing after War: American War Fiction from Realism to Postmodernism.* New York: Oxford University Press, 1994.

Longyear, Christopher Rudston. *Linguistically Determined Categories of Meaning—A Comparative Analysis of Meaning in "The Snows of Kilimanjaro."* The Hague: Mouton, 1971.

Lynn, Kenneth S. *Hemingway.* New York: Simon, 1987.

Mandel, Miriam B. *Reading Hemingway: The Facts in the Fictions.* Metuchen, N.J.: Scarecrow, 1995.

Maziarka, Cynthia, and Donald Vogel, Jr., eds. *Hemingway at Oak Park High: The High School Writings of Ernest Hemingway, 1916–1917.* Oak Park, Ill.: Oak Park and River Forest High School, 1993.

McCaffery, John K. M., ed. *Ernest Hemingway: The Man and His Work.* Cleveland: World, 1950. Re-iss. New York: Cooper Square, 1969.

McIver, Stuart B. *Hemingway's Key West.* Sarasota, Fla: Pineapple, 1993.

McLendon, James. *Papa: Hemingway in Key West.* Miami: Seeman, 1972.

Mellow, James R. *Hemingway: A Life without Consequences.* Boston: Houghton, 1992.

Messent, Peter. *Ernest Hemingway.* Macmillan Modern Novelists. London: Macmillan, 1992.

Meyers, Jeffrey. *Hemingway: A Biography.* New York: Harper, 1985.

———, ed. *Hemingway: The Critical Heritage.* Boston: Routledge, 1982.

Miller, Madelaine Hemingway. *Ernie: Hemingway's Sister "Sunny" Remembers.* New York: Crown, 1975.

Montgomery, Constance Cappel. *Hemingway in Michigan.* New York: Fleet, 1966. Rp, Detroit: Wayne State University Press, 1990.

Moreland, Kim. *The Medievalist Impulse in American Literature: Twain, Adams, Fitzgerald, and Hemingway.* Charlottesville: University Press of Virginia, 1996.

Morgan, Kathleen. *Tales Plainly Told: The Eyewitness Narratives of Hemingway and Homer.* Studies in English and American Literature, Linguistics, and Culture, no. 7. Columbia, S.C.: Camden, 1990.

Naessil, Anders. *Rites and Rhythms: Hemingway—a Genuine Character.* New York: Vantage, 1988.

Nagel, James, ed. *Critical Essays on Ernest Hemingway's "The Sun Also Rises."* New York: Hall, 1995.

————, ed. *Ernest Hemingway: The Oak Park Legacy.* Tuscaloosa: University of Alabama Press, 1996.

————, ed. *Ernest Hemingway: The Writer in Context.* Madison: University of Wisconsin Press, 1984.

Nagel, James, and Henry S. Villard, eds. *Hemingway in Love and War: The Lost Diary of Agnes von Kurowsky, Her Letters & Correspondence of Ernest Hemingway.* Boston: Northeastern University Press, 1989.

Nahal, Chaman. *The Narrative Pattern in Ernest Hemingway's Fiction.* Rutherford, N.J.: Fairleigh Dickinson University Press, 1971.

Nelson, Cary, ed. *Remembering Spain: Hemingway's Civil War Eulogy and the Veterans of the Abraham Lincoln Brigade.* Urbana: University of Illinois Press, 1994.

Nelson, Gerald B., and Glory Jones. *Hemingway: Life and Works.* New York: Facts on File, 1984.

Nelson, Raymond S. *Hemingway: Expressionist Artist.* Ames: Iowa State University Press, 1979.

Noble, Donald R., ed. *Hemingway: A Revaluation.* Troy, N.Y.: Whitston, 1983.

Oberhelman, Harley D. *The Presence of Hemingway in the Short Fiction of Gabriel García Márquez.* Fredericton, N.B., Can.: York, 1994.

Oldsey, Bernard. *Hemingway's Hidden Craft: The Writing of "A Farewell to Arms."* University Park: Pennsylvania State University Press, 1979.

————, ed. *Ernest Hemingway, the Papers of a Writer.* New York: Garland, 1981.

Oliver, Charles M., ed. *A Moving Picture Feast: The Filmgoer's Hemingway.* New York: Praeger, 1989.

Olson, Barbara K. *Authorial Divinity in the Twentieth Century: Omniscient Narration in Woolf, Hemingway, and Others.* Lewisburg, Penn.: Bucknell University Press, 1997.

Pearsall, Robert Brainard. *The Life and Writings of Ernest Hemingway.* Amsterdam: Dodopi, 1973.

Perosa, Sergio, ed. *Hemingway E Venezia.* Florence: Olschki, 1988.

Peterson, Richard K. *Hemingway: Direct and Oblique.* The Hague: Mouton, 1969.

Phillips, Gene D. *Hemingway and Film.* New York: Ungar, 1980.

Phillips, Larry, ed. *Ernest Hemingway on Writing.* New York: Scribner's, 1984.

Pizer, Donald. *American Expatriate Writing and the Paris Moment: Modernism and Place.* Baton Rouge: Louisiana State University Press, 1996.

Raeburn, John. *Fame Became of Him: Hemingway as Public Writer.* Bloomington: Indiana University Press, 1984.

Rao, E. Nageswara. *Ernest Hemingway: A Study of His Rhetoric.* New Delhi: Heinemann, 1983.

Rao, P. G. Rama. *Ernest Hemingway: A Study in Narrative Technique.* New Delhi: Chand, 1980.

Reynolds, Michael S. *Hemingway: The American Homecoming.* Cambridge: Blackwell, 1992.

———. *Hemingway: An Annotated Chronology, an Outline of the Author's Life and Career Detailing Significant Events, Friendships, Travels, and Achievements.* Detroit: Omnigraphics, 1991.

———. *Hemingway: The 1930s.* New York: Norton, 1997.

———. *Hemingway: The Paris Years.* New York: Blackwell, 1989.

———. *Hemingway's First War: The Making of "A Farewell to Arms."* Princeton: Princeton University Press, 1976.

———. *Hemingway's Reading, 1910–1940: An Inventory.* Princeton: Princeton University Press, 1981.

———. *"The Sun Also Rises": A Novel of the Twenties.* Boston: Twayne, 1988.

———. *The Young Hemingway.* New York: Blackwell, 1986.

———, ed. *Critical Essays on Ernest Hemingway's "In Our Time."* Boston: Hall, 1983.

Rogal, Samuel J. *For Whom the Dinner Bell Tolls: The Role and Function of Food and Drink in the Prose of Ernest Hemingway.* Bethesda, Md.: International Scholars, 1997.

Rollyson, Carl. *Nothing Ever Happens to the Brave: The Story of Martha Gellhorn.* New York: St. Martin's, 1990.

Rosen, Kenneth, ed. *Hemingway Repossessed.* Westport, Conn.: Praeger, 1994.

Rovit, Earl. *Ernest Hemingway.* U.S. Authors Series, no. 41. New York:

Twayne, 1963. Rev. ed. ed. by Earl Rovit and Gerry Brenner. 1986.

Rudat, Wolfgang E.H. *Alchemy in "The Sun Also Rises:" Hidden Gold in Hemingway's Narrative.* Lewiston, N.Y.: Mellen, 1992.

———. *A Rotten Way to Be Wounded: The Tragicomedy of "The Sun Also Rises."* New York: Lang, 1991.

Ryan, Frank L. *The Immediate Critical Reception of Ernest Hemingway.* Washington, D.C.: University Press of America, 1980.

Samuelson, Arnold. *With Hemingway: A Year in Key West and Cuba.* New York: Random, 1984.

Sanderson, Rena, ed. *Blowing the Bridge: Essays on Hemingway and "For Whom the Bell Tolls."* Westport, Conn.: Greenwood, 1992.

Sanderson, Stewart F. *Ernest Hemingway.* Writers and Critics Series, no. 7. London: Oliver & Boyd, 1961.

Sanford, Marcelline Hemingway. *At the Hemingways: A Family Portrait.* Boston: Little, 1962.

Sarason, Bertram D., ed. *Hemingway and the Sun Set.* Washington, D.C.: Microcard Editions, 1972.

Scafella, Frank, ed. *Hemingway: Essays of Reassessment.* New York: Oxford University Press, 1991.

Seward, William. *My Friend Ernest Hemingway.* New York: Barnes, 1969.

Shaw, Samuel. *Ernest Hemingway.* New York: Ungar, 1973.

Simmons, Marc et al. *Santiago: Saint of Two Worlds.* Albuquerque: University of New Mexico Press, 1991.

Singer, Kurt D. *Hemingway: Life and Death of a Giant.* Los Angeles: Holloway, 1961.

Smith, Paul. *A Reader's Guide to the Short Stories of Ernest Hemingway.* Boston: Hall, 1989.

Sojka, Gregory S. *Ernest Hemingway: The Angler and Artist.* New York: Lang, 1985.

Spilka, Mark. *Hemingway's Quarrel with Androgyny.* Lincoln: University of Nebraska Press, 1990.

Stanton, Edward F. *Hemingway and Spain: A Pursuit.* Seattle: University of Washington, 1989.

Starrett, Vincent, and Michael Murphy, eds. *Hemingway, a Seventy-fifth Anniversary Tribute.* St. Louis: Autolycus, 1974.

Stephens, Robert O. *Hemingway's Non-Fiction: The Public Voice.* Chapel Hill: University of North Carolina Press, 1968.

————, ed. *Ernest Hemingway: The Critical Reception.* New York: Burt Franklin, 1977.

Stoltzfus, Ben. *Gide and Hemingway: Rebels against God.* Port Washington, N.Y.: Kennikat, 1978.

Sutherland, Fraser. *The Style of Innocence: A Study of Hemingway and Callaghan.* Toronto: Clarke, 1972.

Svoboda, Frederic Joseph. *Hemingway & "The Sun Also Rises:" The Crafting of a Style.* Lawrence: University Press of Kansas, 1983.

Svoboda, Frederic Joseph, and Joseph J. Waldmeir, eds. *Hemingway: Up in Michigan Perspectives.* East Lansing: Michigan State University Press, 1995.

Takigawa, Motoo. *Hemingwei Saiko: Reconsiderations of Hemingway.* Tokyo: Nanundo, 1968.

Tavernier-Courbin, Jacqueline. *Ernest Hemingway's "A Moveable Feast:" The Making of Myth.* Boston: Northeastern University Press, 1991.

Tetlow, Wendolyn E. *Hemingway's "In Our Time:" Lyrical Dimensions.* Lewisburg: Bucknell University Press, 1992.

Unfried, Sarah P. *Man's Place in the Natural Order: A Study of Hemingway's Major Works.* New York: Gordon, 1976.

Wagner, Linda Welshimer. *Ernest Hemingway: A Reference Guide.* Boston: Hall, 1977.

————. *Hemingway and Faulkner: Inventors/Masters.* Metuchen, N.J.: Scarecrow, 1975.

————, ed. *Ernest Hemingway: Five Decades of Criticism.* East Lansing: Michigan State University Press, 1974.

————, ed. *Ernest Hemingway: Six Decades of Criticism.* East Lansing: Michigan State University Press, 1987.

Wagner-Martin, Linda [Wagner, Linda Welshimer]. *The Modern American Novel, 1914–1945: A Critical History.* Boston: Twayne, 1989.

————, ed. *Ernest Hemingway: Seven Decades of Criticism.* East Lansing: Michigan State University Press, 1998.

————, ed. *New Essays on "The Sun Also Rises."* Cambridge: Cambridge University Press, 1987.

Waldhorn, Arthur. *A Reader's Guide to Ernest Hemingway.* New York: Farrar, 1972.

————. ed. *Ernest Hemingway: A Collection of Criticism.* New York: McGraw, 1973.

Watkins, Floyd C. *The Flesh and the Word: Eliot, Hemingway, Faulkner.* Nashville, Tenn.: Vanderbilt University Press, 1971.

Watts, Emily Stipes. *Ernest Hemingway and the Arts.* Urbana: University of Illinois Press, 1971.

Weber, Ronald. *Hemingway's Art of Non-Fiction.* New York: St. Martin's, 1990.

Weeks, Robert P., ed. *Hemingway: A Collection of Critical Essays.* Twentieth Century Views Series. Englewood Cliffs, N.J.: Prentice, 1962.

White, William, ed. *The Merrill Checklist of Ernest Hemingway.* Columbus, Ohio: Merrill, 1970.

————, ed. *The Merrill Studies in "The Sun Also Rises."* Columbus, Ohio: Merrill, 1969.

Whiting, Charles. *Papa Goes to War: Hemingway in Europe, 1944–45.* Ramsbury, Eng.: Crowood, 1990.

Whitlow, Roger. *Cassandra's Daughters: The Women in Hemingway.* Westport, Conn.: Greenwood, 1984.

Wilkinson, Myler. *Hemingway and Turgenev: The Nature of Literary Influence.* Ann Arbor, Mich.: UMI, 1986.

Williams, Wirt. *The Tragic Art of Ernest Hemingway.* Baton Rouge: Louisiana State University Press, 1981.

Workman, Brooke. *In Search of Hemingway: A Model for Teaching a Literature Seminar.* Urbana, Ill.: NCTE, 1979.

Wylder, Delbert E. *Hemingway's Heroes.* Albuquerque: University of New Mexico Press, 1969.

Yang, Renjing. *Hemingway in China.* Xiamen: Xiamen University Press, 1990.

Young, Philip. *Ernest Hemingway.* New York: Rinehart, 1952.

————. *Ernest Hemingway: A Reconsideration.* University Park: Pennsylvania State University Press, 1966.

Young, Philip, and Charles Mann. *The Hemingway Manuscripts: An Inventory.* University Park: Pennsylvania State University Press, 1969.

Contributors

SUSAN F. BEEGEL is Visiting Faculty in English at the University of Idaho and editor of the *Hemingway Review*, the journal of the Ernest Hemingway Society. She is the author of *Hemingway's Craft of Omission: Four Manuscript Examples*, editor of *Hemingway's Neglected Short Fiction: New Perspectives*, and co-editor of *Steinbeck and the Environment: Interdisciplinary Approaches*.

MARILYN ELKINS is Professor of English at California State University, Los Angeles, where she was selected as an Outstanding Professor for 1995–96. She has been a Fulbright Professor at the University Blaise Pascal, Clermont Ferrand, France, and a Distinguished Visiting Professor at the University of Cape Town, Cape Town, South Africa, and the U.S. Military Academy. Her books include *Critical Essays on Kay Boyle, August Wilson: A Casebook,* and *Metamorphosizing the Novel*. Professor Elkins regularly publishes scholarly essays on women writers, fashion, and African American literature, and her writing on the Vietnam War, published in military history journals, is frequently anthologized.

KELLI A. LARSON is an Associate Professor of English at the University of St. Thomas in St. Paul, Minnesota, where she teaches nineteenth- and twentieth-century American literature. She is the author of *Ernest Hemingway: A Reference Guide, 1974–*

1989, *Guide to the Poetry of William Carlos Williams,* and of essays on Hemingway, Eugene O'Neill, Sylvia Beach, and Caroline Kirkland.

FREDERIC J. SVOBODA is Professor and Chair of English at the Flint campus of the University of Michigan. He is the editor (with Joseph Waldmeir) of *Hemingway: Up in Michigan Perspectives* and author of *Hemingway and "The Sun Also Rises": The Crafting of a Style,* as well as a number of articles on the author's work. A charter member of the Ernest Hemingway Society, he currently serves on the society's board of directors. His interests, broadly conceived, are in American Literature and Culture, with an emphasis on the modern period. He currently is editing *Between the Flowers,* a previously unpublished novel by Harriet Arnow, for the Michigan State University Press.

MICHAEL REYNOLDS, Professor Emeritus from North Carolina State University, is the author of a five-volume Hemingway biography—*The Young Hemingway, Hemingway: The Paris Years, Hemingway: The American Homecoming, Hemingway: The 1930s,* and *Hemingway: The Final Years* (1999). He now resides in Santa Fe, New Mexico.

JAMIE BARLOWE is Associate Professor of English and Women's Studies at the University of Toledo. She has been published in the *Hemingway Review,* as well as in *Novel, American Literary History, Studies in the American Renaissance,* and other journals and collections on Hemingway, Nathaniel, Hawthorne, Mary Wollstonecraft, and other feminist writers, on feminist pedagogy and theory, and on women's scholarship. Her book, *The Scarlet Mob of Scribblers,* is forthcoming from Southern Illinois University Press, and her current book project is titled, "'Viewer, I Married Him': The Construction of the Female Spectator in Cinematic Adaptations of Nineteenth- and Early Twentieth-Century Novels by Women."

LINDA WAGNER-MARTIN is Hanes Professor of English at the University of North Carolina, Chapel Hill. She recently served a three-year term as president of the Ernest Hemingway Foundation and Society and has long been active in Hemingway affairs. Besides books on other American modernists such as William Faulkner, John Dos Passos, Gertrude Stein, William Carlos Williams, and others, she has published a number of books and essays on Hemingway's writing. The recipient of grants from the Guggenheim Foundation, the Rockefeller Foundation, the Bunting Institute, and the National Endowment for the Humanities, she has won teaching awards from both UNC and Michigan State University.

Index

Printed in the United States
1983